THE LONG HAUL

First published in 2006 by

WOODFIELD PUBLISHING
Bognor Regis, West Sussex, England
www.woodfieldpublishing.com

© William Bloxham, 2006

The right of William Bloxham
to be identified as Author of this work
has been asserted in accordance with
the Copyright, Designs and Patents Act 1988

ISBN 1-84683-012-5

The Long Haul

Memoirs of a Survivor

To Derek of the 46th!
With good wishes

from

WILLIAM BLOXHAM

William H. Bloxham

Woodfield

06/07

The Author, Aircraft Apprentice, RAF Halton, 1940.

Sweetheart Nita – the love of my life.

In the memory of courageous comrades
who did not survive

Contents

Acknowledgements

My heartfelt thanks to my wife, Nita, son, Philip, and my extended family, who supported me throughout the passage of the last eighty-two years.

To the many friends whose lasting love enriched my life which is still providing today much interest and enjoyment.

I am so grateful to God's messenger who defied danger and dragged me clear of the blazing wreckage in 1942. My most sincere thanks are due to the German medical staff who initially rescued me from death's door. Then the devoted Major Bill Tucker and his colleagues, in captivity themselves, who continued the recovery of my bodily health. This was again achieved in the past ten years by the skill and tenderness of the many doctors and surgeons in my home area to whom I am ever thankful. They have enabled me to express these thanks and tell of the sixty or so years when seeking the truth behind "Operation North Pole".

During this time I have been enlightened by accounts of the operation by German, Dutch and UK sources, but only in recent years have I learned the whole truth enabling me to complete this narrative.

I am also most grateful to Philip and Dermot for their diligence and Elaine, whose typing of the narrative has been superb.

The following poem was included in a wartime newsletter circulated by the Red Cross St John organisation and incorporates the feelings of folks at home in those dark days.

Bill Bloxham
Awbridge, Hampshire
2006

Prisoner of War

You were so young last Christmas
We were all gathered round the fire
When you came in, you had been flying.

Night upon night you had gone out
Into the sea of stars
And e'er you turned again
Had descended under their beauty,
Into Hell.

Yet even so you had not lost your youth.
Your cheeks were still unlined,
Your hands capable and cool.
Your hair smooth, smart, untouched by time
But in your eyes were shades
I shall not forget.

Shadows cast by crushed horror
And the forced assaults on dreams of love and life
That year you shared with us
The children's gaiety and laughter;
(Or did you share? Were you not even then
Imprisoned by your task - Standing apart?

We could not share with you
That strange, ageless detachment
You had learnt, suspended twixt heaven and hell.
But you were there
And you laughed and talked with us
Apparently carefree.)

This year we shall not see you.,
But we shall remember.
We shall think of you in prison
For their sakes and for ours
We shall think of you in bonds
That through your lack
Our liberty should stand.

~ The Long Haul ~

That through your chains
We might preserve those things
Without which love and laughter
And children's play
Are meaningless and void

Youth like a garment
Drops within prison walls
And years spell decades,
When you - no longer young - come back
To Britain and to us.

God help us not to fail you
In your need
May you find people
Standing straight amidst the ruins.

But when you look upon us, your people,
May you know that Britain's heart
Though bleeding, is not dead.
May you know through us,
That hope and faith and strong endeavour
Have been kept and nurtured for this hope
Of new beginnings,
To which our nation's womb of suffering
Must give faith.

God help us not to fail you in your need
And may you find your people
Standing straight among the ruins.

1.   Moonlight Tragedy

There was a full moon as we took off from our base at RAF Tempsford at 22.45 on December 22nd 1942, to carry out operation 'Marrow 12', a clandestine mission required by Special Operations Executive (SOE). We flew at low level from our airfield in Bedfordshire, crossing Cambridgeshire and the Wash. The bright moon cast the shadow of our 138 (Special Duties) Squadron Halifax on the water, as we crossed the North Sea.

Our target was isolated heathland, flanked by a farm track on one side and woodland on the other, near the quiet village of Ijhorst in Northern Holland. This was the dropping zone for our cargo of arms and explosives, to aid Dutch resistance agents operating in that area. Our bomb racks were full of canisters designed for such low-level parachute drops of vital equipment to assist in the build-up of resistance organisations in countries then occupied by the Germans.

Flying into enemy-occupied territory at very low level was always dangerous, especially with a heavy, four-engined aircraft, requiring the light of the moon to help us to find our small target at night. Our hearts were stepped up a gear and thumped as we avoided the dreaded enemy flak ships off the Dutch coast. Their Radar detection ability was minimised by our flying at low-level throughout the operation. As Flight Engineer I was pleased to hear the rhythmic sound of the four Rolls-Royce Merlin engines, sounding and performing as well as they had done when we completed a successful air test earlier in the day.

We shared Tempsford with 161 (SD) Squadron, which was carrying out similar activities. Whilst it was 'business as usual' for the operational squadrons, support personnel at the station were busy with Christmas preparations in their spare time. Such matters, however, were far from our minds as we nervously concentrated on our dangerous mission.

As we crossed Northern Holland, our experienced navigator, Tony Howard, directed us towards our target area. As we approached the dropping zone we climbed to about 3,000 feet, a safe height from which to drop our canisters, and set our four propellers into fine pitch, enabling our skipper, Francis New-port-Tinley, to maintain forward momentum as we circled, just above stalling speed.

We were relieved when we saw torch-lights on the ground, spaced out in their normal positions, acknowledging our arrival, which was spot-on at 0100 hours. As we circled slowly to our correct line of approach, I was asked by the skipper to go to the rear of the aircraft and help our dispatcher, Cliff Hayes, to manhandle two large canvas bags of further supplies for the underground resistance organisation. These were to be dropped at the same time as the canisters were released from the bomb racks; a green warning light from the cockpit would signal the correct timing.

Our squadron aircraft were especially modified for secret op-erations, without mid-upper or front gun turrets but with a double-door hatch located near the rear of the aircraft, through which resistance agents were parachuted on their dangerous missions. There Cliff and I sat on the floor, facing each other, our feet poised to push the bags through the opened hatch. It was a very tense time as I listened to the high pitch of the revving engines, awaiting the signal from the cockpit. This came within a second or two and our bags and canisters were disgorged, hopefully undamaged and in the right area.

Suddenly, the area around the target erupted with anti-aircraft fire and the skipper called "Let's get out of here!" The aircraft banked hard to port as he executed an emergency climbing turn, and I knew that the co-pilot, Ben Pick, would be at hand to open the throttles to full power, while the enemy attempted to shoot us out of the sky. The next moment I was hit hard on my left leg and immediately lost consciousness...

When I came round, I was still in the rear of the aircraft and must have been severely concussed. I realised that the doomed aircraft must have burst into flames and crashed from no more than about 3,000 feet. Being in the rear of the aircraft had per-haps saved me from instant death. I learned later that the five crewmembers stationed further forward in the aircraft had been killed. Cliff Hayes, the dispatcher who had been sitting within a yard of me near the rear hatch just a few moments ago, had also lost his life. Strangely, I found myself wondering what had happened to our homing pigeons, due to be released at the same time by the dispatcher. I hoped that they had managed to get away and were able to fly back to England, confirming that our delivery had been accomplished.

I regained consciousness whilst the aircraft blazed around me and I could feel that I was badly burned on my buttocks and my left hand. I tried desperately to move away from the flames, which were engulfing me, but I could not move my legs which were badly damaged. I knew I was in mortal danger and cried for help. Having been brought up as a staunch member of the Christian church I was also desperately calling for the Lord's intervention.

The next thing I recall is a large figure suddenly appearing through the smoke and flames. He seemed to be dressed in a dark overcoat and large hat. He grabbed hold of me by my parachute harness, where the webbing crossed my chest, and dragged me clear of the wreckage. My back made contact with pieces of the doomed aircraft and the ground, which was quite painful, but, fortunately, his action extinguished the flames on the back of the trousers and long flying underwear I was wearing. He left me lying on the cold, frosty heath, some distance from the burning wreckage. Then, after dragging Frank Tierney, our Canadian rear gunner, to lie alongside me, he suddenly disappeared. This led me to believe that he was a member of the Dutch resistance, who left quickly because of the proximity of enemy forces. I was relieved to see that Frank was alive. The rear turret had apparently broken away from the crashed wreckage and Frank had been thrown clear on impact. He was not burnt but he had bleeding head wounds and what appeared to be a broken ankle. He was also in shock and shivering from the cold after the appalling crash we had experienced.

As the aircraft blazed away, I lay on the cold ground, in severe pain from my buttocks and left hand, accompanied by a numb feeling in my left leg, which lay loosely, at a strange angle and was bleeding excessively. I must have again lost consciousness and then revived, briefly, for I recall finding myself shivering and vomiting and feeling my end was near. I prayed again and asked God to give me strength of body and will to sustain me through my predicament and whatever lay ahead.

When I next opened my eyes I saw a pair of jackboots and looked up to see that a few German soldiers appeared to be standing guard over Frank and me. In a dazed state of mind I said to Frank that I could not understand why the Germans were present as this area had been chosen as a lonely spot in the countryside. I also thought I had been dragged clear by a member of the resistance. With my limited knowledge of the German language, learned at school, I was able to converse a little with our guards and was told that there were no other survivors. Frank and I were deeply distressed by this tragic news, which only added to the wretched state in which we found ourselves.

Our crewmates, who had paid the supreme sacrifice in such a worthy cause were:

Flying Officer G.F.B. Newport-Tinley, DFC
Warrant Officer C.A. Howard, DFM
Flight Sergeant H.C. Taylor
Sergeant B.M. Pick
Sergeant B.S. Nixon
Sergeant C.C. Hayes

They were an experienced crew, having previously completed many operations flying Whitley aircraft, with which 138 Squadron had been equipped before converting to the larger Halifax bombers, which were already in service when, later, I joined the Squadron from the Flight Engineering School at RAF St Athan in South Wales.

How long we lay on the ground, under guard and shivering with cold and fear, I cannot recall, but I do remember that the pain from the burns was severe, although the bleeding in my left leg had stopped. However, I was unable to feel any movement and was terrified that I might be paralysed or have lost my lower limb. In the moonlight I was able to detect a flying boot on my right foot only and I was still wearing my flying jacket under my parachute harness. The pain from my burns suggested that the seat of my battle dress and long flying underwear had burnt away and I was lying exposed on the cold, frosty ground.

I was desperate for help and prayed to my Father in heaven to come to my aid. My thoughts turned also to my home in the village of Cadoxlon-juxta-Neath in Wales where my dear mother, father and family would be preparing for Christmas. December 22nd was Mother's birthday and I hoped my greetings and letter, regretting that I was not able to join the family this year, had arrived. My thoughts also turned to my lovely sweetheart, Nita, had been so disappointed that I was not coming home for Christmas. We had enjoyed such a wonderful time at the two previous Christmases since our courtship had begun in

1940. I hoped that the customary telegram, informing them at home of my misfortune, would not cause too much distress and destroy their festive season. Yet, I was confident that all at home would seek God's comfort and pray for my survival. I cried with anguish and these loving thoughts were drowned by pain and fear over the awful predicament in which I found myself.

Both Frank and I knew that in view of the secret nature of our operations there was a danger that we could be shot for aiding resistors to the German occupation. How much had "Jerry" known about the flight? Were they in the dropping area by chance? Such thoughts were running through my mind as I again lost consciousness, only to be disturbed by movement and flashing lights. Help had arrived and I was relieved to find figures moving around me. By the light of their torches I saw uniformed soldiers, in their jackboots, carrying stretchers towards us. I suffered sharp pain as they strapped my legs together but I was relieved to see my left foot again. The pain in my buttocks was severe as they wrapped a blanket under me and lifted me slowly onto a stretcher. Poor Frank was also lying on a stretcher beside me, close enough to have a quiet conversation. He told me how sad he felt because his wife Maureen, at home in Poole, was pregnant with their first child. I could only think, "Oh Lord, why are we being punished like this?" I felt sad for Frank and Maureen and prayed for their deliverance from this ordeal. However, it was so difficult to see a way out of our desperate plight in enemy hands.

The stretchers were carried some distance across the heathland, where the burnt-out wreckage of our Halifax was still smouldering. This was now the graveyard of my unfortunate crewmates. They had been so young and full of enthusiasm for life, despite the dangerous missions we were called upon to undertake. However, we had become apprehensive about flights over Holland, as we knew it to be heavily defended by light and heavy anti-aircraft guns and German night-fighter squadrons. This was the usual route in for Bomber Command attacks on enemy industry in the Rhur, where a large amount of their weaponry and tanks were manufactured. Both 138 and 161 squadrons had suffered higher losses on special missions to Holland compared to similar operations to France, Belgium, Denmark, Norway and even the more distant targets of Poland and Czechoslovakia.

Our stretchers were loaded into an ambulance, which was parked on a roadway at the edge of the field, and strapped into position by the military ambulance staff. The doors were closed and we drove off, under armed guard. When I asked the guard where they were taking us, he replied, 'to a Kriegsmarine hospital at Leeuwarden, near the coast of Northern Holland.' I shuddered to think that this would be a long journey, and so it was, over rough, cobbled, roads with the ambulance slowing down at frequent intervals, presumably to negotiate the many dykes that are a feature of the Dutch landscape. After a while I must have fallen asleep again, only to be awakened when the doors of the ambulance were opened.

In the early light of a cold December morning, we were loaded onto hospital trolleys and wheeled into the reception area of the country hospital. There we were offered coffee with bread and sausage, but I felt sick and, still suffering from shock, managed only a small sip of warm, strange-tasting coffee. I felt I was in urgent need of medical treatment and something to relieve me of the pain and discomfort. I was also very dirty with oil and grime. Our presence drew the attention of inquisitive German military patients who had gathered, in their hospital suits, at an overlooking balcony. The nursing staff appeared to be nuns, who were ordered away from the stretchers by the German guards.

Then, suddenly, there appeared a tall member of the Abwehr, or possibly Gestapo, in dark civilian clothes, who questioned me about the objective of the flight and the base in England from which we were operating. We were in no fit state to answer questions and knew that under the Geneva Convention we were expected to give only our names and Royal Air Force service number. He didn't threaten me, and soon gave up his questioning and moved on to Frank, who was lying on a trolley on the other side of the reception area. No attempt was made to give us medical treatment or to clean up the mess of dried blood or the dirt and grime of the air crash.

A Luftwaffe officer arrived later and told us we would be taken by train to a major hospital, under their control, at Amsterdam. Some hours later, and still with no treatment of our wounds, we received a pain-killing injection and were loaded into an ambulance for the short journey to a railway station.

A train soon arrived and we were placed on the floor, in neighbouring compartments, each with an armed guard. No other passengers entered these compartments throughout the journey, which took what seemed to be many hours, before we arrived at Amsterdam station. There we were carried by German Luftwaffe personnel, in blue uniform, to the waiting room and, on stretchers, lay on the floor, looking up at a large photograph of Hitler, flanked by Swastika flags.

The word *'Kriegsgefangener'*, spoken by the milling crowd of German military and a smattering of civilians, brought home the horrible truth that, at the age of nineteen years and three months, my youthful aviation adventures had come to a sudden halt. I was now a prisoner of war and I shuddered at the thought of what the future held in store for me.

But as I lay there, in complete helplessness and terror, I closed my eyes and recalled my usual pre-flight prayer, asking God to protect me from danger. Somehow, despite the misery and pain I was experiencing, I thanked God for my preservation and asked for further help to sustain me through the dangers that lay ahead.

2. Hospitals & Interrogation – a Battle for Heart, Mind and Body

I had no idea of time as I lay on the stretcher, subjected to hateful remarks from passing travellers, who referred to Frank and me as *"Terror Fliegers"* and other defamatory expressions. I also detected a look of superior disdain, when some Luftwaffe personnel stopped to gaze at the enemy they had brought down.

In due course, Luftwaffe medical orderlies arrived and carried us outside to our ambulance. We were then driven off through the darkened streets of Amsterdam. It must have been late evening by the time we arrived at the hospital, where I was soon taken to a small room. I was stripped and washed of all the grime and hydraulic oil from the burning wreckage. A young doctor, who spoke good English, arrived and quickly realised I was in much pain as I lay, now in a hospital shirt and a clean bed. He said he was a Luftwaffe doctor and carried out an examination of my condition. He was then joined by another more senior doctor or surgeon and his orderlies, one of whom made notes for him. I was told that my injuries were serious, requiring immediate surgery. An injection quickly eased my pain and sent me to sleep.

How long I was under sedation I do not recollect, but I recovered my senses to find myself alone in a small ward. I lay on a sheet, which felt moist and was painful for my posterior burns. I was still unable to feel my left leg, which had now been lifted onto a platform, inclined at an angle to my knee and then horizontally to the foot of the bed. I could see my left foot above the bedclothes, but there was no feeling and I could not move it. This puzzled me, but I was somewhat relieved that there had been no amputation. I could move my badly-bruised right leg and right arm with pain, but my left hand was heavily bandaged and sore. I realised that I was connected to drip-feeds of blood and some other substance. I felt clean and thanked God that I was being kept alive.

I remember coming round during the night and, very thirsty, calling out many times for water. Luckily I remembered the German words *"wasser bitte"*. After dawn, an orderly arrived.

He was an older man and greeted me with *"Gut morgen Tommy"* From then on, I realised that they called all British servicemen 'Tommy', a nametag that had stuck since the First World War. He brought me some strange-tasting hot coffee with bread and jam, but I was not hungry. He spoke no English, but with my limited German I was able to glean his name, Adam, and that he came from Berlin. He said he was a fruiterer and had volunteered for medical duties in the Luftwaffe whilst his son served on flying duties in the west. He said he was against the war and the bombing. Adam was to prove a helpful friend during my stay in Amsterdam.

Later that morning the older doctor, clearly the surgeon in charge of my case, accompanied by the doctor who had injected me the previous night, examined my wounds thoroughly. He gave instructions, which were noted by three young colleagues. He did not speak to me other than when he stuck a sharp needle into my left foot several times and remarked *"Haben zie fuhlend?"* (have you feeling?). I replied *"nien"*. That was his only conversation with me. He gave his instructions to his younger colleague and left the room, leaving the doctor in charge of my case with me.

He told me that I had a serious, complicated fracture of my left tibia and fibula and that there had been much loss of bone. He explained that I was in traction with a weight of 13 kilogrammes hanging over the end of the bed. I couldn't see this, but I understood the connecting wire was attached to my left ankle by a stirrup-like fitting, the ends of which were linked to a steel rod, drilled laterally through my heel. He explained that the burns on my posterior had been treated with a healing solution, but warned me that the process would be slow because I was forced to lie on my back due to my leg injuries; the proximity of burnt flesh to my genitals added to the difficulties.

In the afternoon I was visited by a man in civilian clothes, who I thought was either from the Gestapo or the Abwehr. He questioned me about my flight, squadron, airbase and the names of my flight and squadron commanders. I was sufficiently alert to give negative and evasive replies to all these questions, but from a file he was able to tell me that the aircraft wreckage indicated we were from 138 Squadron and that German intelligence knew the names of our station and squadron commanders at RAF Tempsford in Bedfordshire. He was also able to tell me much about 161 Squadron. All this was presumably meant to undermine my confidence and morale and convince me of the invincibility of the Germans, who were "bound to win the war". He also advised, "for you, the war is over".

He produced a form, headed by a Red Cross, requiring me to complete answers to many questions, which he said would enable the German authorities to advise the Red Cross and my parents of my capture and describe the nature of my injuries. Many of the questions were about my family, home address and religion, but he also required details of my flight and the base from which we flew.

I was very tired and told the interrogator I was not well and asked him to call the doctor. Lying on my back, I feigned sleep and after a while I heard him depart, threatening to be back. This left me uneasy for my future as I tried to recall the appalling events of the last forty-eight hours or so. My mind was in a whirl. Afraid and very nervous, I had difficulty in resting, but after a little supper of bread and *wurst* (sausage), brought in by Adam, I felt more at ease and, thanking God for his mercy, eventually fell asleep.

Later than night I was awakened by the sound of singing coming through the open door of my room. Carols were being sung, which produced tears as my thoughts turned to my family home and Christmas. A feeling of despair, and longing to be with my sweetheart, Nita, then turned my thoughts to our village church, where we were both in the choir, and of our many friends attending the midnight service on Christmas Eve. I was very thirsty and kept calling for a drink, but to no avail. A desperate feeling of loneliness crept over me. I turned to my prayers for help before falling asleep.

I was greeted with, *"Gut morgen Christmas Frolich, Tommy,"* as Adam arrived early with a drink of coffee and a bowl of warm water to wash me. This brought a little cheer on Christmas morning. After he had attended to me, he was joined by a pretty young nurse, known as Schwester Jette, who checked my wound dressings with tender efficiency. She reminded me of the nursing sisters of Princess Mary's Hospital at RAF Halton, where I did my engineering training. In the next few weeks I was to depend upon both Adam and the sister for my medical recovery. She told me that she was married to a Luftwaffe Lieutenant on anti-aircraft duties in Cologne. She showed no sign of anger with me, despite the heavy bombing of the earlier 'Thousand Bomber Raid' on that city. She thought I was young to be flying on operations. When I enquired about Frank, and asked to convey a Christmas greeting to him, I was told that his damaged leg was in plaster and he was being sent to Dulagluft, the Luftwaffe interrogation centre near Frankfurt-am-Main. I prayed for his safety and trusted that he could cope with his questioners.

The rest of Christmas Day passed without any celebration as I lay, most of the time, reminiscing about our annual festivities on Christmas Day at my Aunt Nan's home in our village. She and her husband, Dan, were the village grocers. Then, on Boxing Day, they all joined us at our house. They were great times, which in the past two years had been enriched by the company of my dear Nita. I felt much anguish for her now.

At intervals my thoughts turned to the predicament I was in. Were the Germans going to treat me as a spy due to my activities on secret flights for the resistance? However, they were treating my extensive injuries well, so there was hope that my life was going to be spared.

A day or two after Christmas I had some more visitors, this time two Luftwaffe officers came to interrogate me. Their initial approach was friendly and they spoke of my misfortune in being their prisoner. They referred to my apparent youth and quizzed me on my previous operations with 138 Squadron. They produced a file which contained much information about the senior officers at Tempsford, mentioning the names of the station and squadron commanders. They were clearly trying to break down my silence and confidence with their depth of knowledge.

Speaking excellent English, as they had both been educated in England, they asked why I had not completed the Red Cross form left behind by the German official. Hinting at the threat of my being handed over to the Gestapo, they said it would be best for me to be in a Stalagluft when I had recovered from my injuries. There were many questions about my home and family and they made favourable remarks about the young lady whose photograph I carried in the pocket of my battledress. I remember asking for my wristwatch but was told that I was not wearing one when first examined at the Leeuwarden hospital. I protested and said it must have been removed at an earlier stage of my capture.

They then asked if there was any way in which they could help me. I asked for something to read and expected a negative response from the two officers, who were becoming impatient at my evasiveness. They were obviously seeking confirmation regarding my squadron's activities and present conditions in Britain. They said they would see about reading material and left with the Red Cross form, partially completed with only my personal details and my parents' address. To my surprise they returned the next day with some copies of *Der Adler* (The Eagle) an air force magazine, and I was impressed with the colour photographs of Luftwaffe activity in Greece. My limited knowledge of German enabled me to read most of the articles, which were clearly written to convince German readers of their air supremacy in all theatres of war. The magazines were dated late summer 1942 and therefore made no reference to the German defeat at El-Alamein or the retreat of the Afrika Korps and the Italians, which had occurred a month or so before my last flight.

The German interrogators had boasted of their invincibility, citing British defeats in Norway, the Low Countries and France and the massive German advances into Poland, the Baltic States, the Soviet Union and the Balkans. They said that events in Africa would be reversed, as they had been in earlier battles, and that they would soon take not only North Africa but also Egypt. They said that in due course their armies in Southern Russia and the Balkans would drive through and meet up with Rommel's forces in the Middle East. At that time the German defeat at Stalingrad was just a few weeks ago and pro-Nazi newspapers like the *Völkischer Beobachter*, which I was allowed to read, were still playing down the defeat and the withdrawal of the German armies in that area.

The papers tended to stress the continuing increase in shipping sunk by the U-Boat fleet and the large number of British bombers shot down in raids on Germany and occupied Europe. At the same time, I was increasingly aware of the back page memorial notices of Germans, many with awards for success in battle, who had lost their lives for the Fuhrer. Clearly, they were not having it all their own way.

To one of the interrogator's assertions that the Luftwaffe was invincible, I asked them to remember the Battle of Britain, when our Fighter Command tactics and deployment of Radar, along with the outstanding performance of our pilots, had forced the withdrawal of the Luftwaffe to defend their occupied territories to the west from low-level attacks by our bomber forces.

They were emphatic that their fighters had completely defeated our light bombers, such as the Fairey Battle and Bristol Blenheim, along with our Hurricane fighters operating from French bases in the defeat of 1940. To this I retorted that new aircraft such as the Beaufighter and Mosquito would not be so easy for the Luftwaffe to deal with. They were particularly interested in any knowledge I had of the Mosquito and its manufacturing sources, as this successful aircraft had begun to cause much concern to the enemy. I was careful not to divulge anything that could be useful to them.

They said that I was in no position to defend myself, that my life was in their hands and if I wanted to see my family again, I would have to be more co-operative. This threat ended the interrogation and the two Luftwaffe officers left me, defenceless in bed, with serious injuries, and terrified about my future.

A day or two later I was feeling better and I began to take note of my environment. The room was larger than I had at first thought and was also used for storage of medical supplies. Through the only window, I occasionally heard the sound of troops on the march, singing rousing songs. I was quite moved, but not able to grasp the words, which was just as well, as later in my captivity I understood the words of the stirring marching song *"Gegen England"* and was able to join fellow prisoners with our own words, which ended "England is Nicht kaputt – up your shoot!" This was at Stalagluft 6, which follows in a later chapter.

Through the window, I saw seagulls flying around, and with a heavy heart, I wished they could take a message to my loved ones at home, as well as warn 138 Squadron and the SOE Dutch Section of my fate. I now accepted my wretched plight, but still believed we would win the war, although I could not, at that time, see how, exactly, we would be successful. I expected my incarceration to be long and tedious, but realised that I must first concentrate on my physical recovery and keep mentally alert.

I drew some comfort from thoughts of the growing strength of Bomber Command, now supported by the involvement of the US Air Force, in addition to our successes in the Battle of Britain and the Eighth Army's achievements in Africa.

The wailing of air raid sirens on New Year's Eve was followed by some anti-aircraft fire as the German heavy guns opened up. This cheered me up immensely and I prayed that my comrades in Bomber Command would return safely. There was no bombing of Amsterdam and I assumed the aircraft were heading for a target in the Ruhr Valley.

When I had completed my daily ablutions, the burns on my back were treated with some kind of ointment by the sister and, to achieve this, I was lifted tenderly by Adam and another orderly. After about a week, Sister Jetta removed the dressings on my hand and I was shocked to see finger bones and joints through burnt flesh. A doctor was called and, after some discussion, he told me that, with treatment, the flesh should heal, but the fingers may be permanently stiff. This was shattering news. He then said it would be a long process and each day thereafter my hand would be immersed in warm water for a few hours. Soon Adam arrived with the water, coloured by a healing solution. After each session the sister would redress the burnt area. Fortunately, my right hand was only slightly damaged, enabling me to read and eat my meagre meals.

On New Year's Day I had another visit from one of the interrogators, who pursued many sensitive questions without success. He said I was reacting negatively and I reminded him that under the Geneva Convention I was not obliged to answer such questions. He then produced letters and cards so that I could write home. Two letters and two cards were allowed per month and I commenced writing to my parents and to Nita. I was also told that the Red Cross had been notified of my capture and medical condition. I asked for more reading material and a Bible to help pass long tedious hours on my own.

I was told that I was receiving medical treatment courtesy of the Luftwaffe, who were using the Queen Wilhelmina Hospital. Some Dutch civilians were employed as cleaners and other similar tasks but I was forbidden to speak to them and they were very cautious whenever I tried to engage them in conversation. I occasionally managed to let the woman cleaner have some of the food I left behind, as my appetite was poor. The Amsterdam civilians were always pleased to partake of a little extra to supplement their poor food situation under German occupation.

The next day I received a new visitor, this time dressed as a German Naval Officer, who told me he was a padre in the German Navy and had come to bring me good cheer. He showed a lot of interest in my family, my home area and school background. He knew I had been trained at the RAF School of Engineering at Halton after talking to the Luftwaffe officer. I suspected they had knowledge of the special serial numbers of Halton apprentices. There were many follow-up questions about my training as a Flight Engineer, particularly with regard to the Halifax aircraft manufacturer, Handley Page, with whom I received part of my training. Such questions were shrewdly put, as if they already knew much that was going on in England. My confidence and willpower were being severely tested.

I told him that my parents had introduced me to the Christian religion at an early age and that I was a strong believer in Jesus Christ, who was ever present with me. At this point he produced a Bible, which he understood I was seeking. Regrettably, when I looked inside, I realised it was written in German and although I had some knowledge of the language I could not cope with its proper interpretation. I told my interrogator so and asked if I could have a version written in English. He left me, promising to find me a copy, but disappointed me when he did not return to fulfil his promise. So much for the Naval Padre.

After about a week of water treatment, Adam produced an apple, asking me to start gripping it with my damaged fingers whilst immersed in the medicated solution. This was a very painful exercise and the flesh and new skin were breaking down, with bleeding in the area of the joints at the back of my hand. Adam reassured me that, despite the pain, the flesh and skin would again heal. After some weeks, during which he and the sister showed much interest and care, I could see the flesh and skin forming in folds around the joints. I was much indebted to their steadfastness for the return to shape of my damaged hand and today I thank them for their unstinting care, and God for his mercy and protection.

I had been the solitary occupant in the small ward for about three weeks, during which the interrogators made many visits. I found such occasions difficult to handle. Although there had been no threats of a physical nature, or to remove my meagre supply of food, the psychological methods they used to extract information from me were disturbing. On the plus side, I felt I was receiving good medical treatment for my wounds and titbits of inducements in the form of reading material. What little food

I ate, I enjoyed. This was served on hospital quality plates and the room was warm and comfortable. The loneliness became more difficult when Adam let slip that there were a few other British airmen prisoners in the hospital. After many requests to Adam and Sister I eventually was able to have the doctor's agreement to my being moved. This happened after the surgeon's examination. I had been a prisoner for about four weeks when I suddenly found Adam and another orderly wheeling my bed and the traction equipment to a lift for, I think, the third floor. There I was taken, past the armed guard stationed near the door, into a larger ward with iron bars on the windows. There I joined three other bedridden patients, who introduced themselves in turn: Frank Gostling, a sergeant navigator from the south of England with severe leg injuries, sergeant pilot Stan Moss, an Australian with injuries to shoulder and arm, sergeant pilot Kazimeryak, a Pole flying with the Royal Air Force, whose leg had been amputated. I also met sergeants John Banfield and Gordon Marwood, who were not seriously wounded when shot down flying a Lancaster in a raid on Essen on January 3rd. They were the only mobile cases in the ward, and were expecting to be moved to a POW camp at short notice.

There was one other, a Russian sergeant of artillery, who was brought into the ward after me; he arrived in a very poor condition, very thin and his face and arms were covered with round scars, as if he had been burned. Our Polish friend, who acted as a language link with the Russian, understood that, since his capture at Kiev, he had been forced to work in German factories, latterly manufacturing tanks, and the scars came from contact with hot rivets. On arrival he looked very ill and demoralized, suffering with pneumonia, but after a few weeks in clean, warm conditions and amongst friends, he recovered and spoke quite freely with our Polish comrade. Even on meagre German rations he noticeably put on weight and moved around our small room until one morning he was taken out under armed guard. I have often wondered about his fate in the turmoil that followed and prayed for his safekeeping.

When first meeting up with fellow prisoners, after about four weeks on my own, I felt a distinct desire to talk to them and we conversed at length ever mindful that the room we were in was likely to be bugged. Nevertheless, we didn't hold back in our criticism of the enemy or in showing our delight at our victories in the desert and the rout of Rommel's Afrika Korps. In early February, when the news emerged, we revelled in the defeat of the German armies in Stalingrad. It raised our morale and strengthened our resolve to face our uncertain future with greater confidence.

During my service in the Royal Air Force, it had never occurred to me that I would be a prisoner of war. Now finding myself in this predicament, I could not see how I would again find freedom, yet at no time did I think that we British would be defeated. I harboured the thought that, if I recovered my bodily health and my legs were strong again, I would try to escape from captivity. I had no knowledge of foreign languages, except for my scant knowledge of German, so I decided to converse with Adam and the nursing sister as much as possible in their own language, as this would improve my chances if I got out.

I had been in traction for about five weeks and the wound in my leg was healing well, but I still could not feel the pin prick when the surgeon tried to ascertain whether I had any feeling in my left foot. The tibia and fibula had been shattered midway between my knee and ankle, with much loss of bone, and the doctor explained that nerves, muscle and veins had been damaged in that area. They feared that I would have a "dropped" foot, or a kind of paralysis. He said that, in time, I might be able to recover some feeling and a limited ability to move the damaged limb. Nevertheless, the surgeon decided to cease traction and placed my left leg in a plaster cast from my groin down to my foot, with only the toes exposed, and they remained quite stiff when I tried to move them.

I was told that my leg had been saved from amputation and the burns in my lower back and hand were healing. There was reason, therefore, to feel that I had escaped a catastrophic experience without very serious long-term damage and I thanked God for his care and sustenance.

As I lay, taking stock of my situation, my thoughts continually returned to my home in South Wales, where I was born on September 25th 1923. I was a shy child, subject to bronchitis attacks and was quite nervous when sitting school tests and examinations. Nevertheless, I was placed second in the area examinations for entry to the Neath Technical School, where I enjoyed studies in pure and applied mathematics, physics, chemistry and engineering drawing, with excellent exam results. My other studies of geology, geography, history, English, Welsh and German were good enough for me to retain my position within the first three in terminal examinations up to matriculation standard.

My parents, despite their low income, maintained a happy home and our school holidays were mainly spent with relatives of father in his native Oxfordshire. We always saved a small sum at Sunday School for the annual outing, when we and other Church families went by train to Porthcawl. There we spent the day at Rest Bay, a quiet beach with adjoining fields and open countryside. When about six years old I recall being most excited when Alan Cobham used to fly in and land nearby; he would take people for a flight over the bay for the sum of five shillings, but this was far more than my parents could afford. Nevertheless, being only a short distance from the aircraft when it taxied up to change passengers, I was suitably impressed. These were the only flights we saw in South Wales at that time, but they were sufficient to encourage me to read as much as I could about aviation. This sparked a strong desire to be in some way involved with flying when old enough.

In the late 1930s, one read of the growth of the Royal Air Force becoming necessary in view of the rapid expansion of the German and Italian air forces. The radio news and the daily newspapers, which I read avidly, reported on the activities of Mussolini in Abyssinia and increasing German air activity in Spain. There is no doubt that my young mind was much influenced by these events and I heartily supported the enlargement of our own Air Force with new aircraft such as the Hurricane, Spitfire and Wellington bomber. This surge of feeling was enhanced by the events of 1936-39, with the German occupation of the French Rhineland, Austria and Czechoslovakia and their use of air power to invade Poland. These developments contributed to my strong desire to be involved with the Royal Air Force as soon as I was old enough. The declaration of war, on September 3rd, further convinced me that all young Britons should be prepared to prevent the Germans from following their expansive policies.

I had already enjoyed a couple of weeks of my holiday that summer, with older brother Leonard, on my Aunt May and Uncle Norman's farm near Bloxham, Oxfordshire. This break ended abruptly because of the worsening situation at the end of

August. From our coach on the return journey we observed much activity and sandbagging at every town we passed through. There seemed to be an Army presence near all bridges and other strategic locations. The fever of war, and its terrible consequences, built up further feelings of national pride in me, so, on my return home, I spoke at length to my parents about these feelings and discussed with them the options open to me.

Dad, with memories of the First World War, spoke of the appalling carnage and destruction that would result from another war with the revived Germany under the Nazi regime. He reminded me of the loss of his younger brother, William, who was killed at Passchendaele in 1917, to be followed by the untimely death of younger brother, James, from war wounds, in 1922. Father knew that he had two elder sons, Jack and Leonard, of an age when their immediate call to military service was inevitable, and as I was already sixteen years of age, in a further two years my involvement would surely follow. In the event, Jack was called up immediately to serve in the Royal Air Force barrage balloon command, despite offering his services for aircrew. Apparently, with his full-time education terminating when aged 14, his knowledge of mathematics and English was insufficient for entry to aircrew training, but with much diligence and effort he studied hard and was successful in passing the aircrew selection board early in 1942.

By this time there was a much-reduced requirement for barrage balloons to protect the United Kingdom's key installations from air attack and consequently he had no difficulty in being granted his request to be transferred to aircrew duties. By the end of 1942, the various training facilities in the United Kingdom, Canada, Rhodesia and America were producing sufficient pilots and navigators. However, Jack, anxious to play his part in flying activities, accepted training as an air gunner, his youthful involvement with motorcycles and vehicles at speed seeming to influence his desire. Later in this book, I describe Jack's experiences in Bomber Command and his death over Berlin.

Leonard, who was two years older than me, had already matriculated and was about to commence his Civil Engineering degree course at Swansea University. Nevertheless, he attended a call-up medical examination for flying duties but, due to a perforated eardrum, did not meet the medical requirements for aircrew. Much to Mother's satisfaction, and Dad's relief, he continued his university course. Leonard's early wartime involvement was in the Home Guard, both at University and in his home area, with many interesting and often humorous incidents, especially one, when guarding, overnight, the iron bridge at Penscynor, near our home village.

Mother's attitude, when I discussed the options open to me, was very clear. She referred to my excellent school reports and dedication to my studies throughout the previous ten years and to my having reached matriculation standard in the main subjects this year. It was expected that there would be an opportunity to take a graduate course in engineering later. This followed my academic strengths and mother reminded me that she had spoken to the Headmaster of my technical school, Doctor Graham Howell, a brilliant mathematician and teacher. He indicated that I was very studious and had a sound knowledge retention, which should enable me to obtain a place at university, studying engineering subjects, after a further year or so under his tutelage. I felt sufficiently confident that I would be able to cope with such study, but argued that such a course could follow a period of service in the Royal Air Force.

I insisted that I wished both to study aeronautical engineering and to fly. This was quite evident from the amount of reading material I had been engrossed in for the previous few years. I suppose I was to some extent influenced by the considerable amount of literature being distributed by the Air Ministry in its drive to improve recruitment in the late 1930s. Whenever I could afford them, copies of the magazines "Aeroplane" or "Flight" were to be seen in our middle room at home, with its large table. My parents had always retained this as a place to study and do our homework. A copy of the hard cover book entitled "Our Air Force", published by Ward, Lock & Co Ltd in 1940, was favourite reading then, and still commands a place amongst my extensive library of almost 3,500 books today.

I was sixteen within three weeks of the outbreak of the Second World War and received a considerable surge of desire to pursue a career in aeronautical engineering. Then, on the first day of my return to school after the summer holidays, I saw on the noticeboard an Air Ministry notice, inviting students to apply for entry into the Royal Air Force as Aircraft Apprentices. The competitive national examination was open to boys between the ages of fifteen and seventeen and the next date for sitting the examination, which was composed of Mathematics (two papers), Science (two papers) and an English Composition and General Paper, was to be on 5th December 1939, and would cover six hours with a short break between each paper.

Before I left school that evening, I armed myself with the literature and application form for entry to the examinations. My parents were alarmed when I confronted them with the literature and I was much dismayed when they, at first, rejected my request to be allowed to sit the examinations. I persisted, though, indicating that this would entail three years intensive training and study in aeronautical subjects, following which I would be a qualified tradesman. There was also a commitment to serve for twelve years following my eighteenth birthday and this might provide an opportunity to achieve a cadetship at RAF College Cranwell if I reached the necessary level of attainment in my studies at the Royal Air Force Engineering School. It would also allow me to have some flying experience, to which I was much attracted, and I argued that the training period would delay any direct action against the enemy.

Dad had some sympathy with my arguments and could see that the impending war might be concluded without endangering my life. Mother was not convinced, and stressed that the best option would be to complete a university degree before getting involved with the Royal Air Force. I did my homework with a clouded mind that evening and, before going to bed that night, I said I would think matters over and, if possible, discuss the situation with Dr Howell the following day.

Next morning I returned to school, with much foreboding, and saw Doctor Howell later that day. He took a similar line to that taken earlier by my mother. He said he had every confidence in my being able to equal my elder brother, who had already gained his university place at Swansea. I now faced a terrible dilemma, which was emphasised when I heard that three of my class had already submitted their application forms to the Air Ministry. My classmates, Alan Hill, Ellis Morgan and a fellow member of our school first XV, Vernon (Blackie) Smith, had already received parental approval. Although they had not achieved a similar standard to me in the many term examinations we had all taken over the previous two years, they were all very capable chaps who felt confident in succeeding when they sat the Royal Air Force entry examinations.

Eventually, after much further discussion, my parents reluctantly agreed to endorse my application form, although Mother was adamant that I was taking this major step in my life against her better judgement. Likewise, when I produced the endorsed application, the Headmaster reluctantly signed his agreement that I had reached the necessary standard to sit the examination. He said he was sorry I would have to leave his school, but wished me well.

In due course we were each informed by the Air Ministry that we would be required to sit the entrance examination on 5th December 1939. That day, under the invigilation of one of the schoolmasters, we set about a tough set of exam papers, the result of which would have a profound effect on our futures.

In February, a large Air Ministry envelope dropped through our letterbox, addressed to me. With feverish excitement I opened it to read that I had been successful in the entrance examination, placed third in the order of merit of successful candidates for the whole United Kingdom. My three classmates at Neath Technical School had also been successful. This was a good achievement, as the vast majority of the other candidates were Grammar School or Public School educated to matric. standard. When Dr Howell addressed school assembly the next day, he congratulated us all and made particular reference to my achieving third place in the national list of successful candidates. He then wished us God speed with our air force careers.

There were mixed feelings at home; of pride in my success in the examinations, but much trepidation about the future that the war might unfold. My brothers and sisters were happy for me and trusted that I knew what I was doing. Mother showed much strength in holding back her true feelings, but wished me well under God's guidance. Father, in his quiet way, said he prayed that the war would not last long and I would be spared the terrible danger of future fighting. He hoped history would not repeat, this time, the personal sacrifices of his family in a world conflict. He said the quality of engineering training in the Royal Air Force would be good and would start shaping my future career.

When, that evening, I showed my papers to my sweetheart, Nita, she was outwardly happy for me, as she knew this was what I wanted, and was pleased that I had achieved such a high place in the examinations. But there was trepidation and sadness when we fully realised that I would be required to report to a particular platform on Baker Street Station, London, at an appointed time on the morning of March 5th 1940, where I would join the other six hundred or so candidates for a journey to RAF Halton, near Wendover in Buckinghamshire. Then we would be required to take a medical examination for fitness to Royal Air Force standards before final acceptance and signing our entry agreements.

Nita and I had been brought up in the same village and had attended the Cadoxton junior and senior schools before I left for the Technical School. We were also regular members of St Catwg's, a Norman church (but a site of worship since the 6th Century) where both our families were worshippers of the Christian faith. Here, as infants, Nita and I had been introduced to God our Father in baptism and, later, we attended Sunday school and enjoyed many parties and church functions. When we were both about twelve years of age, we were prepared for confirmation by the Reverend T.M. Hughes, a splendid man who was an outstanding parish vicar and, despite having lost a leg in the First World War, was noted for his prodigious parish visits. He studiously led the choir, beating the time for the psalms and hymns on the side of the oak seat adjacent to where I sat as a boy soprano, and occasionally sang solo.

Some time after my becoming a choirboy, young women and girls were introduced to the choir. It was about this time that I became aware of the femininity of girls my age. In particular, a sweet girl soprano, Nita Davies, attracted me, as she was so charming and dressed well. A shy lad, with so much interest in school rugby and cricket, along with my homework, it was only at church on Sundays that I saw her, but, nevertheless, my fondness for her grew. Whenever I saw her, something told me that at some point I should like to get to know her better. She was very fond of her parents, who kept a close eye on their lovely daughter, who was blossoming into a fine personality.

Nita was in a different class from me at school and lived at the other end of the village. She was often conveyed to school in her father's car. In the late 1930s only about three cars were owned by residents of the village and most journeys were by bus. Buses, in fact, which brought children from the outlying villages of Aberdulais, Clifrew, Tonna and Pen-yr-wern.

As I lay in hospital, in enemy hands, my mind recaptured the happy times at school, when I remembered such occasions as sports days, where Nita excelled, with her good turn of speed, at winning points for her house. In a competing house, I was unable to match her excellence in the sprints. She also had a good turn of speed on her bicycle, and I was to find as I chased her and her companion, May Melyn, round the village and beyond, trying to get to know her when in our early teens. On one occasion, the chase ended up with May falling into the Tennant Canal, which followed a course from Neath Abbey to Aberdulais. Built in about 1823 to convey coal and other minerals by horse-drawn barge, it had long since fallen into disuse, but its towpath was popular with young couples for country walks and romantic interludes.

Nita and I became sweethearts but our love for one another remained a secret from our parents for a while, although I expect they could see a fond relationship developing. This was the state of affairs when I left the village to join the Royal Air Force in 1940. We kept in touch by the occasional letter, which removed the cloak of secrecy from Nita's parents and, thanks to the nosey initiative of the village postman, news of our exchange of letters soon spread throughout the community.

Thus, when I arrived home for a week's leave in Easter 1940, after passing my medical examination and within a few weeks of my entry at Halton, I took a courageous but risky step and, with Nita's agreement, sought her parents' permission to take a walk together after the church service on Easter Sunday night. Nita was in the church choir, as usual, and my heart beat hard through the service with joyous contemplation of this step we had taken. Permission was graciously given by her parents, on condition we returned by 9.30 pm. We had an enjoyable stroll together, hand in hand, up Dwr-y-Felin, a quiet road, and allowed ourselves a nervous kiss before returning home.

This, I suppose, was the start of our courtship and the loving relationship I was now missing, after my awful experience over Holland in December 1942 and enforced incarceration since. Oh, how I longed to join the birds that flew past my window as I lay there, and join them in flight back across the Channel to my lovely Nita and my home!

The many periods of longing, "hiraeth" in the Welsh language, were always broken by feeling the pain of my wounds, realising my predicament and wondering whether, at some point, I would be fit enough to escape the clutches of the Germans.

I was always a keen lover of traditional Welsh folk music, taught at school by the capable Miss Webb, and many singing festivals on St David's Day. I also remembered being selected to sing in the Welsh Schools' Choir at the National Eisteddfod of Wales when it was held in Neath in the mid-1930s. My involvement in the church choir, where I was fond of singing the Psalms and my favourite hymns, added to my musical knowledge. But it was the Grand Operas, performed by the Cadoxton Amateur Operatic Society, formed in the late 1920s, which enhanced my knowledge of, and enriched my love for, music. Such were my longing thoughts, only to be interrupted by a German Military Band, whose stirring marching tones occasionally sounded loudly through the open window.

The Cadoxton Amateurs were led under the able baton of Mr Alfred Jones, who also produced the many Grand Operas, performed at the Gnoll Hall, in the neighbouring town of Neath, for seven days each year in the 1930s. The quality of their work attracted excellent audiences to a feast of high-quality singing. The chorus comprised men and women, mainly from the village of Cadoxton, and was strengthened by some splendid solo voices from neighbouring towns and villages. Many of these exceptional voices went on to sing solo parts at the Carl Rosa Opera Company, often leading to BBC engagements.

The Morgan Lloyd orchestra was usually engaged for the week and comprised a nucleus of first-class musicians, led by Morgan Lloyd, a brilliant violinist and member of the BBC Welsh Orchestra. The highly commendable gathering of singers practiced for most of the year with Miss Eileen Gethin, a talented pianist, under their dedicated conductor, who was a self-taught musician. Other enthusiastic help came from local people, including my Uncle, David John Lewis, who, apart from being an active chairman, was also a member of the church bell-ringing team. He was, for some years, their leader, ringing many full peals of intricate change ringing. My father was also a member of this team, which was successful in the annual competitions held between the bell-ringers of the many parish churches in the Swansea and Brecon Diocese. Dad was an accomplished campanologist, who rang his first peal of 5040 changes in 1914. He also wrote the changes and many sextants and taught his first born, Jack, to ring the bells at an early age. Both my sisters, Phyllis and Winifred, were taught piano. Phyllis and her husband, whom she married during my Christmas leave from Halton in 1940, were quite accomplished pianists and often played duets, which were much enjoyed by the rest of the family, particularly at party time. Nita also had a nice touch in her piano playing, which resulted in her success in some of the grade examinations, which were held in Swansea.

Most of the successful young pianists in the village were taught by Miss Gladys Roberts, herself a very knowledgeable and charming musician. Apart from my involvement in the church choir, I took lessons in violin playing whilst at the senior school, but these were abandoned when I moved on to the Technical School. There, I concentrated full time on my studies. However, my ability to read music and elementary knowledge of the violin has resulted in a keen appreciation of orchestral music, retained throughout my life.

Both my elder brother, Jack, and elder sister, Phyllis, were performing in a series of Grand Operas and, as a youngster, I was drawn into the appreciation of the music and drama of Faust, Carmen, Il Trovatore, Tannhauser, La Traviata and other well-known operas. Mother, who was involved back stage with the preparation of refreshments for the performers on certain evenings, used to allow me the time, provided I completed my homework, to accompany her, when I would sell programmes with young friends from the village.

Prior to the war Nita was too young to perform with the operatic group, but she was in great demand when plays and concerts were performed in the village. I remembered her excellent performance when, as a youngster, she played a stunning Cinderella. During the war, with so many of the singers and orchestra away in the forces or on other war work, it was not possible to perform Grand Opera, but Nita, along with a nucleus of the choir, were formed into a singing group by Alfred Jones, which entertained locally-based soldiers of the anti-aircraft batteries and RAF Barrage Balloon personnel.

I had been at Queen Wilhelmina Hospital, Amsterdam, for about three months when I was told by the doctor that my plaster cast was now firmly in place and the burns on my back and left hand were still tender, but healed enough for me to be moved to Germany. Next morning I was dressed in a prison hospital suit, like striped pyjamas, with much rougher material. Over this they put me into a pair of Luftwaffe trousers and issued me with my RAF Battle Dress Jacket, which fortunately had not been burned in the crash. I was provided with a pair of German army socks and a pair of boots, which looked very much like British Army issue, captured by the Germans. Apparently, when the British Army retreated to the French coast at Dunkirk, much kit was left behind and this was made available to prisoners at work camps and the like.

I was carried from the hospital on a stretcher to Amsterdam Station the following morning, covered in a navy blue overcoat, which I assumed was the kind issued to German sailors. Thus clad in a motley uniform, I said cheerio and God speed to my fellow prisoners, who were still bedridden and being treated for their wounds, and also many thanks to the Nursing Sister and Adam. They told me that I was being taken to the Luftwaffe Clinic near Frankfurt-am-Main for further treatment, before being transferred to a prisoner-of-war hospital. As soon as they mentioned Frankfurt, I smelt a rat, because I knew from lectures we had received during training that near Frankfurt was the dreaded Dulagluft, where all shot-down aircrew were taken for interrogation. I assumed, therefore, that I was being sent to the hospital unit attached to the interrogation centre and during the journey spent much time contemplating the further grilling to which I would no doubt be exposed.

I was constantly worried about my future, as I knew from earlier interrogations that the Germans were already aware of my involvement with the Special Duty Squadrons at Tempsford. Their file of knowledge was quite awesome and I assumed they had similar files on other RAF squadrons. I was sure that they were thoroughly searching British newspapers and magazines, which were readily available through the neutral countries. Throughout the war, magazines, such as *Aeroplane*, *Flight* and *The London Gazette,* contained a considerable amount concerning service aviation and aircrew, including RAF Casualty Lists (such as the first list, reproduced overleaf, which was published in *Flight* on 28 September 1939).

German air intelligence would have found such information useful, especially when they were trying to break down a captured airman, whose confidence could be compromised by such exposure being cited by the enemy interrogator.

"Flight" photograph.

DIVE-BOMBERS : Blackburn Skua I fleet-fighter dive-bombers of the Fleet Air Arm. An article on the dive-bombers of the German Air Force appears in this issue.

SERVICE AVIATION

Royal Air Force and Official Announcement : Fleet Air Arm News

Sir R. Brooke-Popham

H.E. AIR CHIEF MARSHAL SIR ROBERT BROOKE-POPHAM, Governor of Kenya since 1937, is relinquishing that appointment in order to take up work with the R.A.F., from which he retired on his appointment as Governor.

C.A.G.s Warned

THE first batch of Civil Air Guard men, below the age of 28 and holders of A licences, have been warned that they will shortly be called up for interview, and may be required for the R.A.F. Other C.A.G. categories have been warned that they will be called up later. Women members are advised to offer themselves for the Women's Auxiliary Air Force.

First R.A.F. Casualty List

THE first casualty list of the War was issued last Tuesday week, when the Air Ministry announced the following R.A.F. casualties : —

Missing (Believed Killed)
549741 A/C.2 K. G. Day.

Missing (Believed Prisoner of War)
561012 Sgt. G. F. Booth; 36187 P/O. L. H. Edwards; 548555 A/C.2 L. J. Slattery.

Missing
34213 Flt. Lt. W. F. Barton; 546005 A/C.1 G. T. Brocking; 531493 L.A/C. H. Dore; 36138 F/O. H. L. Emden; 537287 A/C.1 R. Evans; 505002 Sgt. D. E. Jarvis; 546670 A/C.1 E. W. Lyon; 580695 Sgt. A. S. Prince; 524808 L.A/C. J. Quilter; 510850 Cpl. J. L. Ricketts; 30340 F/O. J. F. Ross; 552231 A/C.1 G. Sheffield; 550292 Act. Sgt. E. G. Walton.

It is reported from Rotterdam that A/C. Day, who was in a machine which was shot down on September 4, was buried with full military honours at Cuxhaven. The body was picked up by a cargo steamer on September 14 between the Elbe Lightships I and II.

The second casualty list to be issued contains the names of three killed; one reported missing (believed killed); and twenty missing. This list will be published in our next issue.

"Follow Your Trade in the R.A.F."

A FEW days ago an appeal was issued by the Ministry of Information to young craftsmen to volunteer for service in the Navy, Army and Air Force. The appeal is directed to young men in the reserved trades who are not now employed on work of national importance.

For the R.A.F. volunteers are sought in the following trades, and must be below the ages given in parentheses: Electricians (25); fitters (including internal combustion engine fitters but not tool fitters) (23); fitter assemblers (25); instrument makers and repairers (23); motor-drivers (with heavy goods licences) (25); motor-drivers (commercial vehicles, 1½-2½ tons) (30); watch and clock makers and repairers (25); wireless operators (non-seagoing) (30).

Much useful information is given in the booklet "Royal Air Force Trade Groups and Rates of Pay," obtainable from H.M. Stationery Office, and volunteers are advised to apply to the nearest recruiting office for particulars of the experience necessary.

The Penetration of Bombs

THE following figures for the depth of penetration of thin-cased bombs in reinforced concrete are taken from a German source:—

Weight of bomb (kg.)	Penetration (cm.)
50	45
100	55
300	80
1,000	125
1,800	150

For soft steel the penetration is one-fifth of the above but for sand it is multiplied by ten.

Royal Air Force Gazette

Air Ministry, Sept. 12

Royal Air Force Reserve

RESERVE OF AIR FORCE OFFICERS
General Duties Branch

T. W. Walker is granted a commission as Flying Officer in Class A with effect from September 1 and with seniority of September 1, 1935; T. B. Byrne is granted a commission as Flying Officer in Class C with effect from August 31 and with seniority of April 14, 1932.

The following are granted commissions in Class CC as Flight Lieutenants on the dates stated:—Flt. Lt. E. E. Ellison (R.A.F.O.) (April 1); F. Marshall, T.D. (April 25); Capt. B. G. St. John-Smith (July 10); Lt.-Cdr. S. R. Sunnucks (R.N., Ret.) (July 24); Capt. C. Barnes (August 8).

Lt. F. R. Alford is granted a commission in Class CC as Flying Officer (February 27); F/O. R. A. Ford is granted the acting rank of Squadron Leader in Class CC (August 23, 1938); F/O. (Honorary Flight Lieutenant) A. M. Butt (R.A.F.O.) relinquishes his honorary rank and is granted a commission in Class CC as Flying Officer with the acting rank of Flight Lieutenant with effect from May 7, 1938, and with seniority of August 3, 1937, and is granted the rank of Flight Lieutenant with effect from December 23, 1938; F/O. W. N. L. Cope is transferred from Class A to Class C (August 29); Flt. Lt. W. R. Cox is transferred from Class C to Class A with effect from August 9; P/O. A. F. L. Bowley resigns his commission (June 12); P/O. W. J. W. Kingston relinquishes his commission on appointment to a short-service commission in the Royal Air Force (August 31).

A page from 'Flight' magazine, showing the first RAF casualty list.

My journey from Amsterdam was spent lying on a stretcher, laid across the compartment, between the seats of a passenger train with an armed escort sitting on one of the seats near the door. It was a bright, sunny day and I had a glimpse of the clear sky and the countryside as we sped along. I made particular note of any Luftwaffe activity and exercised my aircraft identification knowledge. The guard told me that we were due to stop at Cologne, where we would connect with another train for Frankfurt. I assumed, correctly, that our journey would take us through Utrecht and Arnhem before crossing the border into Germany, following the Rhine through Duisburg and Dusseldorf to Cologne. All these towns and their surrounding industrial areas revealed heavy damage from allied bombing attacks, which, in the latter half of 1942, had become more fierce, none more so than the raid on Cologne, where we had a stop of about an hour before resuming our journey to Frankfurt. It was a moving sight to see the twin spires of Cologne cathedral standing, whilst everything around, including the railway station, had been badly damaged. However, it cheered me to think that Germany was now receiving what it had handed out to the Dutch at Rotterdam and to London and other UK cities in 1940 and 1941.

The stop at Cologne enabled the German guard to obtain some soup, which was provided by a Red Cross canteen at the station. This was most welcome, as I was hungry, having had just a slice of bread and jam for breakfast at an early hour.

During the latter half of the journey, my thoughts turned to the probability of being interrogated again. However, I felt stronger and more confident now than I had during the early days at Amsterdam, when my injuries and shock had been very weakening. In this mood, my thoughts once again returned to my home and to Nita. I was reminded of the poem I had written and sent to her some months earlier, when I had completed my Flight Engineering training and was expecting to commence operational flying duties. I knew I was about to embark on dangerous missions, but trusted in God to see me through.

Young Britain

Today the country's all ablaze
With fiery toil and sweat and blood,
As through the darkness and haze
Young Britain emerges as a flood.

To flow freely through post war years
That, though proclaimed an arduous task,
Strong courage, stout heart is all we ask
To prove the vigour of our might.

Today the graves of many a noble youth,
A living memory of the darkest hour,
Prove the urgency of war's demands
Throughout this our own most Gracious land.

Through many long and darkened days
The folk of Britain, young and old,
Have stood with dauntless spirit
Yet undefeated warriors bold.

Through these hours of peril, never to shun
The haunts of fascist and of hun,
Through winter's wind and summer's sun
All heroes world confidence won.

Onward we tread in father's stead
To victory, no one can deny,
With thoughts of freedom, our foes have fled
Before the valour and concord shy.

These words, written in August 1942, reflected the strong patriotic feelings that encouraged me to make the important decision to join the Royal Air Force in 1940. They now reassured me to remain steadfast whatever the future had in store for me.

I wondered how Nita was taking our dramatic separation; it must have been quite a strain, but I knew her strong will would see her through the ordeal. I wondered whether the news of my survival was already known at home and whether any of the letters or postcards I had sent to my parents and Nita had actually reached them. I had received no news from home and was hoping that I would soon hear. In the event, it wasn't until I had been a prisoner for six months that I received any communication at all. Then, within two or three days, I received twelve letters and a few postcards, some written by my mother, others in Nita's fair hand. I noted that Nita was using foolscap sheets for her letters, the maximum size of paper allowed, in order to contain as much news from her as possible.

It was dark when we pulled into Frankfurt-am-Main station, where Hitler's photograph stared down, with many swastika flags and bunting for company. I felt nervous at the hostility of the many civilians and others in German Army and Luftwaffe uniforms, who gave me disdainful looks as I lay there under German armed guard. After a short wait, I was carried to an ambulance, which took about an hour to reach Oberursel, where my stretcher was carried into a vacant room on the ground floor of a small hospital. I was later to learn that it was a clinic in a wooded area of Hohemark, about ten miles from the centre of Frankfurt.

The clinic, under the control of the Luftwaffe, was run by nuns. It had high ceilings and the handles on the doors and windows were all curved downwards. I formed the impression that this had previously been a place where mental patients were incarcerated before its present use, confining wounded prisoners of war. I was put into a clean comfortable bed and, after a short while, a Luftwaffe officer arrived. He explained that he was on the staff at Dulagluft, a hutted camp about a mile away, mention of which confirmed to me that I was about to be interrogated. Instead, he explained that the staff would be providing me with a meal and he would return later. I was very hungry, as the only food I had eaten was the bowl of soup at Cologne, and I enjoyed what was supplied.

Feeling better, I lay back in my prison-like pyjamas and was dozing off when in walked the Luftwaffe officer, accompanied by a uniformed companion. I was interrogated at length by the two officers, who spoke perfect English. They had, before them, a file of information and endeavoured to undermine my confidence and resistance by telling me they already knew that the Halifax aircraft in which I had been flying was from 138 Squadron, based at Tempsford, on a secret mission to support resistance and sabotage in occupied Holland and that I could be shot for supporting the enemy in this clandestine way.

They said that for me the war was over and stated confidently that the British would be defeated. They claimed that the Luftwaffe was far superior to the Royal Air Force, whose aircraft were being shot down in increasing numbers, whereas the German air force was being equipped with improved aircraft all the time. They pressed me hard on the subject of the De Havilland Mosquito, saying that even this aircraft would be overwhelmed in combat. I knew it would be making its presence felt in increasing numbers, but declined to be drawn when the interrogators persisted with their line of questioning.

I realised that the Germans might know that, as a Flight Engineer, I was trained at RAF St Athan. Using their Junkers JU86 aircraft on high-altitude reconnaissance, they had possibly photographed the station, which had many other functions at that time, apart from the training school. They became somewhat impatient when I told them that I had no knowledge of activities at St Athan other than the Flight Engineers School. I knew, in fact, that St Athan was busily employed in fitting aircraft with up-to-date Radar, ASV and other advanced electronic equipment; there was a constant flow of Coastal Command aircraft, some in white livery and others painted completely black for night fighting and intruder purposes.

They appeared to be experienced interrogators and knew much of the activities of the Royal Air Force and made constant reference to the file when they said they knew a great deal of what was going on at Tempsford. They again tested my ability to resist questioning by mentioning the names of the Station Commander and the Squadron and Flight Commanders of 138 and 161 Squadrons. They seemed to require confirmation of titbits of information German intelligence had already learned.

Then they switched again to Flight Engineer training and wished to know the number of aircrew being trained, the length of the course and which aircraft manufacturer had I visited during my training. They gave me the impression that they knew a great deal, but the questioning again indicated that some of it was guesswork requiring me to lower my resistance and 'spill the beans'. It was difficult, again, when they reverted to questions about my family and the sweet young lady on the photograph I had been carrying in the breast pocket of my battledress, seeking a tender spot in my resistance. This was followed by questions about industry in my home area. I was afraid I might fall into the trap of talking too much in rebuking them when they referred to German invincibility and the result of the war being a foregone conclusion, when, naturally, I retorted that Great Britain and her allies would be victorious.

In response to my query about Frank Tierney, they told me that he had passed through Dulagluft before transferring to the POW hospital at Obermassfeld. The persistent interrogators again returned to the Red Cross form and implied that completion of this was essential in order that my family could be informed that I was alive, a prisoner and in hospital. Again, this method of interviewing, exploiting my affection for my family, made it hard to resist.

Meanwhile, life in the clinic at Dulagluft was relatively quiet. I was alone throughout my stay there, except when disturbed by the daily routine cleaning and meals provided by the staff. As mentioned, these were mainly nuns, who also checked on my wounds from time to time. I was able, whilst lying on my bed, to see outside through a large window and admire the beauty of the countryside, which was mainly pine forests, sloping downwards in the distance. There was a light covering of snow for much of the time. The scene always made me homesick, with thoughts of my family and lovely Nita, which brought a lump to my throat and tears to my eyes. This feeling usually resulted in a silent prayer to my God, seeking his help and protection to overcome my anguish.

The sloping woodland scene reminded me of my school holidays, when the local woods – mainly of Oak and Silver Birch with a smattering of Holly and Ivy, climbing vigorously over rocky areas – were the venue for most of our outdoor pursuits. We walked for miles, Dad often making toy whistles from the lower branches of the trees. There was a clearing about a third of the way through the woods, which we called 'The Flat'. That was the rugged area where I learned much of my batting ability. We enjoyed hours of cricket matches, made up of two teams of varying size. Then there was the sloping pathway, down through the trees and the old stumps of fallen trees, where we used to race aboard our four-wheeled scooter, without brakes, and with a rather crude steering of the front wheels, with a rope or wire connected to the front axle. I think it was there that I developed a longing for speed, which developed into my strong interest in aviation, especially when we lay prone, careering head-first down the treacherous course we had mapped out.

Those were happy days, enjoyed amongst friends, all of similar age. Some of my contemporaries were already casualties in the dangerous work of our Navy in the North Atlantic and others in the North African campaign. I often pondered over the possibility of meeting up with Nita's cousin, Flight Lieutenant Clem Hunkin, whom I knew was shot down flying a Wellington bomber in 1941. My thoughts often settled on my eldest brother, Jack, who I knew had already commenced his training as an Air Gunner before the end of 1942 when I met disaster in the air. I fully expected him to move on through his course to an operational training unit, a heavy conversion unit, then on to an operational squadron. It was, I knew, a dangerous path that my dear brother had chosen to take in serving his country; I also knew that it was his ultimate desire to take up pilot training at the first opportunity on completion of his tour of operations. I was dreading the effect the war was having on my parents, particularly mother, and prayed for her strength and religious belief to see her through these anxious times.

Meanwhile, I felt much better in myself in the comparative comfort of the clinic, although I had no feeling yet in the toes of my damaged left leg, encased in plaster from the groin down. I was surprised, and somewhat relieved, when, after about three weeks at the Kurklinik Hohemark, I was told by the doctor that I was being moved early the following morning to a hospital for prisoners of war at Obermassfeld, where there would be British doctors and medical assistants to help deal with my wounds.

Nevertheless, late that afternoon I had a visit from a Luftwaffe engineer in the uniform of a yellow-tabbed Oberfeldwebel. He told me that he was involved in the engine maintenance of aircraft and thought that I would be interested in his work. Early on in our conversation I concluded that he was part of the intelligence-gathering setup at Dulagluft and that I needed to be careful. His questions turned to the Mosquito and the strength of its current involvement in the RAF. When I reported that I had no knowledge or contact with this aircraft, he soon gave up on this line of questioning and attempted to cool the conversation by telling me that I would meet up with many air force comrades who had passed through Dulagluft and on to the Lazarette (hospital) at Obermassfeld.

The questions raised by this interrogation later turned my thoughts to the technical aspects of aviation, especially my Halton training, where I was allocated to the Fitter II Engines Course, but because of war demands we were expected to complete the normal three-year training in two years. This necessitated longer hours in the workshops and schools on weekdays and Saturday mornings. Leave periods were cut and time for sport was reduced.

Despite the tiring basic training, which necessitated standing at the bench for long periods, we became proficient in all kinds of processes with solid steel, brass and sheet metals. Working to tight tolerances, with the aid of micrometers and verniers, we mastered the skill and touch necessary for measuring circular objects to great accuracy. We mastered the techniques of spot and acetylene welding and soldering, and our basic engineering inspection qualities were also tested. We also mastered the technique of pipe-bending.

As an exercise during the sheet metal forming, grinding and welding training, we were requested to produce pikes – to be used by airfield and land defence forces to beat off potential attacks by German invading armies! Such was the shortage of defensive rifles, machine guns and other weapons after the debacle in France and the Low Countries in 1940, when huge quantities of military equipment had to be abandoned as the British Expeditionary force beat a retreat via Dunkirk. What hope for our home defence force, equipped with pikes to face the firepower of the Wehrmacht and Panzer forces in the event of an invasion? Of course, the airborne forces of the Luftwaffe would be well equipped with automatic weapons, which they had used so successfully in the rapid defeat of the Netherlands.

I recall the influx of Royal Air Force ground personnel evacuated in a hurry from France in June 1940. A large area of the camp was hastily prepared for hundreds of bedraggled ground and support airmen, housed under canvas. There the tired survivors relaxed, recovered, and were fed in the dining rooms attached to each wing of the Halton Station. They were soon sent on leave, along with details of their new postings. This was a difficult test of the Royal Air Force administrative machine, which proved itself by efficiently organising the disposition of personnel in time to support the operational squadrons effectively during the Battle of Britain in the summer months of 1940. In addition, there was the concurrent requirement to equip the RAF contingent for the Middle East and Desert campaigns.

We apprentices continued to work hard at our studies of mathematics, metallurgy, engineering drawing, the theory of flight and the physics of heat engines, along with general studies of British involvement in world affairs in the last century. Particular attention was drawn to Empire defensive policies, with lectures centred on our place in India and the many ramifications of the British oil policies in the Middle East. Such involvement meant the presence of our Air Forces in these areas in the 1920s and 1930s. I found such studies most interesting and enjoyed my work.

I found the work in the heat engines laboratory was quite absorbing and was especially impressed with the reference to the Wankel rotary principle. There was also special reference to gas turbine engines, but no mention was made of Frank Whittle's experimental work on jet engines – this development was shrouded in secrecy. I was quite thrilled later to know that he was formerly an aircraft apprentice and to see his endeavours produce such outstanding results.

With the threat of an imminent German invasion, there was an urgent requirement to dig defensive trenches through Halton. Much of our spare time was utilised in this tiring work, but we knew that the enemy was 'at the gate' and all hands were put to the task. We were particularly interested in Fighter Command's efforts to take on the larger strength of the Luftwaffe, but we had great faith in our Hurricanes and Spitfires, and the courage of the Royal Air Force pilots and ground crews.

Despite so many demands on my time throughout the summer and autumn of 1940, I still managed to play some cricket and was quite pleased that my batting talents were recognised and was proud to be selected for both "B" Squadron and No.2 Wing teams. I well recall successfully opening the batting for our Wing XI when, in August 1940, we beat the older apprentices of No.3 Wing in the final of the Barrington-Kennet Cup, which was presented by Air Commodore Sir Oliver Swann KCB CBE, the station commander.

Throughout the winter months of 1940/41 I applied myself to rugby football and proved quite an accomplished outside half for both "B" Squadron and Wing XVs. On sports days, away fixtures took us to many of the public schools in the surrounding area and our team of seventeen-year-olds made a match for school first XVs and also neighbouring RAF Station XVs, although I do remember receiving quite a battering when we played against RAF Bicester, a busy operational training unit which could field an experienced XV of adults. Along with three or four other members of our team, I required a tetanus injection for the many cuts I received from the burly opposition forwards.

It was one of the season's worst defeats, but it gave us much satisfaction when in a home match we later piled up a score of about fifty points against an RAF Police team. Our passing and running completely outplayed the opposition and I remember putting over several conversions and penalties, as well as scoring a couple of tries. I was still growing, but felt rather thin and light when up against hardened, experienced players with big physiques. Nevertheless, with nimble footwork and a good turn of speed, I was able to avoid the hardest knocks most of the time. However, the Bicester match knocked away much of my confidence, and at the end of the 1941/2 season, I was wavering in my desire to continue playing competitive rugby.

As I lay in my sickbed at the Hohemark clinic, I had very serious doubts whether my damaged left leg would enable me to continue playing active games again, and rugby football could certainly not be contemplated. After a period of longing to be free again, I prayed to my Almighty Father that I might be spared serious disability and one day to be returned to my loved ones in distant Wales. These thoughts then turned to my favourite sporting activity, cricket, and I longingly hoped my disability would not prevent me participating again. These were doubts which haunted me from time to time.

My batting performance during my first year at Halton didn't go unnoticed, and in the summer of 1941, my second year, I, along with another talented member of my entry, Hugh Blissett, was selected to play for the Halton command team. We were so thrilled to be playing alongside several players who had success with county sides in the 1930s, amongst them Beveridge of Middlesex, George Mobey, the Surrey wicket-keeper, the Bedser twins, who were both Corporals in the RAF police, and especially W.E.G. Payton, who had a double blue (Hockey and Cricket) at Cambridge and had played as an amateur for Nottingham during university vacations. He was a skilled batsman and had impressed Hugh and me with his technique and sound defence. I found this period had an important influence on my cricketing development and only wished I could have enjoyed a few more years in such company.

Apart from his involvement with the command cricket team, Squadron Leader The Reverend W.E.G. Payton was also a very sincere and active padre at Halton and remained an inspiration to me throughout my life. His broadminded approach to active Christianity was a good example to all who knew him.

During the 1941 cricket season Hugh and I, at the age of seventeen, were too youngsters playing with an experienced group of players, captained by Group Captain Padre Cox, a pre-war member of the Royal Air Force and senior Chaplin at Halton, where there must have been about five thousand personnel stationed. Apart from the four apprentice wings, there were courses for Flight Mechanics, Dentistry and the Princess Mary's Hospital, apart from a large transport department and the tutors at the schools and workshops and the airfield itself. Apart from staffing a very active gymnasium, the physical training and many sports activities also required organisational personnel.

There was also a noticeable presence of RAF Regiment personnel to man the airfield and defences of this large station, nestling closely to the woodland of mature beech trees, sweeping down from the Chiltern Hills. These made a picturesque backdrop to the brick-built barrack blocks. Despite its importance to the Royal Air Force, it had been bombed only once during my time at Halton.

This had been my home for two interesting years, during which time I developed mentally and gained confidence in the presence of such a wide diversity of experienced people. Having completed the very intensive training, I was one of only six apprentices in our entry chosen to interview for an Officer Cadetship at RAF Cranwell. This would have been an outstanding achievement and in the months following our graduation, or 'passing out', I felt there was a chance that the cadetship would materialise.

This, however, did not deter me from my ambition to undertake flying duties and as soon as I was promoted to leading aircraftsman, in the trade Fitter II (engines), whilst carrying out inspection duties at No.32 MU St Athan, my application for transfer to flying duties was accepted, subject to a rigorous medical examination.

3.   Obermassfeld and Kloster Haina (Stalag IX C.A/H)

It was now late March 1943, when, in the early hours, an ambulance came and collected me from the clinic and I was taken in the darkness the short distance to Dulagluft. I noticed that this was mainly a hutted camp with much barbed wire and heavily guarded. When inside the compound my stretcher was loaded on to a small grey-painted military bus, where I joined a few other air force prisoners, all in plaster casts for leg injuries; some using crutches to move around. It was still dark when, with two armed guards as company, we set off on a very noisy and slow journey. We discovered later that the small, uncomfortable bus was powered by burning charcoal from wood chippings. Alongside the road there were, at intervals, piles of chippings for motor vehicles to refuel – another example of German ingenuity, like the ersatz coffee made from crushed acorns, the margarine that was a by-product of the coal industry and the rather unpalatable black bread – all of which were doled out as rations to prisoners of war.

The bus eventually dropped us at Frankfurt Station, where our group was transferred to a passenger train. My companions, Sergeant Howie Copeman and fellow Canadians Bill Thompson and Dick Whitall, had all been shot down in recent months and had been processed through various hospitals in German,y or occupied European countries before moving on to Dulagluft. They were good company as the rather slow train travelled eastwards. The journey to Obermassfeld, only about eighty miles as the crow flies, took many hours, as the train took a tortuous, winding route, requiring several changes and many stops at small, local stations. We travelled all day, without any food, but enjoyed the beautiful, hilly country of Thuringia (*Thüringerwald*) on the second half of the journey.

It was early the following morning when we arrived at Obermassfeld-Grimmenthal railway station. We were now very hungry and tired, as we had had little sleep throughout the night. We had a further wait at the station, while our guard telephoned the hospital to tell them of our arrival. Soon, an ox-drawn cart arrived, with two soldiers, dressed in British Army khaki uniforms. They were older men, both greying, and looked rather thin. I was quite thrilled to discover that they were both from South Wales, serving in the Welsh Guards. They, likewise, were pleased to find out that I was Welsh and were keen to establish the latest situation in the principality, as they had already been prisoners of war in Germany since early June 1940.

They explained that the Welsh Guards, along with the 51st Highland Division, had been involved in the defensive stand at St Valery, near the North French coast, as the rest of our army escaped capture by the efforts of the small boats and the Royal Navy at Dunkirk. I remembered reading that there were many tens of thousands of allied soldiers captured by the Germans during the invasion of France and the Low Countries, as well as those captured in the Norwegian campaign.

I was now meeting two of them, from my native Wales, who, along with about forty thousand others, were marched long distances through France to the German border, then sent hundreds of miles to Eastern Germany and occupied countries to work camps hastily constructed and organised by their German captors. Concurrently, the Germans had tens of thousands of French, Belgian and Dutch soldiers to incarcerate. These, along with many foreign civilian workers, were forced to work for the German economy.

The journey, over rough roads, took about half an hour. Then we turned through iron gates into the forecourt of a large, grey-looking building, on three floors, with gabled windows built into the sloping roof. There were guards on the main gate, a swastika flag and barbed wire everywhere. I noticed that all windows were barred. The place had been used as a factory, an agricultural school and, at one time, an SS Barracks. It was a depressing-looking building, near two branches of the River Werra, one of which was diverted under a wing of the building. This powered a small electric generating plant, which, with its rhythmic noise, disturbed sleep in some of the rooms.

I lay on a stretcher in the forecourt, looking up towards the building. The windows were crowded with patients, clad in their striped hospital suits, which I was soon to discover were rough, thick and consequently rather uncomfortable.

As soon as the escorting guards handed over the relevant identity documents to the German staff, the two guardsmen picked up the stretcher and I was carried up to the first floor. There, much to my surprise and despair, I entered Ward 3, a crowded, smelly room where the two rows of bunks were stacked two-high, with a central passageway in between. In the centre of the passage was a long table, at which sat some of the inmates, some in hospital garb, others in an assortment of khaki army uniforms and a few in RAF blue battledress tops over their hospital garb. They were a motley lot and shouted greetings to Dick Withall, Bill Thompson and me. We were allocated bunks on the lower level. All of us had leg injuries, the other two with lesser complications than me, but they were already using crutches, as they had been at Dulagluft.

I had become used to the unpleasant smell of my own burnt flesh, but was appalled by the foul odour in the ward, which I learnt was the combined effect of burnt flesh and broken bones infected with the crippling disease osteomyelitis. Regrettably, many of the patients with fractured limbs were stricken with this disease, which penetrated their plaster casts and resulted in a reddish-brown discolouration as well as the putrid odour. I was told later, when discussing my own fractures with a doctor, that there was no immediate cure for someone infected by the disease and the orthopaedic surgeon, Major W.E. Tucker, was trying to defeat its effects by chipping away areas of infected bone and then replastering the limb, hoping all the infection had been removed. There were no antibiotics available, which would have produced a much more favourable response to the treatment. There were many cases of patients suffering in this way in the ward and I was told there were more serious cases in Ward 1, where I was myself transferred later.

The room was not large and housed sixty chaps, of whom about forty were British army men, captured in France in 1940 or in the North African desert. Some were Australians and New Zealanders, taken during the Greece and Crete battles. In addition, there were a couple of East European Serbs, who, like many of the army men, were suffering serious debilitating illnesses incurred whilst working for the Germans in salt mines, coal mines or other work camps. Some of the British army men were still suffering serious effects from the 1940 battles in France. The Air Force patients, numbering about twenty, were mainly shot down operating with Bomber Command, although there were a few fighter boys and one or two fortunate survivors of air battles in the Mediterranean area.

The two Welsh guardsmen, Wacky Thomas and Tom Evans, lifted me from the stretcher and I lay on a lower bunk, mid-way down the ward, noticing a palliasse of sack material, filled with wood shavings, underneath me. They sat on the bunk and were clearly trying to cheer me from my rather nervous and tired condition. They explained that they had been taken on the working staff at the hospital after they had recovered from typhus they had both contracted whilst in a work camp to which they had been sent following their. I was humbled on hearing their story and in a quiet moment thanked God for being merciful to me.

Soon, a hospital orderly came with two sheets and a pillow, along with a mess tin and a set of army cutlery. He explained that these captured items from the French campaign were now being issued by the Germans for use at prisoner of war camps and hospitals. The senior ward orderly, also from the RAMC (Royal Army Medical Corps), explained a few simple rules and made notes about my injuries and earlier treatment at Amsterdam and the Hohemark Clinic.

Amidst the noise and chatter of my sixty roommates, I tried to rest, only to be disturbed by the two guardsmen, who brought a packet of cigarettes, firmly believing that smoking them would bring some relief to the stressed condition in which they had found me that morning. I told them I was a non-smoker, but they insisted that I try, as they could bring me some respite. I tried, but after a few puffs I gave up, as I didn't enjoy the sensation at all. It was with much trepidation that I returned the remainder of the packet to my kind benefactors, who, I think, understood my aversion to smoking, which has stayed with me throughout my life.

I was later issued with my daily ration of one seventh of a loaf of black bread, a hard, sawdust-like, crust and a small portion of ersatz margarine. This, with a tin cup of acorn coffee, was for breakfast, followed later by two hot potatoes, placed in my mess tin at the end of my bed.

An army ward orderly introduced himself and produced a pair of striped prisoner-of-war pyjama-like trousers and jacket. The clothes in which I was clad when I left Amsterdam were hung behind my bed, including the navy blue overcoat. I was told I would be having "X" rays of my left leg and would soon be seen by the orthopaedic surgeon.

Despite my initial shock when faced with the prevailing conditions, I lay back on my bunk, feeling cleaner after a wash, helped by one of the orderlies, and for the first time since my capture I felt I was with friends, most of whom had survived the horror of imprisonment in the hands of the enemy for more than two years. I thanked God, my saviour, for his hand in bringing me round from the despair I had withstood for the past three months, when there seemed to be no let-up from the pain I had suffered, the many interrogation sessions and the lack of contact with folks at home.

My spirits were improved by the many visits I had in the next few days from fellow Royal Air Force POWs. Some had already been at Obermassfeld for many months and knew the ropes. Among them was Don Coleman, a Sergeant Wireless Operator, whose 150 Squadron Wellington was shot down during the return flight after a raid on industrial targets in the Duisburg area on 21st July. Don, though wounded, bailed out over Holland and suffered a multiple fracture in his right leg and serious head injuries in the descent. Two of his crew were killed and are buried at Bergen Op-Zoom.

Don had left his signature on some of the reading material at Queen Wilhelmina Hospital in Amsterdam, then later in the Hohemark Kirk Clinic, so it was no surprise to learn, on meeting him at Obermassfeld, that we had shared similar experiences since the tragic events that had ended our respective operational flying careers. He had preceded me by a few months and was now walking with the aid of crutches. He asked me to join him and combine our meagre food supplies, a practice generally adopted by small groups of POWs, which meant a more efficient use of the small supply of German rations and of the more varied and nourishing contents of the Red Cross parcels with which we were issued at regular intervals.

Unfortunately, there were no cooking facilities for the tinned contents of the parcels. We thus resorted to warming them on a central heating pipe near the floor behind our bunks. Many hours later, a pudding or a tin of bacon would be eaten with relish, despite the fact that the special treat was not piping hot.

My friendship with Don, which lasted until he died a few years ago, was forged in hardship, surviving many unpleasant experiences in our old factory building, minimally converted for prisoner of war hospital usage in this remote area of Thuringia.

I was soon x-rayed and next morning, when the senior orderly brought around the negatives and laid them on the bunks, he told me that the bone specialist, Major Tucker, was due to examine me that morning. I had mixed feelings when contemplating whether the work done on my leg in Amsterdam had been successful. Would further surgery be required to bring about an improved result? I looked at the x-rays and saw the fractured pieces of bone on the tibia, but the fibula was not fragmented and the fractured ends were slightly overlapping and had started to fuse in that state.

Major Tucker was a large, ruddy-faced, smiling person and, with a few words, put me completely at ease. I then related a summary of events of the fateful night and my subsequent treatment at Amsterdam and the Hohemark Clinic. With large hands he studied the x-rays and lifted my plastered leg by the heel. When he looked at my wasting thigh he said the sooner I exercised the offending leg the better and advised immediate physiotherapy and the use of crutches to keep my limb moving. I had been confined to hospital beds for about three months, so was overjoyed with Bill Tucker's prognosis. Later that day a Staff Sergeant of the Black Watch regiment, who was the physiotherapist working with the surgeons, came, complete with a pair of crutches, and I was able to stand between the beds, feeling rather giddy, but soon mastered the use of the crutches, which were to be my means of mobility for the next nine months.

Getting on my feet was a bit taxing, but I was soon putting a boot on my right foot and started to reconnoitre the ward and the adjoining washhouse, supplied with cold running water. Standing on my good leg, I was able to do my daily ablutions. This was a big step forward and moving around amongst the other prisoners was a tonic.

The overcrowded ward was occupied mainly by British and Commonwealth Army personnel up to sergeant-major rank. Many were pre-war regular army soldiers, covered from head to foot with tattoos of varied designs, many of them acquired in the fleshpots of Egypt and India. These unfortunate chaps, who had been in captivity since May 1940, were still critical of the lack of air support in the battle for France and in Low Countries. As a newcomer in their midst, and from the junior service, I was forcibly asked on many occasions: "Where were the RAF at Dunkirk and the earlier defensive battles, when we were facing the onslaught of the Panzer attacks?"

I explained to them, as no doubt others before me had, that throughout the battles for France and the Low Countries, RAF Fighter Command, with limited resources of aircraft and pilots, had conserved their major fighter strength in order to be able to defend the British Isles – as they later did so successfully in the Battle of Britain. I also pointed out that events showed how weak the air forces of France, Belgium and Holland were when faced by the modern Luftwaffe *blitzkrieg* tactics, so the RAF Hurricane squadrons, based in France, at the time had little support and suffered heavy casualties. I was also strong in my support of the bomber aircraft which, following the allied retreat in France and evacuation to the UK, were continually involved in daylight attacks on the channel ports, where there was a progressive build-up of barges and flak ships, preparing for the invasion of the British Isles.

Operation 'Sea-lion' – the German codename for the invasion – was eventually called off by the Germans after suffering loss of air superiority and many losses of their invasion craft and navy support. I think that, with this knowledge, I was able to cool those chaps, whose knowledge of events in 1940, and subsequently had been blurred by the effects of captivity and imprisonment, subject only to the German point of view.

Some of the army patients to whom I spoke had been in work camps, on farms, or in coal and salt mines in Eastern Germany for the three years since they had been captured.

Many of the patients at Obermassfeld were there having treatment for serious ulcers and malnutrition, caused by the poor working conditions in the salt mines. Along with the many seriously wounded cases, they were all suffering, but their spirit was not deflated.

It wasn't long before I found myself playing crib and draughts and, in partnership with Don Coleman, taking on all-comers at bridge and whist. Our winnings were usually in cigarettes – the recognised currency amongst POWs. As I was a non-smoker, and despite Don's affection for the weed, we were able to build up a small capital, always useful to occasionally trade for some food or other requirements.

I had, slowly, shared experiences with the other air force in-mates, who, without exception, had survived the terrible ordeal of being shot down by enemy flak or Luftwaffe fighter activity. Most were Bomber Command casualties and in the majority of cases were the only survivors of their crew. In many cases, the changeable weather over Europe had contributed to the dreadful conditions in which they operated.

Within a few days I received an unexpected visitor from an-other ward. He was wearing an RAF battledress jacket, display-ing the rank of Pilot Officer and pilots wings. One of his arms was in plaster. He said his name was Bill Davies and we ex-changed experiences. He explained that the main reason for his visit was highly confidential and asked for complete secrecy regarding the remainder of our conversation. He said that he had been informed that I was clad in a navy blue overcoat when I arrived at the hospital and asked if I could confirm that I still possessed the coat. This I did, saying how stupid the Germans had been at Amsterdam in kitting me out with the garment before I left on a stretcher. Furthermore, I explained that those Luftwaffe intelligence officers at the Hohemark Clinic had been remiss in allowing me to move on from there to Obermassfeld, clad still in the navy-coloured overcoat. I said that such a coat would be a useful piece of clothing in the event of a future escape, which I would contemplate if my physical recovery would allow me to participate.

He said that such a recovery appeared to be some time ahead and asked whether I would be prepared to allow the coat to be used for an earlier escape attempt. He said he could not divulge any further details, but he assured me that the coat would soon be used if I would be prepared to part with it. In my present state I could not speculate on my future prospects for escape and felt if I could help a fellow prisoner to do so it would be my duty. I immediately agreed to trade my navy coat for an Army Officer's greatcoat and I was given two hundred cigarettes as well, which added to the combine's assets.

It so happened that a few months later I was able to exchange the two hundred cigarettes for an American airman's shirt. This was successful trading, as the garment was well used for the rest of my POW confinement. Likewise, the army greatcoat became vital when I became more mobile, and a godsend to keep out the winter cold on my journeys through Poland and East Prussia and Lithuania in January/February 1944.

A few months after I exchanged coats, I learned that two army captains had made a clean breakout from the officers' ward and had evaded the patrolling guards. They had, apparently, climbed out of a window and scaled down a wall, supported by tied blankets. This courageous action enlivened the inmates, all but a few exceptions, who felt that it was incorrect to escape from a prisoner-of-war hospital, where the medical staff and certain prisoners, under the care of RAMC staff, had the privilege of walks outside under parole conditions. They argued that the enemy could cancel such privileges at the slightest provocation.

The daring bomber raid of May 16th/17th 1943 by 617 Squadron Lancasters on the Ruhr dams raised our spirits considerably. The German authorities decided to punish us and decided to cut off all water supplies to the hospital, despite the fact that our water was not provided by the dams that had been broken. We estimated that we were well over one hundred miles from the Eder dam, which appeared to be the nearest to our hospital.

Obermassfeld Hospital was situated on an island astride the River Werra, which flowed quickly either side. As described earlier, one branch of the river had been diverted under a part of the hospital that adjoined a small electricity generating plant. This water-powered generator must have provided power for the small village of Obermassfeld, situated a mile or two from the picturesque town of Meiningen along the Werra.

Whilst we air force and army POWs were quite excited and proud of the outstanding raid, which caused such a stir amongst the German authorities, we were mildly rebuked by our medical staff, who lost all their privilege walks and swimming sessions in the river. They were also faced with the awful task of running a hospital, where they were continually struggling to defeat the constant infections from which the patients suffered. This they did, without antibiotics, which were unavailable at that time. Regrettably, Major Henderson, the brain specialist who was the British doctor in charge, and his two colleagues, Major Tucker, the orthopaedic specialist, and Major Smyth, the physician, who functioned under the overall control of the German Colonel Doctor, were unable to carry out operations. Additionally, the sanitation conditions were appalling for many weeks whilst the Germans imposed the restriction. This allowed minimal water for drinking and very limited personal washing. Conditions in the toilets worsened every day and the smell throughout was terrible.

Obviously, such conditions could not be allowed to continue and, after a week or two of suffering, Major Henderson, who spent part of his medical training pre-war in Germany, and had connections with senior medical people in Berlin, made a telephone call. Fortunately for many urgent cases, Henderson's telephone call enabled the local commandant to allow water for medical operations, although a restriction of supply was maintained a little longer for sanitation and personal hygiene purposes. Meanwhile, we inmates were on the receiving end, not only of German invective, but also the atmosphere in the hospital was dreadful.

The adverse hygiene conditions in the hospital were compounded by the antiquated method employed for the sterilisation of dressings and the other medical supplies available. At the rear of the hospital was a small exercise yard, where I was allowed out in the fresh air once I was competent with the use of crutches. I enjoyed many an hour there on fine mornings, when I was able to talk more freely with fellow prisoners, including chaps in the other wards.

Standing in the corner of the yard was a steam engine, resting on four wheels; a maker's plate on the side of the machine indicating that it was manufactured in Slovakia in the late 1890s. On most mornings the engine was fired up by the two Welsh Guardsmen who had carried me on the stretcher when I arrived at the hospital, who were employed as *arbeiters* (workers). They proceeded to place the material for sterilisation into a space in the boiler. This was later removed and used for medical operations and other treatment. Little wonder that the dreaded osteomyelitis was so prevalent![1]

---

[1] Particularly amongst RAF aircrew, many of whom suffered leg or ankle fractures after baling out of their stricken aircraft, mostly in darkness. Post war information released by the authorities indicated that out of total bomber crews of 125,000 (who were all volunteers) the casualties were 55,573 dead, 9,838 prisoners of war, 8,403 wounded. Total casualties were 73,814 – 59% of those who volunteered for Bomber Command operational duties – a high price paid by a young, educated group of dedicated airmen.

Within a few weeks of my arrival at Obermassfeld I was capable of wandering on my crutches around the ward and beyond into Ward 1, where all the critical cases, and those awaiting urgent operations, were lying in bed. Amongst them was a former Manchester Pilot, Warrant Officer Stan Packard, with whom I became friendly. He had a serious leg wound and suffered greatly and was eventually repatriated in an exchange of the seriously wounded.

Whilst in the exercise yard one morning I had the pleasure to meet with Flight Lieutenant Don Morrison, a Canadian pilot with 401 Squadron. Whilst flying a Spitfire Mark 9 aircraft in combat with a bunch of Focke-Wulf 190s over the Pas de Calais area, his right leg was hit by a cannon shell, but despite his terrible wounds he managed to bale out, leaving the bottom half of his leg in the aircraft.

He was taken into the German Hospital at Sainte Omer, not far from the Luftwaffe fighter station where the 190s were based. I learned that Don, who had earlier been awarded the DFM and DFC for gallantry in action, was in a critical condition for many days. Before he was taken into Sainte Omer hospital he was first carried across a narrow canal by a French farm worker and then driven about two miles, laid across a German army side-car unit. Later in this book, I recount that, with our wives, Don and I revisited the location and tracked down the Frenchman who had saved Don's life initially, as well as meeting other civilians, who recounted events of 8th November 1942.

On that day, Don told me that 401 Squadron, along with five other squadrons, had been escorting American B17 Fortresses, who were attacking a target in North East France. His hospital experience started before mine, and our meeting at Obermassfeld and resulted in a long and happy friendship, which lasted throughout the years until his death in February 1994. In November 1943 he was repatriated with the first batch of seriously wounded Allied servicemen, exchanged with a similar number of wounded Germans. Don was an athletic chap and I recall many a race through Ward 1 and out into the exercise yard on our crutches, which he invariably won.

By the time Easter arrived, late in April 1943, I was already well used to walking with the aid of crutches, although the plaster cast throughout the length of my left leg and the built up plaster heel were quite a heavy weight to carry along. Nevertheless, I was feeling much more confident and proceeded to the ground floor and out into the forecourt where I, along with fellow inmates, was photographed.

I was able also to climb a narrow stairway to a small room which was used as a dental surgery. There, I recall, on Easter Sunday morning, along with a couple of others, I attended Holy Communion, administered by the studious army POW padre attached to the hospital. This was an uplifting experience, but later that day, whilst lying quietly on my bed, thoughts turned to my home church and of my parents and family and dear Nita, attending the usual Easter services. These were always well attended, complete with the ladies wearing a new bonnet on Easter day. I longed to be with them, but thanked God for my improving health and the care of Major Bill Tucker and his team, who, with daily bed exercises, had got me on my feet again.

That Easter we at Obermassfeld were treated to a splendid cabaret called "Makers of Magic", written and produced by Doctor Silvester of our medical staff. He was the talented brother of bandleader Victor Silvester, whose orchestra was popular in England during the war. I enjoyed Dr Silvester's amusing show, which he had cleverly scripted to include scenes and dialogue for the consumption of a group of male prisoners of war. It was a great success and was followed later in the year by a show called "Alice in Wonderland", culminating on December 27th 1943 with a "Christmas Cabaret", presented by corporal Roland Egan, a very talented medical orderly in the RAMC. I remember this included a competent orchestra with original music and orchestration by Guy Boyd of the medical staff. Fellow combine member Don Coleman had the pleasure of playing the double bass in this show, which he performed with his usual aplomb.

These concerts, which occupied a great deal of time and skill in writing, also involved others in costume preparation and were very successfully produced by the medical staff and other workers, all of them prisoners who had already spent three years incarcerated by the Germans. It must have helped them combat the awful tedium of prison camp life. At the same time, they were a great morale booster and source of much pleasure for those of us who were suffering from wounds, depression or other illnesses. I will be forever grateful for their outstanding contribution.

I spent as much time as I was allowed by the German authorities outside during that hot summer of 1943. There I was able to breathe fresh air and avoid the obnoxious smell of rotting bone and burnt flesh. During one morning session I had the first of many conversations with Group Captain H.M. Massey, who was more than twice my age and old enough to be my father. His DSO and MC ribbons were awarded for outstanding service in the Royal Flying Corps in the First World War and I was intrigued by the presence of such a senior officer in our midst, sharing all the misery and deprivation of prisoner of war hospital life. He told me of his participation in the heavy Bomber Command raid on Essen on June 1st and 2nd 1942, which was "Bomber" Harris's follow-up raid to the previous night's 1,000-bomber raid on Cologne. Whilst Group Captains were not usually included in Bomber Command operational crews, I understood that G/C Massey had hitched a ride with the Flight Commander on No.7 Squadron, flying Stirling aircraft. He told me that he was the Commanding Officer of an Operational Training Unit and had been appointed to take up new duties with the Royal Air Force training programme in the United States of America. He wished to savour the atmosphere and action of Bomber Command on an intensive raid over Germany and decided on the 7 Squadron flight to Essen.

The enemy night fighter and flak defences were licking their wounds following the impressive involvement of force the night before on the 1,000 Bomber Cologne raid, when 3.9% of Bomber and Training Commands were lost. Then, on the Essen raid, 31 aircraft or 3.2% of the 956 aircraft taking part from Bomber and Flying Training Commands were missing. Amongst these was the sole loss of 7 Squadron aircraft, with Group Captain Massey aboard as an observer. I note in William Chorley's *Bomber Command Losses, Volume 3* that all of Massey's crew, captained by Flight Lieutenant Winch, baled out safely and became prisoners of war.

Nevertheless, after Obermassfeld, still with the ill effects of his damaged leg, Group Captain Massey moved on and became the Senior British Officer at Stalagluft 3, from whence he was repatriated in the exchange of wounded in April 1944. I recall being outside in the exercise yard with the Group Captain and a few others on a clear warm day, early in August 1943, when high up to the south, in the distance, we saw the vapour trails of large aircraft flying in formation. The sight of an American daylight attack deep inside Germany was most exciting and drew many morale-boosting remarks from the prisoners. The German guards looked upon this intrusion with despondency, which, following the earlier remarkable raid of the Rhur dams, set them back on their heels. It showed a further decline in their morale, which was so encouraging to us prisoners. We remember seeing enemy fighters, darting like flies through the bomber formations, and significant puffs of smoke, which then dropped earthwards.

The navigators amongst us were fairly certain that the bombers were attacking Schweinfurt, about forty miles due south of Obermassfeld, a strategically important centre for the manufacture of ball and roller bearings, which were vital components for aero engines and other moving parts necessary for a great deal of the enemy war machine. We knew that there was a tough battle being fought over enemy skies and some wounded American aircrew, who were prisoners with us in the hospital, gave us a candid account of the hazardous daylight operations of the 8th Air Force. Many of our American friends had been taken completely by surprise at the extent of enemy resistance, both from anti-aircraft gunfire and the Messerschmitt 109 and Focke-Wulf 190 fighters of the Luftwaffe. However, the episode, on that clear day in August 1943, provided a great boost to our morale.

To me, it was a firm indication that the Lord God was providing some answers to my daily prayers. This was a notable comfort to me. These prayers had also been answered earlier in June 1943, when I had the outstanding surprise and great pleasure of receiving mail for the first time after my capture, six months earlier. I had just returned to my bed, after my morning adventure to the exercise yard, when the ward orderly arrived with the daily mail distribution. We were about sixty prisoners in Ward 2 and there were practically always some lucky chaps on the receiving end of news from home ... and some unlucky ones receiving "Dear John" letters. On that morning, it was my delight to receive eight letters and eight postcards, sent by my parents and Nita during the period from January to May. There was no explanation of the delay in receiving my first mail, but I suspected that the German censor was trying to establish whether my letters incorporated some kind of code system. Nita's letters were written on the two sides of foolscap paper, which provided more space than a normal prisoner of war letter post form. She quickly grasped that the use of foolscap was permissible and I benefited from the receipt of much local news as well as comforting words from my sweetheart.

I also received one letter from my eldest sister, Phyllis, which, regrettably, had been severely censored by the British censor. (After my return home I discovered she had been writing to tell me of the removal of a large number of trees from woodland near our home, which had changed the nature of the landscape. Presumably, such information was considered useful to a potential enemy invader.) Nevertheless, letters from home were a great comfort and it was pleasing to know that they were receiving letters and cards regularly from me.

During those hot summer months of 1943, I was able to get around on my crutches and also had regained my general health and confidence. I developed a strong attraction to the countryside around Obermassfeld, a beautiful part of Thuringia, with hilly slopes of various evergreen trees. I noted that the road signs, on the corner, near the bridge over the river Werra, pointed to Meiningen, the nearest town, and to Coburg, Bamberg, Suhl and Badsalzungen. The area of Thuringia was steeped in a historical connection with England. This stemmed from the marriage of the Duke of Clarence to the Princess Adelaide from the small state of Meiningen. She was later to become Queen Consort of England when the Duke became King William IV in 1831. The charm of the Thuringian countryside, and the large area of forests, provided an attraction to the wealthy visitors and boar hunters of the time. Such views from the many hospital windows often induced a yearning for freedom to wander and take in the pleasant surroundings. Oh, I longed to be out, enjoying this lovely countryside, away from the smell and depressing hospital environment!

My leg had been in plaster for about four months and during this time, despite the regular exercises, specified by Major Tucker and the physio, there was a definite wasting of the encased thigh muscles. During these hot months, in the crowded accommodation, there was a progressive irritation around the hollow area between the heel and the rear of my ankle. This was getting worse and one of my Polish air force friends fashioned a kind of claw at the end of a long thin wooden stick, which I was able to squeeze down in the space between my thinning leg and the plaster. This provided much laughter for my friends, but, along with some powder which a kind medical orderly supplied, it brought some relief. In due course, Major Tucker decided on a further x-ray, which unfortunately showed that the fractured area of the tibia was not reforming as it should. A closer examination of the leg was necessary to see if a bone graft or possible amputation of the lower leg would be required. When the plaster was bi-valved, the wasting leg looked a sorry sight, with skin infection, especially around the ankle and the heel. The surgeon was, therefore, unable to carry out any surgery and was disappointed with my progress. I was likewise depressed at this setback in my recovery.

There were no antibiotics available to treat the infected area but, after a clean up and some treatment, Bill Tucker decided to put the leg back into the two halves of the plaster and bind them tightly together, so that the broken limb was in a contained state throughout its length. He explained that he would closely monitor any progress. I had already been moved from Ward 3 to Ward 1 for the intended bone graft, where I stayed for many weeks. When one moved from one bed to another, the chalked nameplate was also moved and placed, outward facing, at the foot of the bed.

This move resulted in a very strange story with a regrettably sad conclusion. A patient in Ward 2 was a young army private from Melyncrythan near Neath, my home town. He had been badly wounded when the lower half of his face was shot away in the Battle for France in 1940. For the next three years he was a patient, requiring major surgery, and I met him at Obermassfeld early in 1943, whilst I was in Ward 3. He often walked through Ward 1 to the exercise yard, his face heavily bandaged and his speech adversely affected. That September, when passing through Ward 1, he noticed the name 'Bloxham' on the bed where I was now awaiting surgery for a bone graft. He didn't stop to talk to me but somehow assumed that the person now in Ward 1 was another 'Bloxham'. A couple of months later he returned to the United Kingdom on the first repatriation of the severely wounded, exchanged for a similar number of wounded Germans held prisoner in the UK. His homecoming was mentioned in the local newspaper and my mother, accompanied by

Nita, went to see him at Neath Hospital. They were appalled at his wounded face and difficulty in speaking. However he happened to say that he had met two people named Bloxham at Obermassfeld hospital. This information was a comfort for them to hear at first hand about me, but for Mother it also raised the hope that her eldest son Jack, who had been shot down on a raid on Berlin at the end of August, was alive, although regrettably in hospital. This conversation prompted mother to write to me, asking if I had met Jack and if he was he badly wounded. On receipt of this letter from home some weeks later, I enquired if it was true that there were two Bloxhams in the hospital. As I suspected, the answer was negative, but, of course, I was greatly concerned to establish what had happened to my brother.

Prior to the terrible events that had overtaken me the previous December, I knew that Jack had been accepted for aircrew training and had commenced an air gunnery course. Since then I had received no further news and knowing only too well the danger involved in wartime operational flying, I was always concerned about him. Some time in June, in one of her letters, mother informed me in a coded message that Jack was busy in his profession but had moved to a new address: 90 New Street, Cambridge. I thus concluded Jack was now on operations with 90 Squadron, based in Cambridgeshire. There were frequent new arrivals at Obermassfeld of unfortunate Bomber Command casualties and I sought the first opportunity of establishing their squadron's number. I remember being very relieved to meet a navigator who had been flying Stirling aircraft with 90 Squadron from their base at Wratting Common in Cambridgeshire. He had severe arm injuries, sustained when baling out of a crippled bomber. He told me that he knew Jack, who was well and very actively involved with the squadron, which had been involved in the very intensive bombing campaign throughout the summer of 1943. My informant thought Jack, who flew in Warrant Officer Callaway's crew, had completed more than twenty operations and was near the completion of his tour. It was therefore with much apprehension that I pondered Jack's safety and prayed to God to help and protect him in his courageous endeavour. I knew from bitter experience that he was endangering his life each time he flew in the face of the flak and fighters of a determined enemy.

I had been in Ward 1 for only a couple of weeks when it was necessary for my bed to be occupied by an airman who arrived in a very bad state and surgery was urgent to save his life. In view of the lack of progress with my fractured leg, which was also infected, I was afraid that I too might succumb to osteomyelitis, which would be a serious setback. This resulted in my being depressed and worried about my future. At this point Major Tucker decided that, because he could not operate, he would send me to another POW hospital at Kloster Haina, which housed an overspill of patients from Obermassfeld. So, early one morning at the end of September, the orderlies roused me and, along with Don Coleman and about twelve other patients, who were all capable of walking with aid of crutches, I was taken by German army truck to Obermassfeld railway station. Two armed guards were assigned to accompany us and we had been supplied with some bread and sausage for our sustenance. This was just as well, because it took about twelve hours, on a meandering route, to reach our destination.

This, for me, was an exciting journey, because I was able to sit up and see the countryside as the slow train wound its way, with many stopping points, through the very pleasant countryside of central Germany. We wound our way north to change trains at a sizeable junction, Eisenach, where we saw much military movement and some industry. Our small group consisted of some army and air force patients with leg, arm or shoulder injuries. We all had plasters or similar dressings, so none was in a fit state to escape. At each change or stopping point we attracted the attention of the many civilians and enemy soldiers, who seemed sullen, appeared to detest us and would no doubt have given vent to their feelings if we had not been guarded.

From Eisenach I remember the route took us towards Kassel, but we again changed at a small station and junction a few miles to the south. Whilst waiting on this small platform I noticed that the German trains were all marked with bold lettering along their locomotive boilers *"Radden mussen rollen fur den sieg"* which I took to mean "Wheels must roll for victory". This was one of Dr Goebbels' propaganda slogans, seen all over Germany and the occupied countries.

Our arrival at a large hospital, built around an old monastery in the hills near Haina, was soon noted by the inmates many of whom we knew. When we had been searched and processed by the security guards, Don Coleman and I were assigned to a ward that contained many of our many air force chums who had passed through Obermassfeld. I was also able to catch up with Frank Tierney who I hadn't seen since the previous December at Amsterdam. He had recovered from his injuries and felt much better, finding life at Haina more tolerable. We were able to converse quite freely in the open spaces around the wards, where there were pleasant grass areas on which we were able to relax and where sometimes the very large contingent of leg amputees used to enjoy football matches and other exercises, despite the disability of being on one peg leg. The limbless were not provided with artificial limbs by the enemy. Nevertheless, they had become quite mobile after, in many cases, more than three years since they were wounded and captured in France.

There were also more than a hundred blind cases who, despite their severe disability and the extra difficulties it imposed on them compared to other prisoners, kept quite cheerful. Their ability to cope and maintain a positive demeanour, had a profound effect on my feelings and I thanked God for my life and for not being as badly handicapped as so many of my compatriots. I appealed to my Lord and master to comfort them in their disabled condition.

Both Frank and I had not met up with anyone else from the Squadrons based at Tempsford. Therefore, we were both still uncertain whether or not we had flown into a prepared trap set by the Germans on our last fateful flight together. It was pleasing to hear that Frank had been receiving regular mail for many months and that Maureen had produced a healthy child, despite the adverse effect of Frank being reported missing. I understood that Maureen and the boy were both getting on favourably, despite having no father around. They were living with Maureen's parents near Poole and did not have the added involvement of Frank's family, who lived in Brockville, a small town near the Saint Lawrence River in far-off Canada.

Within a week or so Frank and I were again separated when he was discharged from hospital. Along with a few other air force and American comrades who had recovered sufficiently from their wounds, he was sent to Stalagluft VI, situated near the East Prussian border in Lithuania, thought by the Germans to be too remote for anyone to successfully escape from.

Later in October there was a great buzz of excitement that all the patients, who had already been certified by the medical commission, were to be repatriated. This was the first exchange of wounded in World War Two, organised by the Swiss government, acting as the protecting power. Along with the two belligerent powers, they had set up a commission which inspected the prisoner-of-war hospitals and camps many months earlier and selected about 3,000 of the worst cases – prisoners who were blind or suffering with very serious diseases, or with leg or arm amputations – to be included in the first exchange.

Within this number were many unfortunate chaps who had originally been selected for repatriation in 1941. Some had travelled from hospitals or camps, with great hopes of returning home and to their loved ones. Some were even on board a hospital ship in a French Mediterranean port when the repatriation was cancelled. Their return to prison conditions was a bitter disappointment, never to be forgotten, but their spirits were again raised as they left Haina for the repatriation centre late in October 1943.

Amongst those who set out from Sagan (Stalagluft III) was my Canadian friend Flt/Lieutenant Don Morrison, who told me later that the hospital ships finally docked with the wounded passengers in November. Everyone, including Don, was exuberant with joy and in his case amongst the many instructions awaiting him was a request to report to Buckingham Palace, where he was awarded the DFC and DFM for gallantry whilst flying with 401 Squadron – a great honour for a good and very courageous guy. Don's return to Canada was therefore delayed slightly, but he returned to a great welcome at his home near Toronto and to his longstanding sweetheart, Jean. Having no time to arrange for an artificial leg, he walked to the altar on crutches when he and Jean were married on December 28th 1943.

The departure of the repatriated from Kloster Haina left the remainder of us feeling quite down, but within a day or two a further group arrived from Obermassfeld, with much news about their own experiences and of the medical progress of many friends, but sadly with none of my brother Jack.

I felt much better in the Haina environment, away from the smell and confinement of Obermassfeld Hospital. This was a good psychological move by Major Tucker, which was later to produce favourable results. Whilst taking a walk outside with Don Coleman and a few other air force chums one day in late October, I was thrilled to hear the familiar roar of Rolls-Royce Merlin engines. Looking up, we spotted three Mosquitos, flying fast, in close formation. They appeared to be no more than about 3,000 feet above us. Seeing these aircraft in broad daylight, flying on an operational mission deep over enemy territory, thus indicating our ascendancy in the air battle against the Germans, was a great boost to our morale.

At the end of October about ten of us were told to be up and ready early the following morning for a move back to Obermassfeld. Armed with just my crutches and a small bag, I, along with my colleagues was duly loaded on a German army lorry next morning and, accompanied by two armed guards, we were taken about a mile to the nearest railway station. I remember the weather was fine and there was much bustle as the locals from nearby Haina village were setting out. Soon we boarded a section of a passenger train and settled down to a pleasant journey through beautiful countryside. It was a slow trip, stopping at all the local stations, until we pulled up at a junction a few miles south of Kassel. There we detrained, awaiting a connection to take us on to Eisenach.

Whilst waiting on the platform a number of trainloads of people, mainly women and children, came from the direction of Kassel. Some of the passengers left at our station were carrying heavy bags and other belongings. They were angry and when it become known that we were British Prisoners of War, some in RAF uniform, a crowd of them moved threateningly in our direction. Quickly realising our danger, we immediately formed our group into an outward facing square with our crutches and sticks at the ready to defend ourselves. Our two guards, with rifles at the ready, stood their ground and defended us. I remember one of our party was a Major in the Canadian Army, badly wounded in a shoulder and an arm during the landing at Dieppe the previous year. He was able to advise us airmen, who were in the majority, how best to beat off the threatening horde. When the next train came in we were hustled aboard, having just avoided a serious threat to our lives.

The guards explained that the angry crowds were being evacuated from nearby Kassel which had been heavily bombed a few nights previously, following a previous raid by our bomber force earlier in the month. Kassel was a sizeable manufacturing town which, according to my Bomber Command friends, had been targeted for a raid, especially on the Henschel factories, making "V" flying bomb weapons and other related industries.

It was a terrifying experience and the tension was only relieved when our train moved off. Regrettably, what we had witnessed was a natural reaction of the civilian population to being involved in a 'total war'. Yet the efforts of our bomber forces were vital in defeating a Germany under the control of a regime prepared to use any methods to achieve European, and possibly worldwide, domination. Subsequent revelations confirmed what a terrible enemy we were facing.

During the few rail journeys I undertook as a prisoner of war, I witnessed many trains of cattle-type enclosed wagons, carrying large numbers of people, presumably to work or death camps. When these trainloads of victims halted, sometimes adjacent to our own prison wagons, the smell and cries of the anguished was clearly apparent. I shuddered to think that our lot as prisoners of war in the hands of the enemy was very precarious. It seemed that many of the enemy-occupied working populations and their families were being conveyed to work for Germany or something more sinister. In time the world would know the truth...

Meanwhile, our journey back to Obermassfeld continued through the pleasant autumn countryside of the Thuringwald. My diary of events indicated that we covered a little over one hundred miles and it took about twelve hours, due to our meandering route through the hills and the many scheduled stops. Apart from the unpleasant attitude of the populace, I enjoyed the comparative freedom of sitting up and viewing what I could, and in quiet contemplation I closed my eyes with a prayer of thankfulness for the Lord's mercy.

Darkness had set in by the time we arrived back at Obermassfeld and again having to clear all the German security checks including fingerprints and photographs. After tucking into our Red Cross food supplies, Don Coleman and I were again allocated to Ward 3, where we met up with former fellow patients and some new Royal Air Force and American Air Force wounded. It was good to hear news from home and of the continuing success of air operations over Germany and the occupied countries. It was encouraging to hear of successful raids on Berlin and other important targets, especially the pranging of

Peenemunde, in August 1943, where the "V" weapons were being developed and tested, and Hamburg, in July, with its proliferation of submarine manufacture and other important industries.

I was particularly impressed and excited to hear first-hand of the success of OBOE and H2S as navigational aids, which had been introduced to our bomber force after I was shot down. It was also good news to hear of the outstanding success the first time 'window' was used in the Hamburg raids. The American airmen I met were full of their achievements in daylight operations, although one of their B17 Fortress crewmen told me there were heavy casualties in the raid on the industrial town of Schweinfurt, due to the extremely active enemy fighters. This would have been the raid we were watching in the distance from the Obermassfeld exercise yard earlier in the year. Regrettably, there was no one in the new intake of patients from either 138 Squadron or Jack's 90 Squadron and I continued to be increasingly worried about him. The bombing campaign had been stepped up a gear or two in 1943 and there were increasing numbers of casualties coming into Obermassfeld each few weeks. The proportion of air force casualties at the hospital was increasing all the time.

The day after we returned to Obermassfeld, Major Tucker arranged an x-ray and examination of my leg and he was very happy to convey good news. He said that during my stay at Kloster Haina there had been some bone growth around the fractures in my left tibia and the fractured fibula, which seemed to have united in an overlapping of the bone structure. Furthermore, the skin infections of my leg and foot had healed. It was therefore decided to continue to support the leg in the bi-valved plaster, which was bound tightly, and I was encouraged to exercise the limb as much as possible.

I was particularly pleased that I was now able to move my toes slightly in the damaged leg, which indicated that the threat of paralysis of the ankle and foot was subsiding. After a few weeks, a further x-ray indicated sufficient recovery of bone formation to remove the bi-valved plaster and, with much physiotherapy and exercise, I was able to walk slowly, initially with the aid of crutches, then to much joy I used two sticks to get around the hospital. The physiotherapist, a Captain in a Scots Regiment, was most helpful and advised me on each step of recovery. He said I would always have the left leg shorter by about half an inch than the right, but by careful control of my walking I could overcome the need of having a built-up shoe. I was encouraged to walk facing a long mirror and soon was perambulating with care.

Although housed in the miserable conditions of Obermass-feld, I had a much more enjoyable Christmas in 1943 than a year earlier. To me, the highlight was the Holy Communion service, conducted by the residential Army Padre in the room normally used by the army dentist. It was attended by a few of the hospital patients and staff and the Padre had scrounged some wine and a morsel of black bread, which sufficed as the sacrament, given in the name of Jesus. I felt uplifted and prepared to face the future with more confidence.

Don Coleman and I had saved some food from our Red Cross supplies and we shared a tin of bacon and some hard tack biscuits crushed up and made a kind of 'cake'. There was a drop of illicit wine, prepared from potatoes or other scrounged material, which was rather potent, but on Christmas day was the source of much merriment (and in many cases the overindulgent were sick). Our capable concert party also produced an amusing cabaret. We used to troop across the road, carefully guarded, to a small hall, which allowed an audience of about two hundred to enjoy a couple of hours of revelry and break the tedium of prison life.

Invariably when airmen were deemed by the medical authorities to be fit enough or beyond cure due to the limited resources available, they were moved on to a Stalagluft. These camps were run by the Luftwaffe and so towards the end of January 1944, along with seven other Royal Air Force comrades I was told one evening that I must be up and away by 6 am to be escorted to Stalagluft VI at Heydekrug, just over the East Prussian border, in Lithuania. It was a most agonising journey, with our wagon appended to a series of freight trains, in the depths of winter, through Eastern Germany, Poland and East Prussia.

After passing through the endless petrochemical complex of Halle and Leipzig, we stopped on the first night for some ersatz soup at Cottbus, in South East Berlin. On the stone platform we were prevented from sleeping by the intense cold and the continuing wrath of passing civilians. In the early hours we were shunted onto the end of a goods train and through heavy snow continued this unhappy journey as far as Thorn in Poland. There we halted for a few hours alongside a Wehrmacht Training Camp, seeing the very sorry sight of ill-clad Cossacks, who had been won over and were now in training for service in mounted battalions of the German army. There was also much Luftwaffe activity in the area.

After a freezing third day in the unheated wagon, we were shunted into the sidings at Insterburg, a major staging post in East Prussia for the northern sector of the Russian front, and near Hitler's Command Headquarters, where the July 1944 an attempt on his life took place.

By this time we were suffering with dysentery and very depressed. To crown this misery, we were marched in darkness through the snow for about a mile to a transit camp where, exhausted, we stopped for the night. How we made that walk using our sticks, some with crutches, still haunts me, but I recall arriving at our destination in complete darkness, where, stumbling about, we found an unheated hut, with wooden bunks three high, and a bowl of the inevitable tasteless soup. We were exhausted and tried to sleep, only to be bitten alive by lice, which emerged from the bags of wood shavings on which we lay. The following morning we were given a slice of black bread and a cup of acorn coffee. We then struggled back in the snow to the railhead.

Returning to the terrible wagon, which appeared to have square wheels, we continued for a further eight hours, during which we were attacked by Russian aircraft. After travelling for many miles along the Baltic Coast we were impressed with the large numbers of storks flying around in the marshes that flanked the railway.

Eventually, we de-trained and were conveyed about three miles in a horse-drawn wagon through the sandy forest to Stalagluft VI, where our smelly, bedraggled group found relief in the comparative warmth of the very crowded Luftwaffe Prison Camp where six thousand Air Force compatriots were detained. But how glad we were to be with our own once again! It marked the end of a nightmare.

4.   Stalagluft VI (Heydekrug)

It was bitterly cold and snowing on February 2nd 1944 when our bedraggled group arrived at Stalagluft VI. We passed through the guarded gates of an outer barbed wire enclosure. There, we were taken to the camp commander's administration hut, where the escorting guard handed over our small group to the Luftwaffe staff, who proceeded to check our papers. We were then searched, fingerprinted and photographed. This was the fifth occasion that I had been subjected to these measures, which seemed to be a wasteful procedure and showed a lack of cohesion between different administration sections of the German army and air force.

It was late in the day when these formalities were completed and we were escorted into A (Lager) Compound, where a small crowd of RAF prisoners, which included some who had been with me at Obermassfeld, waved their greeting as we were taken to the Compound Office. There, we were greeted warmly by Dixie Dean, the Camp Leader, and Ron Mogg. After careful questioning they were satisfied with our bona fides and after a brief explanation of the camp rules they allocated us rooms. Because of our particular disabilities, Don Coleman and I were allotted ground level bunks in hut A6, which we found without too much difficulty.

Stalagluft VI was a large Luftwaffe prisoner of war camp with approximately 6,000 British, Commonwealth and American airmen. 'A' Lager contained 2,500 British and Commonwealth, 'K' Lager about 1500 British and Commonwealth, with about 2,000 Americans in 'C' Lager. It was situated about three miles inland of the Eastern Baltic Coast in Lithuania, near the isthmus that thrust itself out from the northern coast of East Prussia into the Baltic Sea. The camp was built in 1943 by the Todt organisation, using forced labour groups of Russian prisoners of war.

The site, in an isolated area near a pine forest, was clearly chosen by the Germans to be away from the civilian population and because the loose sandy soil made tunnelling very difficult, even with the aid of a few tools. These were usually available and were, principally, shovels and odd implements, stolen from the Russian Compound, or left deliberately by our Russian comrades when they came into our Compound under armed guard to work on the buildings or site drainage problems.

There were thirty-six rooms, each with sixty NCO airmen crowded in each room, with wooden bunks, three bunks high in the centre, tapering down to two bunks high towards the sides. There was a central stove and weak electric lighting, which was completely inadequate to read by after the sun went down and the shutters were closed on the outside of the small windows at each end of the living space. Throughout the time until doors and shutters were opened at about 7 am each morning, the only toilet arrangement in each room consisted of a bucket, used for all sanitary purposes and emptied by prisoners in rotation. This was carried to the communal toilet, which comprised two lines of planks facing each other, about six feet apart, below which was a smelly, slow-running stream of water and excrement. Approximately thirty prisoners could sit down at a time to do their ablutions, quite an unpleasant set of circumstances, also humiliating, as no toilet paper was provided.

Despite the very crude conditions, spirits amongst my new roommates were high. They were a mixed bunch of pilots, navigators, engineers, wireless operators, bomb aimers and gunners and had been flying a range of aircraft, in the different air commands, from the UK and in other theatres of war. They were mainly composed of 1,700 NCOs who had arrived from Stalaluft III in June 1943, followed closely by some American NCO airmen. (At the time, Stalagluft III, at Sagan in Poland, was being used as a prison camp for officers of the British and American Air Forces.)

Some of the Royal Air Force contingent had been prisoners a long time, including Larry Slattery and George Booth, who had been shot down on a daylight armed reconnaissance raid on the Schilling Roads, near Wilhelmshaven, on 4th September 1939. They became the first unfortunate airmen to become prisoners in World War Two. Whilst they were both wounded on capture, the pilot of their Blenheim Mark IV fighter, Bomber Sergeant A.S. Prince, was killed, along with all nine aircrew manning the three other 107 Squadron aircraft shot down over the target area. I understand the raid was carried out at the request of the Admiralty, who wished to obtain an accurate report on the disposition of the German capital ships at the outbreak of war. It proved a disastrous result for the top brass of Royal Air Force, who were forced to review their daylight bomber operations so early in the campaign.

When I met Larry and George, at Stalagluft VI, they were surprisingly fit and mentally alert, despite having been confined for four and a half years already. Larry, an Irishman by birth, had a splendid sense of humour; that, and his favourite indulgence, of playing the violin, helped him maintain his equilibrium. His splendid constitution and mental alertness was a great help in postwar years, when he was a most loyal and hardworking secretary of the Royal Air Forces Ex Prisoner of War Association. It also served him well during the untimely death of his wife, whom he had married before the commencement of hostilities in September 1939. George Booth survived the terrible ordeal of more than five and a half years imprisonment reasonably well, and, at some stage, decided to enjoy his postwar years in a sunny Mediterranean location. He later returned to his home country. He died a few years ago.

The remainder of prisoners – including many who had spent some years away from their families in enforced captivity behind the wire – were a cheerful collection of resourceful young airmen from the Mother Country and the Commonwealth. In addition, there were many from occupied European countries who, after escaping the German occupation, joined the Royal Air Force to take the fight to the fearsome enemy who had occupied their home countries. The Polish and Czech airmen were well represented in our operational squadrons and many had the misfortune to suffer the same fate as we from the UK had experienced in becoming POWs.

It was a very crowded camp, though initially there was some space between the four rows of huts and a pathway had been trodden just inside the tripwire around the huts. It was, therefore, possible to exercise and simultaneously have a conversation with a fellow prisoner, without being overheard by any "bugging" contrived by the Germans.

At intervals around the barbed wire security fence the enemy installed loudspeakers to broadcast their never-ending propaganda and news bulletins. The prisoners took no notice of this crude activity; they received their news from home via the BBC, using their own, secretly assembled, radio receiver. This was taken down in shorthand, quickly typed up in the camp office and read out by volunteers, who had their own specific rooms to service each day. Peter Thomas, a Sergeant Pilot, later to become a barrister, MP and Minister of State for Wales, was the newsreader for our hut. The radio receiver was secretly dismantled after each daily broadcast and the components well hidden from the prying eyes of the 'ferrets' and Gestapo agents when they frequently carried out searches.

In October 1943, the NCO fliers from Stalagluft I at Barth in Northern Germany moved into 'K' Lager, a further compound built at Heydekrug. They numbered about 1,500 and contained chaps, mainly from the UK, with a good representation from the Commonwealth countries, particularly Canada, Australia and New Zealand. There were also men from most of the occupied countries, who lived in constant fear for the safety of their families with the possibility that German intelligence could ascertain their home locations.

When I arrived at Heydekrug, early in February 1944, I had great joy in rejoining our rear gunner Frank Tierney, who I last saw at Kloster Haina. He was confined to 'K' Lager, along with the others, when they were moved from Stalagluft I (Barth). He had been checking the lists of new arrivals at Heydekrug ever since and his vigilance was rewarded when my name appeared on the list for 'A' Lager. He was soon able to get a message to me by the daily movement of special representatives between compounds and we met at the adjoining barbed wire and warning fences one morning. We had to converse with raised voices, as we were about twenty-five yards apart, so remained guarded in the content of our conversation, as we knew that the Germans had incorporated bugging devices in the security fence at intervals, along with the loudspeaker system that surrounded each compound.

It was a wonderful experience meeting up again and seeing Frank quite fit and in good spirits. He apparently had experienced a tough interrogation at Dulagluft, when he was surprised at the extent of the German knowledge. This, presumably, was along similar lines to my grilling by the interrogators at Hohemark. After Dulagluft he spent some time at both Obermassfeld and Kloster Haina, in both cases preceding my admission to these hospitals. His broken ankle and other facial wounds had recovered well, thus enabling him to progress more quickly than I was able to. We parted, having agreed to rendezvous, at the same time and place, in three days. We also committed ourselves to seek an opportunity to cross through the barbed wire gates with one of the work parties moving between compounds.

With our bag of wood shavings and two rather coarse German army blankets, we were expected to rest ourselves in a dark room with sixty fellow prisoners and no source of fresh air. It was an unpleasant environment at nighttimes, particularly when my body warmed up and the lice sought human flesh, leaving many small red marks on my skin as I inspected their blood sucking intrusions. It was also a necessary routine to shake my blankets each morning, when the insects were released from the sanctuary of the previous night.

I had arrived at the camp very tired after the four nights unpleasant journey from Obermassfeld, but I was not able to settle down to a good night's sleep for some weeks. I found that, despite the noise and constant movements by the inmates of room A6, I managed to sleep occasionally in the daytime.

Our food situation depended on Red Cross parcels, there being no facilities for individual cooking, only a communal facility available in the cookhouse. This was sited some distance from our living accommodation, requiring volunteers, under a rota system, each day to convey the warm tea, coffee or hot food in buckets. The Germans rations were minimal and consisted of a small ration of low-quality potatoes normally each lunchtime, with a daily issue of one seventh of a loaf of black bread, which had a powdery crust like sawdust. Once a week, a minute ration of ersatz margarine and a spoonful of jam were added. I am convinced that without the British and Canadian Red Cross parcels, serious malnutrition and other diseases would have resulted in a high degree of starvation and death amongst prisoners in the German-controlled camps.

It is an interesting reflection that thoughts of good food and having a good meal were the favourite subjects of conversation amongst my comrades, as we ate our meagre daily intake. Each day a team of two from each room was required to clean potatoes for the sixty occupants. We presented ourselves at the cookhouse with stools to sit on and a knife each. The potatoes were weighed out in a bucket, depending on the number to be fed. On completion, the peelings were then weighed and the percentage of waste posted up on a board in the cookhouse for all to see. The couple with the highest percentage were then sent back by their room mates the following day, until they ceased to be the biggest waste producers. This was a useful endeavour, devised by the prisoners, to minimise the waste each day and thus marginally improve the number of grammes available for consumption.

I was always bothered by the inferior quality of the potatoes, which had far too many eyes and other skin blemishes, but Don Coleman and I were never top of the waste list and we always had help to take our stools with us, because of our leg disabilities. We were also fortunate to be provided with a signed chit from the camp doctor, to be excused APPEL, the twice-daily count of inmates, which the Germans carried out in the open area provided for physical exercises and competitive games of all kinds. The rugger matches were the most physical on the hard, grass-free pitches. I remember seeing one of the players, sporting a Wasps jersey, being carried off one day. Gladly, it was not a serious injury.

Life amongst two thousand young airmen was never dull, despite most having lost members of their crew when they suffered the wretched experience of baling out, or crashing in enemy occupied territory, or when their squadron members were killed in action. We who survived such terrifying experiences thanked God for his mercy and intervention, many saying how lucky we were. Most of the men with whom I had much contact were Christian minded and the Sunday services, held by the camp padre, were usually well attended. We often sung one of my favourite hymns to absent friends:

> *Holy Father in Thy mercy*
> *Hear our anxious prayers*
> *Keep our loved ones, now far distant,*
> *Neath Thy care.*

> *Jesus Saviour, let Thy presence*
> *Be their light and guide*
> *Keep, oh keep them, in their weakness,*
> *At Thy side.*

> *When in sorrow, when in danger,*
> *When in loneliness,*
> *In Thy love look down and comfort*
> *Their distress.*

May the joy of Thy salvation
Be their strength and stay
May they love and may they praise Thee
Day by day.

Holy Spirit, let Thy teaching
Sanctify their life
Send Thy grace, that they may conquer
In the strife.

Father, Son and Holy Spirit
God the One in Three
Bless them, guide them, save them, keep them
Near to Thee.

These words were so moving to us, who were forcibly separated from our loved ones. We yearned for their presence and each time we sung the hymn I was left with tears in my eyes and a large lump in my throat.

Apart from the enriching Christian worship, there was much cultural activity at the camp. There was a library of over 5,000 books and a large quantity of gramophone records, supplied mainly by the British Red Cross and St John War Organisation, supplemented by items sent to individual prisoners by their families. The average age of airmen prisoners would have been in the early twenties, but there were quite a few older chaps, who had been in the regular air force and were flying at the outset of hostilities. These, and others in their late twenties, were usually qualified in a profession or trade and were sufficiently competent in their subjects to hold lectures and classes, which were thoroughly organised to enable other prisoners to study and reach professional examination status.

The examinations were held under the supervision of the Education Committee of E. Alderton, C.J. Springett and G. Higginbottom, all men qualified in their professions and approved by the authorities in England to invigilate at the examinations. Overall responsibility was held by James (Dixie) Deans, a member of the UK Civil Service before he became a Sergeant Pilot in Bomber Command, and a very efficient and capable prison camp leader. His knowledge of the German language and courageous handling of enemy officers inspired fellow prisoners to withstand the ordeal and kept their morale at a high level.

The school at Stalagluft VI was an outstanding achievement and described, in their publication of January 1945, by the Educational Books Section, Prisoner of War Department Organisation of the British Red Cross Society and Order of St John of Jerusalem New Bodleian, Oxford as follows:

> *"It is clear that more than ordinary willpower is needed to enable men to concentrate under the distracting and unnatural conditions of prison life, and those who make this effort (whether they achieve success in examinations or not) give proof of that strength of character and stability which, the war won, will help us keep the peace."*

With much enthusiasm, I attended lectures in mathematics, engineering and economics. The latter introduced new thinking, as, hitherto, my education had been technically orientated, but I was greatly influenced by reading the economics and commerce textbooks of a roommate, who was taking examinations for the Chartered Institute of Secretaries. These provided an insight into the theory of corporate and global economics, which had so far eluded me in my educational development.

I was worried at the extent of my leg disability, which, at that stage, was painful to stand on or to walk distances of more than two hundred yards or so, without the aid of a walking stick. This condition put doubt in my mind about my future career, which, hitherto, was to have been in aeronautical engineering. I was only in my 20th year, committed to the Royal Air Force for a further 10 years, but without a clear sense that my service career could continue, due to my injuries.

I was also still in the dark with regard to circumstances of my aircraft being shot down on December 23rd 1942. Conversations with Frank had not clarified matters, nor had I met any other members of my squadron whilst in captivity, with whom I could compare experiences, which might have led to some understanding of the situation. Nevertheless, I was resolved to discover the truth, if possible, one day…

Within a few days of my arrival in hut A6 I noticed that Nat Leaman, a Sergeant Navigator, whose bunk was on ground level, about ten feet from mine, was engaged in deep conversation with one of the Luftwaffe staff. On closer examination I could see he was an Unter Officer, equivalent to a corporal in our air force, and not wearing an overall suit, as worn by the German security men, who patrolled and probed in the sandy soil around and under the prison huts. They were speaking quietly in German, but at times this became more intense. Inquisitively, I enquired of other roommates what Nat was up to, and was told that he was a leading member of the "Tally-Ho Club", the camp counter security and escape organisation, which was quite active. Many of the prisoners at Heydedrug had been at Sagan and were aware of the Tally Ho Club, which had been formed there, gaining a great deal of experience of escape attempts and the preparation and organisation necessary to perpetrate them.

I was soon briefed on the activities of the organisation at Heydekrug by friends in our room and volunteered to help in any way that my limited knowledge of the German language would allow. My services as a stooge were soon put to use and I was sent to sit at various vantage points, observing the movement of the German security "ferrets" when they approached a sensitive area where map-making, forgeries of German documents or the designing and sewing of escape garments was being undertaken.

The escape organisation, controlled by Dixie Deans, Jack Alexander and Alan Morris, had already had some success in masterminding escapes and an essential requirement of their plans was to achieve complete infiltration of the German security system. Nat Leaman was allocated the responsibility of bribing the guards and ferrets with coffee, cigarettes, chocolate and other items not easily obtainable in the Reich. Such exchanges of maps, uniforms, badges, cameras and radio components for our goodies was particularly attractive to the Germans just before they went on leave.

Some of the security staff, like Adolf Munkert (the security man who was deep in conversation in A6 with Nat Leaman) had not only fallen for the goodies, it transpired they were actually anti Hitler and the Nazis. Munkert proved very useful to the Tally Ho organisation, believing that he would be "looked after" at the cessation of hostilities. In the event, Munkert, Sommers (the camp photographer) and others were later eliminated by the Gestapo. The German counter-intelligence organisation (*Abwehr*) was much involved in tracking down those who had escaped using the assistance of Munkert, who provided much that was needed to break out. He also acted as a means of communication from Danzig, and other areas, to report back on the escapees' progress to "Tally Ho".

The most active escaper from Stalagluft 6 was George Grimson, who had been a prisoner since July 1940, having been shot down flying a Wellington bomber in the Middle East. He had made several unsuccessful escape attempts from previous camps in which he had been incarcerated, the most recent disguised as a Luftwaffe electrician from Stalagluft III at Sagan. He was recaptured after five days of eventful freedom, but he was soon escaping again, within a few weeks of being transferred with the NCO contingent to Heydekrug.

His escape from Luft 6 in January 1944 was well planned and organised by the Tally Ho organisation. Grimson, by now well-spoken in German, was disguised as a Luftwaffe camp guard. Off duty and relaxed he mingled with the other guards as they passed through the security gates at the end of their day's duty. He was provided by fellow Kriegie Wilfred Harrison with a key to the hut, about a mile from the camp, which held an overflow of prisoners' possessions. Harrison had earlier craftily engineered his appointment as camp storekeeper for the issue of cutlery, bowls, etc to fellow prisoners. Along with a few other "Kriegies", under armed guard, he would, at intervals, push a handcart containing such possessions, in named Red Cross boxes. On one such journey a set of civilian clothes was taken and secreted in the hut, awaiting Grimson, who changed from his Luftwaffe uniform, which was then returned to the camp with the next load of possessions to be made available for a further escape. Grimson, now dressed as a dock worker, made for the port area of Danzig, where he was to find a safe house and establish an escape line from Heydekrug and guide following escapees to a safe ship, destined for Sweden.

This dangerous mission was particularly successful and Grimson continued to communicate with Tally Ho using the co-operative Munkert, who was risking everything in this bold venture. Following Grimson, the indefatigable Bruce Flockhart escaped, disguised as a well-dressed surveyor and, despite the icy wintry weather, met up with Grimson in the Danzig area. There he was guided to a place to stay and disguised with overalls and seaman's cap he temporarily became a Swedish seaman. Despite the intensive attention of the dockside guards and the strong presence of Gestapo agents, he managed to crawl through a gap that had been prepared in the dock fence and was guided to a Swedish ship, soon to be sailing to a neutral Swedish port. From Sweden he was flown by Mosquito to safety in the UK. This was a magnificent effort, in which Grimson excelled. Awarded a DCM for his bold escape and promoted to Squadron Leader, Paddy Flockhart continued to assist air force prisoners of war from the UK.

Meanwhile, Jock Callender was next out. When clear of the camp he made his way to Danzig and spoke to a Polish underground worker there, but failed to contact Grimson. Nothing more was heard of him and it was concluded that he fell into the hands of the alert Gestapo and was eliminated. The same fate awaited the next escaper to travel down the escape line to Danzig, Townsend-Coles. He left Heydekrug dressed smartly as a civilian, accompanied by fellow kriegie Jack Gilbert. After a couple of weeks hidden in a Polish workers camp, by coded message they met up with Grimson, who took them to a safe house in Gdynia. There Grimson aided them to board a Swedish ship due to sail shortly. Gilbert was successful in boarding and stowed in a locker until sailing safely to Sweden. Regrettably, Townsend-Coles was spotted by a dockside sentry as he stood on the first rung of the gangway. Rearrested, he was handed over to the Gestapo and was reported shot dead on July 15th 1944 "while offering resistance". Such a statement was also used by the enemy when fifty RAF officers and NCOs were murdered by the Gestapo at Stalagluft III, Sagan in March 1944. It was the usual declaration by the cold-blooded murderers after they had carried out their treacherous acts. It would appear also that George Grimson was recaptured, and murdered by the Gestapo at this stage.

The 'Great Escape' from Stalagluft III on the night of March 24th was a tremendous feat of long-term planning, using three tunnels – Tom, Dick and Harry. German ferrets discovered Tom, then Dick became unusable due to the construction of a new compound in the area chosen for the break out of the tunnel, so all effort was then concentrated on the completion of Harry prior to a moonless period when it was planned that eighty-seven prisoners would escape. In the event, seventy-six determined young airmen cleared the tunnel outside the prison fence, before an unexpected air raid alarm siren sounded, indicating the impending arrival of Royal Air Force aircraft in the neighbour-hood. All lights in the camp were extinguished, including those secretly installed in the tunnel.

There was some delay whilst emergency oil lamps were brought into use. This added to the delays already experienced in accommodating the early escapees, many of whom had suitcases larger than expected. Number eighty-seven on the escape list had no sooner entered the tunnel when, at 5:00 am, there was a rifle shot, fired by a guard who had discovered the exit. Those still in the tunnel scrambled back to the entrance and quickly dispersed. Daylight was slowly emerging and, about an hour later, a heavily-armed German riot squad entered the compound. This heralded the long process of counting and searching whilst the greatly agitated Commandant and staff tried to recover some semblance of control.

Of the seventy-six prisoners who cleared the camp, three es-caped to England and seventy-three were recaptured, some of them well dispersed throughout Germany. Five of them were sent to Sachsenhausen concentration camp, three to Stalagluft 1 at Barth and fifteen returned to Stalagluft III at Sagan. The remaining fifty were shot, at different locations, by the Gestapo, on direct orders from Hitler. This was callous murder, despite the misleading reports put out by the Germans that they were shot whilst attempting further escape after arrest. There were no wounded escapees, all were killed.

This information was conveyed to Group Captain Massey, the camp senior officer, in three stages, firstly, when forty-one prisoners were shot (later the number was increased to forty-seven) then, finally, on May 25 the bulletin issued by the enemy announced the deaths of three more making the final total of fifty. These were gallant young men killed whilst seeking free-dom from the tedium and discomfort of imprisonment by a ruthless enemy. Included in the total of determined fliers from twelve different countries were: twenty-three from Great Britain, six from Canada and Poland, three from Australia and South Africa, two from New Zealand and Norway, one each from Belgium, France, Holland, Lithuania and Norway. This cosmo-politan group was representative of the volunteers from these countries who had been successfully moulded into an efficient fighting unit by the Royal Air Force, with much credit to their commanders and the training schemes employed during the war.

Within a few days of the startling events at Stalagluft III, we at Luft 6, including the disabled prisoners, were ordered out on to the playing area and rounded up by a vigorous show of force by a contingent of the Gestapo, armed with heavy machine guns and rifles, who marched threateningly into the compound. There we were addressed by the camp Commandant, who spelt out the broad details of the escape and then informed us of the death of fifty prisoners who were "shot trying to escape". This statement was met by a resounding shout of dismay by us, who then booed the Commandant and his staff as well as the large number of Gestapo officials, who were becoming very agitated and jumpy as the noisy reaction continued. A rifle shot soon cooled down the situation and we were counted and recounted several times before being dismissed by Dixie Dean.

The shock of the fiasco at Sagan was the subject of much discussion amongst us, but it did not deter the continued activity of the Tally-Ho organisation, despite the loss of some of the less important items of escape equipment, which had been deliberately left in vulnerable locations to satisfy the prying eyes of the Gestapo group.

The next out from Heydekrug was Flight Sergeant E.P. (Taff) Lewis, a wireless operator, shot down when flying in a Whitley V aircraft of 10 Squadron in a raid on Bremen on 27th/28th June 1941. I met Taffy Lewis on March 1st 1944, at our very moving celebration of Saint David's Day, with a concert, at which each of us Welshmen were accompanied by a friend of another nationality, with much boisterous singing. This included the Welsh National Anthem, in the presence of the Commandant and his immediate staff, who unexpectedly clapped their appreciation of the entertainment provided by our determined group of about thirty Welsh voices and our guests.

Within a few days Taffy Lewis broke out of our compound through a trench, left unfinished by a Russian forced labourer, behind a newly-built wash-house. Taffy cleared the camp, but it was later reported that he had been recaptured during the Gestapo blitz in the Danzig area in July. He was soon handed over to the SS and shot along, with Grimson, Townsend-Coles and Jock Callender.

On 12th April, Nat Leaman left our room and made his escape attempt, disguised as a 'ferret', in overalls and a Luftwaffe cap. He passed through the gate guard at the northern fence, but the guard shouted after him to book out at the nearby guardroom. Nat protested, but relented when the guard showed a determined stance. On reporting in German to the guardroom sergeant, who examined his forged pass, Nat was asked to state which Company he was attached to. His reply "Third Company" and the sergeant's inquisitiveness, resulted in Nat being arrested and interrogated in the security office. Incriminating evidence was discovered and Nat was detained in the cooler and subjected to a further grilling by the Gestapo. For Nat, a London born Jew, the situation was desperately serious. His predicament was relayed back to us through Munkert and the Tally Ho organisation. In his determined way, he bluffed one of the friendly guards to collect his uniform, and we in A6 thankfully obliged. Now, Nat again became Sergeant Leaman of the Royal Air Force and not the German ferret he had pretended to be. He was then subjected to his sentence of a long stay in the cooler.

He was lucky, as the Germans were desperate in their attitude to Jews of all nationalities. I was very fond of Nat and admired his self-confidence and his determination to inflict as much trouble on the Germans as he possibly could. There was a great deal of fear left in our room concerning his probable fate.

The Germans had made much headway in breaking the Tally Ho escape line in Danzig and there was much tension throughout the camp as the Gestapo arrested fifteen of their camp staff, in addition to the elimination of Munkert and Sommers. It was during this period that a new figure appeared at the compound gate, accompanied by a guard. There was nothing strange about the man, as he was dressed in a mixture of army and air force uniforms, typical of the rest of us in the camp. But, unusually, the guard carried his rifle over his left shoulder, and a model aircraft and the prisoner's kitbag in his hands.

The prisoner was Sergeant Navigator R.B. Pape, with a model of a Short Stirling bomber, of 15 Squadron, in which Richard Pape was flying when he was shot down in September 1941. He turned out to be an inveterate escaper in the two and a half years since his capture. He had mastered the German language and had already compromised the guard, who had accompanied him from German army Stalag VIII B in south-eastern Germany. There, his change of identity with an army private had been discovered by the Germans, which resulted in a stretch of confinement in the "cooler" and subsequent transfer to the Luftwaffe camp.

In due time "Ginger" Pape's escapades whilst a prisoner in a number of work camps became known amongst a number of prisoners, revealing him as a very resilient and determined man who hated his captors. He was not injured when he and the rest of the crew survived when their Stirling I crashed in northern Holland after being hit by flak on a Berlin raid. His daring life as a POW is well documented in his bestseller *Boldness Be My Friend*, published in 1947. Whilst at Stalagluft VI he was seen to be very friendly with Polish airmen in our midst. Some of his escapes had been assisted by Poles, both from their forces and civilian resistance members, who had provided support and guidance when he escaped from Stalag VIII B, situated near the Polish border.

I had known 'Ginger' for only a few weeks when we were thrust together in a venture, which, I believe, was his most daring and risky escape attempt. Due to my injuries and their adverse effect whilst walking and standing, the camp doctor Captain Forest-Hay at Stalagluft VI examined me thoroughly and recommended that I should go before the impending visit of the Repatriation Commission. In the event, on 4th May 1944, we were about thirty prisoners whose injuries and general health were examined by the Commission, headed by a senior German army doctor, which included other German doctors, our camp doctor and a civilian diplomat representing the Swedish Government, who were the protecting power under the Geneva Convention. Some of those approved by the camp doctor were with me at Obermassfeld, including Don Coleman, but there were a few others who had come through other Stalags and hospitals who I didn't know so well. They included many badly wounded cases as well as some unfortunate prisoners who had contracted serious medical or mental conditions.

To my great surprise and amazement I found Richard Pape in line to go before the Commission. He was very agitated and running a high temperature, his ankles were very swollen and there was some frothing of his mouth. He looked and sounded a very sick man and he told me he had a spot on a lung following an attack of pneumonia and pleurisy, which he contacted whilst out working in a Silesian coal mine. This was prior to one of his escape attempts whilst using the identity of Private Winston Yeatman, a New Zealander and inmate of Stalag VIII B.

What was more amazing, as we sat waiting to be called before the Commission, I realised that Ginger was about to embark on one of his boldest escape attempts. He was sufficiently confident, yet reckless enough, to make himself temporarily ill with severe breathlessness and high blood pressure. He had practised self-inflicted pain and weight loss and prepared a carefully planned strategy to convince, initially, the camp doctor that he was suffering with debilitating disease, Nephritis. This was a serious disease of the kidneys and he was prepared to produce a urine sample before the Commission.

To achieve this exceptional ruse, he had fashioned a lifelike rubber penis, with a central hole, connected to a rubber tube containing urine, which was wrapped around his waist. He was fortunate enough to have obtained the sample from a Polish friend he had met in the camp, who was indeed suffering with Nephritis. He went behind a temporary screen to produce his sample and at no time was he asked to drop his pants during the medical examination. It was a high-risk deceptive plan and we were all relieved when he emerged wearing his signed repatriation certificate.[2]

Along with most of the others who went before the Commission, I was feeling "over the moon", having obtained my own certificate. These were all awarded to genuine cases of those wounded in action or suffering a debilitating condition, requiring urgent medical or neurological treatment or medicines not available in a prisoner of war camp in Germany at that time. But we had just come through a terrible ordeal of fear that Ginger's feigning of Nephritis, if discovered by the Commission, would have negated our repatriation claims.

At this time, the enemy was on the defensive, having sustained losses in their Mediterranean and North African campaigns. They were also retreating on the Russian front and being heavily bombed from the air. In addition, there was a feverish expectation of an invasion of the Atlantic Wall. There had developed a highly sensitive and tense demeanour among the German officers and men.

---

[2] See my copy of the repatriation certificate in the photo section.

It was hard to guess what might happen. We could not outwardly show our concern, so thankfully dispersed with our certificates, thanking God for his merciful help. My room mates were quite thrilled at the success of Don and I in being certified for freedom. We said nothing about Ginger; there were too many ferrets and other spies, and we shuddered with the thought of how serious the consequences would have been if his ruse had been discovered. The camp doctor's credibility would have been destroyed and the repatriation jeopardised.

Such was the dangerously exciting and highly-strung Ginger Pape, who I was later to know much better, when we shared a room with forty prisoners at the Annaburg repatriation centre, to which we were sent later in that year…

Meanwhile, tensions inside the compound were at a high level because in addition to the furore caused by the activities of the Tally Ho organisation and the many escapes in recent weeks, there was increasing speculation about the effects of the spectacular Russian advances on the Eastern front. Popular opinion anticipated a northern thrust, cutting off the three Baltic States, Estonia, Latvia and Lithuania. The BBC news at that time was indicating such a threat to the German forces in the Baltic States and then on to the stronghold of East Prussia, where Hitler's Eastern Front Command Centre was located.

As a result, all prisoners at Stalagluft VI were advised through notices from Dixie Dean, the camp leader, to have an emergency pack of essentials ready, in case a speedy evacuation was ordered by the Germans. We were also requested to use any spare clothing to prepare emergency medical kits as a precaution against the inevitable casualties that would result if the camp area was caught up in a Russian bombing attack, or if fighting ensued from a rapid advance of Russian armour in the flat plain of the Belarusian area and Northern Poland.

The tensions of April and May 1944 were suddenly increased, with the BBC radio announcement on June 6th of the long awaited Allied invasion of the Hitler's West Wall. We at Luft VI had been expecting such an announcement, as recent arrivals from both Fighter and Bomber Commands had informed us that such a move was imminent. The intensive activity over Western France and the Pas-De-Calais area involved high RAF and American Air Force losses, which resulted in many prisoners arriving in Stalagluft VI. The increasing number of arrivals in

the early months of 1944 required the building of tented accommodation on the sports area and in other spaces between the
hutted accommodations.

The camp was now overcrowded. Amongst those survivors
from the wretched experience of being shot down was Dick
Twine, who was a great chum of mine at Halton and a very
capable fast bowler in our successful wing cricket eleven. He
was a Flight Engineer on 35 Squadron, shot down in flames by a
night fighter whilst flying a Halifax Mark III on February 19/20
1944, on a heavy raid on Leipzig. Dick told me that there was a
high degree of activity by the German defences. I note that post
war records indicate that 82 aircraft of Bomber Command failed
to return from this raid on a vital centre of the petrochemicals
industry located in the Leipzig-Halle area. I recalled seeing
miles and miles of tall chimneys piercing the skyline when I had
passed through that area earlier.

In his outstanding publication, *Royal Air Force Bomber
Command Losses,* W.R.Chorley lists a total of 140 airmen who
became POWs that night, which amounted to 24% of the aircrew
shot down in the raid. Regrettably, 434, or 76%, were fatal
casualties. Of the 823 aircraft that set out to attack Leipzig, 9.5%
were lost, due to inclement winds and alert German defences.

During this time of increasing tension the food situation in the
camp deteriorated, with even smaller German rations and fewer
Red Cross parcels getting through, as the rail network throughout Germany and occupied Europe was suffering much damage
in the highly intensive bombing. Apart from some loss of weight
I developed a troublesome rash at the back of my head and neck.
Consequently, on the camp doctor's advice, I asked a colleague
to shave my head, which left me feeling the cold and generally
uncomfortable. In no time, one of my Polish friends crocheted a
cap with the wool from an old jersey. This did the trick, but
caused a great deal of laughter when I next presented myself for
a cross wire conversation with Frank in 'K' Lager and Don, who
was in the sick compound with a severe cold. Nevertheless, the
cap provided much comfort until the weather warmed up and my
hair started to grow again.

Nita also sent me splendid knitted headgear, which was well
scented and provided a pleasing reminder of her each time it was
worn. I used to lay my head on it each night as I said my prayers
and yearned for her company. The headgear was contained in a

personal parcel containing pyjamas, jersey and underwear, along with some soap and chocolate. These welcome items provided comfort and joy and I was greatly thankful when such a splendid gift from home arrived. The official allowance was two parcels a year, but I was fortunate to receive even one, considering the appalling deterioration in the German rail system from the middle of 1943.

Throughout the war, the wellbeing and requirements of POWs were not treated with any degree of priority by our German captors and the situation became progressively worse as the Axis forces suffered increasing loss of territory and industrial areas of Germany were subjected to intense bombing attacks by the British and American air forces. We could see the changing attitude of our captors, which became more obvious after D-Day in 1944, when only the fanatical SS and Gestapo personnel reflected Nazi determination to inflict maximum damage to the Allies. With the fall of Rome and the arrest of Mussolini, one could feel a change of attitude amongst many of our camp guards and their officers, who now sought a favourable reaction from the prisoners that might help on the cessation of hostilities.

The Lithuanian summer of 1944 was warm and we sought as much fresh air as was available in our crowded camp in the daytime. The onset of nightfall meant closing down the shutters, whereupon the atmosphere became intolerable in our rooms, which were now accommodating the maximum number of prisoners.

We followed the advances of the Allies in France and the dramatic advances of the Russians as they re-occupied the central plain and then crossed into Polish territory, where the dreadful atrocities of the German occupiers were being exposed. There was a growing opinion, expressed by many, that the war might be over and we would be free again to return home by Christmas 1944. There certainly was much excitement as everyone, particularly those who had spent three or four years behind the wire, began to sense the likelihood of freedom soon.

The hold up of our invasion forces around Caen caused some disappointment, but did not quell the feeling of confidence and anticipation of eventual victory. Whilst I was caught up in the enthusiastic fervour, my main thoughts were about the medical repatriation that was pending and as the weeks passed by, so the tension grew. Each night my prayers embraced the longing to see my loved ones again and I trusted God to help me overcome the trials, tribulations and pensive moods that prevailed.

The thought of the impending repatriation occupied a great deal of time between Don Coleman and myself during the exciting summer months after the Commission had granted our certificates, which felt like gold, to be safeguarded all hours. Meanwhile, I was studying advanced mathematics and economics as I began to appreciate what made the business world tick.

Then, in the darkness of my bug-ridden bunk, I would always think of Nita and my home village. These thoughts always led me to think of my uncertain future, as I was still walking with a stick to overcome the minimum movement of my left foot, which kept striking slightly raised obstacles. At the same time there seemed to be excessive movement of the left knee, which suggested a loss of stability, normally provided by the ligaments. There was clearly both ligament and cartilage stretch in the damaged leg, which was not helped by the knee and thigh muscles, which were still wasted, despite the regular exercise of the offending limb whilst laying down on my back.

My thought processes then led me back to the dreadful experience of December 23rd 1942, which had left me with so much uncertainty about the circumstances that led to the downing of our aircraft and the tragic loss of my fellow crewmembers. I resolved that one day I would find out what brought the enemy gunfire to that remote part of Holland. Could there have been a failure in the intelligence activity of MI6 and the Netherlands branch of SOE? This was a terrifying prospect. I had been a prisoner for more than eighteen months but was still none the wiser, as I had not met any other prisoner from the Tempsford squadrons other than Frank Tierney, who was equally baffled by the unexpected experience we had shared on that fateful night. Should I send a secret message through Tally Ho to avoid further losses in the Netherlands? I pondered this, but felt I had insufficient knowledge and firm evidence to alert our own intelligence service and especially the Dutch section of SOE. I had been kept well in the dark by the Germans during the interrogation sessions in Leeuwarden, Amsterdam and eventually at Dulagluft.

The onset of the defeat of the U-Boat campaign in the Atlantic, the defeats of the Germans in North Africa, Tunisia, Sicily and now the successes in Italy were good news, followed by the more recent successes in Normandy and the spectacular advances of the Russians on the Eastern Front.

This encouraging BBC news, received via the clandestine radio amazingly engineered by Alec Bristow, which included the continuing success of our bombing campaign, had partially overcome the fears and worries I had about events in Holland. I did not wish to compromise the hard work of the splendid Tally Ho organisation by getting them involved, with such limited evidence to support my doubts. I thus decided to await my return to England before pursuing the mystery.

5. Repatriation – Stalag IV DZ

Notwithstanding the dirt, discomfort and terrible overcrowding of Stalagluft VI in early July 1944, the warm sunshine added to our already greatly increased confidence as we contemplated our possible release from confinement. My daily prayers helped to calm my inner excitement and, to my great joy, I, along with about twenty other fortunate souls, received notice, on July 11th, to be up and ready to move out to a repatriation centre at 6.30am the following morning.

Hastily, I completed a task I had started a few weeks earlier, of compiling a list of names, addresses and messages to the next of kin from the many friends I was leaving behind to face the dangers and frustrations that inevitably lay in store for them. Without exception, when I said my goodbyes, my friends expressed great joy for me, including Frank, who shouted across from "A" Lager to wish me good luck and bade me give his love to his wife Maureen and their son, whom he had not yet seen. I was so sorry that Frank was not coming back with me and for a moment thought that we could change places. But this, I knew, would not be possible. So we said cheerio and God speed.

The 11th passed quickly as I packed together my few possessions and handed on some textbooks I had received earlier during my captivity. That night I had little sleep, but lay thinking of being reunited with my family and Nita in the not too distant future. These were wonderful thoughts, tempered by anxiety about my future career in the Royal Air Force. I asked God to provide me with a safe journey tomorrow.

In the morning Don and I were up early. A quick wash in the nearby washhouse, a slice of bread and jam for breakfast and a cup of tea provided our sustenance. We said our last goodbyes to our roommates, then, each carrying a small rucksack and a walking stick, we presented ourselves at the compound gate at the allotted time, where we met up with our fellow airmen, each carrying their ticket to freedom, signed by the Commission.

Two armed guards came from the German administration compound and conducted us to a room, where we were searched thoroughly, our identities verified, and we were issued with a casualty label, which was attached to a buttonhole in our jackets.

The German camp adjutant then read out a statement that we were being sent to a repatriation centre at Annaberg, situated between Berlin and Leipzig. He also warned us against any escape attempts or misconduct on the journey, as this might jeopardise our eventual repatriation. In due course, we were herded on to a small army bus, powered by a charcoal burner, and in great excitement and with much chatter, particularly from Richard Pape, we moved slowly out of the camp. This raised a great cheer from our friends behind the wire and we were jumping with joy and shouting our delight inside the bus. This was not yet freedom, but it was the first stage in being released from the wretched experience of being imprisoned.

As the bus chugged along through the sandy, undulating, countryside, we soon cleared the woodland area and reached the small railway station, where the guards kept us together, away from the few passengers and staff at this early hour. Then, with a thunderous roar, a train approached at a high speed from a northerly direction. As it passed, we had a fleeting glance, which indicated that it was an armed military command train. There were anti-aircraft guns on platforms to the front and the rear of the short train, with one enclosed carriage and on the open wagons behind, tired and injured bodies lay sprawed across a large table on which maps were spread, some spilled on the floor. The light anti-aircraft guns were poised at different angles and we formed the view that this was a commander's train rapidly retreating from the direction of Riga, in Latvia, which was being shelled and bombed by the approaching Russian forces.

To us, it was a startling example of the precarious state of the German army, as we noted senior officers' stripes on the trousers of some of the casualties, as they passed close to where we stood on the platform. We were quite thrilled at the spectacle, and yet we feared that the train we were awaiting would, itself, be bombed by the Russians when we left Lithuania and crossed into East Prussia. It was, therefore, with mixed feelings of joy and trepidation that we boarded our train when it steamed up to the platform a short time later.

The Luftwaffe guards shepherded us into what was, clearly, a wagon designed for conveying foreign workers and their families or prisoners being consigned to concentration camps. In Germany and the occupied countries there was much demand for such wagons with such large numbers on the move. The short wagon had hard wooden seating across each end with an open space in between. The guards sat on opposite corners of the wooden seats, each near a windowed door. The floor space was bare wooden planks, where we prisoners were expected to sit down in rows. We decided that we would take turns for some of our number to sit on the benches alongside the guards for a limited time and alternately lie on the floor like sardines in a tin. Our motley group was composed of about ten from 'A' Lager, whom we knew quite well, and a further ten made up of about half from 'K' Lager and half from the American compound. There was much conversation for a while, but then groups settled in and slept on the floor.

When it became my turn to lie on the hard planks I was kept awake as our poorly sprung wagon clunked over the large gaps between the rails on its badly worn wheels. I was to get little sleep during the three days and nights we travelled in a southerly direction. When taking my turn at sitting up, despite the hard seats, it was more relaxing, especially when the guard stood up to stretch his legs. Through the window I could view the passing countryside and saw many storks in flight, with others resting on the chimneys of houses near the railway.

After crossing the uninteresting flatlands of East Prussia we arrived at Insterburg at about midday. Here we witnessed a considerable military presence, in the form of Germany Army and SS units. Luftwaffe personnel were also on the move, this being one of the important links between Germany and the northern section of the Eastern Front in their battle with the advancing Russians. Hitler's northern HQ, "The Wolf's Lair" was situated in the nearby forest. There was also much evidence of the civilian population on the move as the enemy was now apparently within 150 kilometres. Nevertheless, our guard was successful in scrounging some soup, prepared by the German Red Cross staff at the station.

Our journey continued across East Prussia, crossing the Polish border on to Thorn (or Torun, as it was previously named) on a stretch of flat plain, studded with clumps of silver birch, broken by many small villages and farms. Our wagon, now hitched to a goods train, made slow progress and halted at nightfall. There seemed to be much traffic moving in the opposite direction throughout the night, obviously conveying the military being pressed into defence of the northern sector. We moved slowly onward, eventually arriving at Poznan (or Posen, which was its previous name). Here there were signs of panic, as this again was an important military staging post for the Eastern front.

It was exceptionally hot and stuffy in our wagon during the daytime, but it turned very cold at night, when I found my army overcoat a blessing. With the inevitable filling up of the can in the corner, the smell became intolerable at times. The knowledge that we were heading for repatriation held off any thoughts of escape from this wagon, even by Ginger Pape, whose banter we found amusing. His hatred of the enemy was profound but potentially dangerous for his safety in the presence of the guards, who understood some of our language.

At Poznan, our guard was able to obtain some coffee, which staved off the hunger we felt. We left the flat, uninteresting countryside of central Poland, crossed the Oder at Frankfurt and then, connected to another train, moved on to Cottbus. At both of these busy junctions one experienced the feverish movement of large numbers of military personnel, who seemed to be getting into place for the impending thrust of the Russian army. We again were shunted onto another train at Cottbus, which took us in the direction of Finsterwalde and on to Falkenburg, where yet another train took us on to Annaberg. At these junctions, we heard cries coming from trainloads of foreign workers and their families, clearly in distress, locked in wagons that were not even fit for the carriage of animals.

Annaberg, a provincial village, is roughly midway between Berlin and Leipzig, in the south and not far removed from the Elbe at Torgau. A short army bus ride from the station took us to an imposing-looking castle with a swastika flag flying aloft. The guard at the gate and the barbed wire surrounding the open area indicated that this was our repatriation centre – Heilag Stalag (IVDZ).

After the formalities of identification and security checks we twenty airmen were allotted a room on the second floor, with a tall window overlooking a cobblestone yard, with a grassed and sandy area beyond. It was now July 15th and very hot, but we were allowed to have the windows open at night time. My room mates, many of whom I had known at Obermassfeld, included Don Coleman and Ginger Pape, who continued to be a lively extrovert and found it difficult to remain a captive, despite the prospect of our repatriation in the not too distant future. Within a day or so, he had reconnoitred much of the four floors, the cellar and the gabled rooms in the roof of the large castle. He discovered that, although it was manned by the German army, there seemed to be a team of Luftwaffe personnel in charge of a large number of carrier pigeons.

After a couple of days watching their movements away from the castle, and their return some hours later, he concluded that they were being used as silent conveyers of messages for the enemy military units. In this way the very efficient interception measures, adopted by the allies, were being avoided. This had become increasingly important, as the Germans were now transferring fighting units between the three fronts on which they were now fighting. Then the inevitable happened. Ginger and an army companion forced their way into the wired enclosure housing the pigeons, killing some of them and bringing back the deceased to our room, which temporarily supplemented our food rations. Actually, our meals were not too bad and perhaps reflected the German desire to improve their treatment of captives who were shortly to be freed.

In our room we were also fortunate to have an occasional loaf of white bread, which Ginger secreted under his shirt before returning from a working party that went under guard to collect the daily rations in the local village. He was a man who took many risks. It created a serious stir when the Commandant's investigations failed to find the perpetrators of the pigeon fiasco. There was talk that this episode could jeopardize our repatriation and have serious consequences between the Allies, Germany and neutral Sweden, which had negotiated the agreement, but somehow the event passed without retribution. Nevertheless, it highlighted to his room-mates how adventurous a character Ginger Pape was.

Then, on 20th July, news of the attempt on Hitler's life was broken and caused quite a stir, both to the Germans and their captives. We thought that this could have ended the war before our repatriation was concluded. There seemed to be a fearful reaction amongst the guards and castle staff, and I and my perplexed companions found much inner joy that the perpetrators were German officers at the "Wolf's Lair" in East Prussia, where we had only recently passed through. We had access to the mouthpiece of the Nazi's, the *Volkischer Beobachter*, which made a great play on the efforts to arrest and condemn the high level organisers of the revolt. This included the enforced 'suicide' of Rommel and the hanging of hundreds of other senior officers and public leaders rounded up by the Gestapo.

We were also supplied with a copy of "The Camp". This was distributed to all camps in which British prisoners were incarcerated and was written in English but edited by the Germans and, I understood, printed by British prisoners at one of the camps. It was essentially an enemy propaganda medium, containing emphasis on Allied losses at sea, aircraft shot down and the German point of view concerning the land battles on all three fronts. It also attempted to portray the good treatment of prisoners of war by focussing on their involvement with camp stage shows and sports activities. I recall one issue of "The Camp" when the Germans scored an own goal. On the front page was a photograph of a happy concert party in their costumes at one of the Stalags. Little did the German editor realise that across the front of the stage were the five lines and four spaces of musical notation, containing the notes of the first line of "There'll always be an England". This was one of many such morale boosters, unintentionally published by the Germans.

All the prisoners at Annaburg were in a high state of anxiety as we waited, day after day, for information of our impending repatriation. But some among us were being returned home because of mental disorder and they were exceptionally morose in their behaviour, requiring a great deal of discretion on our part. They tended to keep themselves to themselves and were still anxious about being behind barbed wire. They became impatient and some even attempted to escape, especially those who had spent more than four years as captives. Regrettably, one of our number was killed, by a camp guard's rifle shot, whilst climbing the wire.

By now, most Germans were beginning to realise that they were not going to win the war, the German senior staff at Annaburg being amongst them. To show that they were still blessed with a degree of human decency the Camp Commandant agreed to a very dignified and solemn burial for our army private, who was conveyed on a grand horse-drawn hearse, flanked and followed by a parade of uniformed POWs.

Life was quite tense as the rest of July and August passed slowly on. Don and I continued our Bridge partnership, that is, when he was not taking on all-comers at Poker, following a reckless urge to increase his supply of cigarettes.

The senior officer commanding the repatrées, Lieutenant Colonel Lester Le Sauef, of the Australian Army Medical Corps, was a keen cricketer and somehow managed to get hold of a few cricket bats, balls and stumps. He decided, in this very hot spell of weather, to keep us occupied by organising a competition between the representatives of the cricket playing commonwealth countries – Australia, New Zealand, South Africa, Rhodesia and the British Isles.

The knock-out competition, of limited overs, was very hard fought and I had much satisfaction in being material in defeating the Aussies in the final. It was good fun and drew a crowd comprising most of our 3,000 inmates. We played with a hard cricket ball, but had no pads for wicket keeping or batting. However, we were all disabled to some degree, so there was no one fit enough to bowl fast. I couldn't run, but managed a few steps and bowled a good off-break, which brought the downfall of the star Aussie batsman in the final match. Then, with a patient twenty-odd runs, accompanied by a dextrous army officer, batting with one arm, we were victorious. I cannot recall the winning trophy, but Colonel Le Sauef gave me a signed photograph, dated 3rd September 1944, with which to register our ascendancy over the Aussies at Stalag IV.

We were also treated to a theatre performance by the inmates, which brightened our lives.

We were very much on tenterhooks until 5th September, when we were told that we would be leaving early the following morning, by hospital trains, for the Baltic coast, where we would embark on a sea ferry to Sweden. Amidst great excitement, we put together our few belongings and, with loving prayers and thoughts of Nita and my parents, the warm night passed slowly without much sleep. A great deal of smoking and chatter heralded the dawn, when we were up and ready, contemplating our journey through central and northern Germany, now the regular hunting ground of British and American bombers and long-range fighters. I prayed for God's protection in the coming days.

With my heart pumping, we set out by army coach to the railhead near the village, where hospital trains with red crosses were awaiting us. Soon we were checked aboard and, with our limited guard accompaniment, we sat comfortably, six to each compartment, with a corridor connection to the toilet. This seemed like complete luxury and raised our hopes as we set out. For several hours, the train seemed to be going in a westerly direction, through Wittenberg and Magdeburg, and we enjoyed the relative freedom and views of open countryside. The train stopped many times and after dark that evening we pulled up in the countryside outside Braunswerg as there had been an air raid warning.

Thankfully, the railway line north, towards the Baltic, was traversable and at daylight on 7th September we were passing through Schwerin and the flat countryside to Stralsund. Then, as we crossed the island of Rugen, we had glimpses of the Baltic Sea before we reached the ferry port of Sassnitz. This brought much relief and thankfulness as we left the train and were guided to the ferry boats awaiting our group of 3,000 tired prisoners, now about to leave our captors behind.

These were wonderful moments as we boarded the Swedish ferry, leaving our armed guard on the dockside. Don Coleman and I, along with some air force chums, were allocated a space on the deck, and we soon, amidst great cheering from everyone on board, set sail on a northerly course across the Baltic. We left the German coast behind with a wonderful feeling of being free at last, but ever-conscious of the fact that the war was raging at its fiercest and from our knowledge of RAF activities we knew that areas of the Baltic Sea were being continually laid with mines. In a silent moment I again had time for a prayer of thankfulness and joy at my release and for a safe journey to Sweden and, later, my homeland.

The weather was fine and fresh for our eventful journey and after a sandwich and a drink we were able to wander around. Everyone was in high spirits except the Poles and Czechs amongst us, some of whom were very wary of the presence on board of Russian agents, who had attempted to obtain their home addresses in the countries from which they had fled in 1939/40, before volunteering their services to the Royal Air Force. There were also journalists on board and a number of stories of POW exploits appeared in the next day's editions of the Swedish newspapers.

During the journey I spent much time in conversation with Richard (Ginger) Pape, who by now had overcome the strains he had put on his body during the inspection by the repatriation commission. Now in the Baltic, bound for neutral Sweden he was more relaxed and talkative, relieved of the pressures he had suffered during three years of captivity. No longer thinking of escape and overjoyed that his deception had succeeded, he talked freely about his experiences as a reporter working for the *Yorkshire Post* and his youthful experiences with a son of Lord Harewood and his many visits to Harewood House. Coincidentally, the future Earl of Harewood had also suffered incarceration after the short battle and fall of France in 1940. With his background as a newspaper writer and an exceptionally daring time as a prisoner of war, it is no wonder that within a few years of the end of hostilities Ginger wrote his book *Boldness Be My Friend*.

Some hours later a cheer again went up as we approached the welcome sight of the Swedish coastline and I felt greatly relieved as we drew alongside the quay to an awaiting group of officers. It was a very moving occasion, only to be surpassed in intensity of feeling when we eventually arrived safely in the UK a week or so later. In the meantime, we quickly disembarked at Trelleborg, on the southern coast of Sweden, and were directed onto special trains awaiting us nearby. There, some of us airmen were together in a comfortable compartment, where we were served with Swedish open sandwiches and coffee and advised that we would be travelling overnight to the port of Gothenberg. This meant we would be following the west coast line near the Kattegat, the main waterway separating Denmark and Sweden. As the train sped north, the agricultural countryside looked prosperous and the villages clean and orderly.

It was soon dark and, feeling very tired after two days of exuberant joy and much travel, sleep overcame me with the rhythmic rocking of the train. When I awoke some hours later, dawn was breaking as we followed the coastline to the west through the rolling country of the Gatland area. It was still early morning when we approached the busy port of Gothenburg and it was quite a change to see a city at peace with the world. I admired, then, the Swedes for pursuing a neutral policy during two world wars. The train pulled into a crowded platform of officials, pressmen and representatives from the British Embassy and, after short speeches of welcome, we in our carriage were asked to follow two uniformed guides, who led us onto a bus, where we were met by someone from the Swedish navy.

En route he told us that we would be spending two nights in a yacht in the harbour. He issued us with an envelope containing some details of Gothenburg and its history, along with a résumé of what they had in store for us during our stay. When we arrived at the vessel we were greeted warmly by a smart orderly, who led us through to our cabins, passing a luxuriously fitted hallway, far removed from the drab, uncomfortable environment of the prisoner of war accommodation we had left behind. I was allowed to bathe and clean up as best I could, in a well-furnished cabin; a welcome change from the primitive and crude conditions for ablutions provided for us in Germany.

We soon realised that this was a yacht owned by royalty, or someone similarly endowed with wealth and grandeur, and the twenty or so of us were treated splendidly. The food and wine were superb and we wondered why we had been singled out for such excellent treatment when told that the rest of the repatrées were housed in a local military hospital, which had been cleared for the occasion. Apparently, the railway coach in which we had travelled from Trelleborg had been chosen at random when we arrived at Gothenburg, so we were lucky with our royal treatment.

We were so sorry that, without money or other wealth, we were unable to show our thanks, other than in words of appreciation for the Swedish authorities arranging the repatriation and our wonderful reception in their country.

The combined effect of wine, a superb dinner and much exuberant chatter soon led me to my cabin, where I made up for much of my accumulative sleeplessness and with my usual humble prayer, coupled with an outstanding feeling of being free again, I slept soundly.

After an early call on 9th September, and a wonderful breakfast, we were soon leaving the yacht and were being conveyed by coach to the dock area, where three liners were berthed. Our coach party was led through a checkpoint before going aboard the *Arundel Castle*, which had been converted into a hospital ship. Painted with a prominent Red Cross, it was berthed near the two Swedish liners, *Drottingholm* and *Gripsholm*, also suitably converted. It didn't take long before the three thousand of us were safely counted aboard and with a great deal of merriment we cast off, to loud hailers of farewell from the very hospitable Swedes. On board, we were allotted cabins and issued with a set of instructions and, amidst a welter of excitement, we slowly moved into the Skagerrak, as we left the friendly Swedish coastline behind, with Denmark to port and the rugged Norwegian coast to our starboard.

We felt thrilled, yet a little apprehensive of striking an errant mine, as we knew that these waters, through which we were passing, had been subject to many minelaying operations by Bomber Command. There was always the possibility of mines straying from their intended areas as the high north-westerly gales blew from the North Sea into the Skagerrak. Some of us feared such a catastrophic event as we ploughed our way through rough seas.

I soon retired to my cabin and, after a silent prayer, when I placed myself into God's care, I settled down to read and write a few postcards I had obtained at Gothenburg. We were well cared for on board, with good meals and much entertainment. I was able to sleep, despite the incessant vibration as the ship rounded the southern coast of Norway and steered a northerly course, with the rugged coastline to our starboard. At night the three ships in our convoy were well illuminated with floodlights and by the second day our confidence in the safety of the journey was growing.

During the journey north, towards the Norwegian Sea, I learned that the convoy was planning to steam towards the 65 degree latitude line before steering to port, north of the Shetlands, towards Iceland, then to be followed by a further turn to port, sailing south in the Atlantic, west of the Hebrides, into the Irish Sea, before reaching our destination, Liverpool. We guessed then that we would be several days at sea through the North Atlantic.

As the journey progressed through the rough waters, many on board succumbed to the inevitable periods of seasickness, which resulted in a settling down of the noisy enthusiasm at the commencement of the journey. I was able to avoid any adverse stomach reaction and continued to read as much as I could, but found it difficult to concentrate. Thoughts of soon returning to my loved ones surmounted all other feelings. I was also praying for God's guidance, as my future service in the Royal Air Force was in doubt, due to the disability I now suffered. I was still walking with the aid of a stick and found difficulty in climbing the many steps between decks.

There was much excitement on board when we spotted a large convoy of ships, with Royal Navy escort, in the distance. We put up a great cheer as a Coastal Command Liberator, painted completely white, flew near us. Such events raised our morale to dazzling heights. This was particularly noticeable amongst the soldiers on board, many of whom had been prisoners for more than four years. Then came the announcement that there was every expectation we would be docking the following day.

On 14th September 1944, those of us who managed some sleep awoke at daybreak to find the ship had stopped and was lying at anchor many miles from the shore. With much nervous enthusiasm, I quickly washed, collected my few belongings and with much difficulty managed a very light breakfast of toast and coffee before making my way to the top deck. There, I joined many others of all three services. The ship's crew told me that our liner, *Arundel Castle*, would dock first, followed by the Swedish liner *Drottingholm* and later the *Gripsholm* would be called in.

Some two or three hours passed slowly as we became impatient just standing offshore. Then, with a loud hailing, the ship moved slowly the last few miles, as the beloved shoreline of our homeland loomed ever nearer. We passed many vessels of all kinds, including the rusty grey hulls of naval destroyers and frigates, which had been escorting convoys through the dangerous U-Boat hunting grounds of the North Sea and Arctic waters.

Eventually, in late morning, we approached a gaily-decorated landing stage and, as we nudged forwards, we could hear the strains of a military band playing stirring music. At this point my cheers were drowned in tears and my thoughts and prayers were of thankfulness. I felt truly safe for the first time since the terrible experiences I had suffered nearly two years earlier.

When the *Arundel Castle* had berthed, an Army general relayed on a loudhailer a gracious message of welcome from the King and Queen. I learned later that he was General Sir Ronald Adam, Adjutant General, and he was accompanied by a large official reception party, amongst whom I recognised Air Commodore Dacre, who had been the station commander at Halton before I completed my engineering training in 1942. These were moments of great joy, which brought on more tears as I grappled with my emotions, awaiting the turn of the Royal Air Force contingent to be called. But first came the blind and the stretcher cases. It brought a lump to my throat as I contemplated their fate. They had left their homeland fit and active, called upon to defend the values of peace and freedom; now they were returning, their bodies crippled. But their spirits were high. Soon they would be joining loving families and sweethearts, who were anxiously waiting their return.

Amongst the reception party we spotted a lady in the uniform of a Red Cross Officer and gave a great cheer when the Commandant of the Red Cross, Mrs Bromley-Davenport, came aboard to warmly welcome us. Our hearts were as one as we reflected on the wonderful parcels we had received from her organisation. We knew that many of us would have succumbed to malnutrition and starvation had it not been for the Red Cross and order of St John parcels. This organisation would remain one of my favourite charities throughout my life.

I now realised how lucky I was to have been to be saved from the jaws of death when our aircraft was shot from the skies in flames, ending the lives of six of my friends. There would be no homecoming for them, no greetings from a loving family, but they were now in God's hands, where their gallant souls were preserved. I reflected on the fate of Frank, our admirable rear gunner, to whom, with heavy heart, I had said "cheerio for now". Just a few months earlier I prayed that he would also return safely to these shores and be with his loving Maureen and newborn son, with whom he had not yet shared the joys of a father-and-son relationship.

There was a great buzz of anticipation as the soldiers and sailors were marshalled slowly down the gangplank. Many had succumbed to mental illness after prolonged periods of captivity. Each needed a medical escort to guide them, hopefully towards a full recovery at some point in the future.

Then came the turn of the walking-wounded of the Royal Air Force contingent. Hastily grabbing my small kit bag, and carefully watching my footing, I remember my heart was thumping with great joy as I waved to the official reception party and groups of dockworkers, who had gathered on the quayside. This was another great moment in my life. In the presence of Jesus that morning, I felt that, despite all the aggressive anxiety in the world, there was also much love and compassion. I had come through the hell of bondage safely and returned to my homeland.

I was delighted to receive an English newspaper and read of the thrust of our army into southern Holland after a dash from the successes of the Normandy landings. After heavy fighting in the Normandy *bocage*, the heavy German defeat in the 'Falaise gap' was great news and it was good to read the Allied point of view for a change, after being subjected to the biased news reported in the *Volkischer Beobachter*. It was also quite thrilling to note the latest positions of the Russian forces in their advance towards East Prussia and my thoughts immediately turned to the possible evacuation of the colleagues I had left behind at Stalagluft VI in July. As yet, no news of their fate had been released to the public. I was also impressed with the Russian advances into southern Poland. Such news left me optimistic regarding the war situation and my thoughts now turned to my own future as I sat in the coach, awaiting our departure to the Royal Air Force hospital near Blackpool.

We left the dockside to a great cheer from the many official well-wishers who had gathered, and quickly moved through the much-damaged streets of Liverpool. The German air attacks on this important dock city in 1940 and 1941 had severely damaged civilian and business premises, as well as the infrastructure, and I felt firm justification for the counter-attacks that I and my colleagues in Bomber Command and the American Eighth Air Force had inflicted in retaliation on the enemy.

During the coach journey we passed through many villages and towns in bright sunshine and my thoughts turned towards my home village, where I would soon be reunited with my family, Nita, her loving parents and the villagers; a wonderful prospect, soon to be realised. It was refreshing to appreciate God's hand in events leading up to my return. My silent prayers now turned to the future, which I found difficult to contemplate. I wondered what the reaction of the Royal Air Force would be; would my disability prevent me continuing my service agreement? With my twenty-first birthday approaching I had the minimum of nine more years to serve. If the Air Force found me unfit, what then should I do? Such thoughts were going to occupy much of my time when I returned home.

When the coach passed near Preston, I knew it would be a short distance to RAF Weeton, our destination. We stepped off the coach to a warm reception from the station hospital staff, who plied us with refreshments. We were allocated beds in wards that had been cleared to accommodate the variety of medical cases that now descended on them. We all stripped off, were deloused and had a most welcome shower. Thus cleansed, we dressed in temporary hospital garb, whilst our prison camp clothing was sent for incineration, although we hung on to a few personal belongings. We were then measured and kitted out with new uniforms. I was pleased to note I had been awarded the 1939/45 star, my first medal, and I also received confirmation of my promotion to Flight Sergeant whilst a prisoner. I was delighted with this news, coupled with the information that I was soon expected to be promoted to Warrant Officer.

A medical examination was quickly followed by a debriefing, at which I explained how puzzled I was with events of nearly two years previously, when our aircraft had been shot out of the sky over Holland. I also advised the interviewing officer of the tragic death of my six crewmates and my having met up with our rear gunner, Frank Tierney, who had recovered well from his wounds. I was also able to give a summary of my treatment by the Germans. Like many of my colleagues, I confirmed that I had been treated better by Luftwaffe personnel than by their Wehrmacht or Gestapo counterparts.

However, during our conversation the interviewing officer gave me no explanation for the surprise attack on Halifax 'R' for Robert over Holland. I was assured that clarification would follow when the battle to free the Netherlands and SOE's work with the resistance in Europe was completed.

However, my thoughts at this time were focussed on my homecoming, so solving of the mystery that had haunted me throughout my incarceration was put aside… at least for now.

Everyone I spoke to was overjoyed at the spectacular British and American advances following the breakout in Normandy and with our establishment of air superiority, which was paramount to this success. However, there was now a major difficulty in the supply of fuel and armaments, due to continued German resistance at vital ports, which meant a supply-line many hundreds of miles long, from Cherbourg and the temporary 'Mulberry' harbour in Normandy.

That evening of Friday September 14th, I was able to contact my Aunt Nan, who lived in my home village and was one of a small minority with a telephone at that time. She was relieved to hear that I was free again and feeling reasonably well. She was overjoyed to tell me how thrilled my parents and family and Nita and her family would be to know of my safe arrival. This was great news and I asked if all the family and Nita could assemble there on Sunday evening after church, when we could converse. I would then be able to tell them a firm date, early the following week, when I expected to be cleared of all the formalities and could enjoy some leave at home.

That following Sunday evening I had a great reunion with my parents and Nita over the telephone. I was able to tell them that I expected to be cleared for a month's leave by Monday morning, following which I had been requested to report back for further treatment at RAF Weeton hospital. I was so thrilled to hear their voices again, particularly that of Nita, who was overcome with joy and a little emotional as we exchanged loving greetings in the presence of the family gathering. I was very disturbed, however, to be told that my brother Jack had been missing since a raid on Berlin on August 31st 1943, although mother had hinted at this in our earlier correspondence.

That Sunday was exceptionally busy. I was issued with an advance of pay and a travel warrant. I was also able to have fitting adjustments for my new uniform, with flying badge and medal ribbon in place. The Royal Air Force had also arranged a church service at the hospital, when we all thanked God for his mercy in saving us from captivity and prayed for the safe return of friends left behind and a successful end to hostilities.

A restless night was followed by early breakfast and a short coach journey before I entrained at Blackpool and, with nervous anticipation of the eventful day ahead, settled down for a few hours journey south to Cardiff. After leaving the industrial area of Lancashire, the countryside was beautiful as we sped through Cheshire and Herefordshire and on to Cardiff, where I was due to change trains for the final leg of my journey.

I was pleasantly surprised to be met by uncles, John and Dan, who had travelled up to Cardiff to assist in the change and accompany me to Neath. During the hour-long journey I was told to prepare myself for the meeting with my parents, who were grief-stricken following the loss of Jack a year earlier. They also gave me some insight into the reception awaiting me in my home village. I was so excited as I stepped off the train at Neath, where Nita and a few other members of the family greeted me warmly. After a loving embrace from Nita I was thrilled as we shared a conversation in the taxi. For the last mile the village of Cadoxton was bedecked with flags and bunting and we waved to many friends before pulling up at my home, where a neighbour had made a sign which read: "Welcome home Billy". There, at last, with warm tears of greeting, were Mum and Dad, who had bravely overcome much tribulation in the past two years. We shared tears of joy and sorrow and they told me of Jack's fateful last sortie and the communications they had subsequently received from 90 Squadron and the Air Ministry.

Jack, the firstborn of a family of two girls and four boys, was now tragically missed by us all, particularly by my parents. Their profound love reflected the regard we all had for Jack's wonderful personality and Christian awareness. He was highly regarded in our home village, where he was a respected member of the church bell-ringing team and a bass member of the Operatic Chorus. I remember so well his repeated rendering of the Anvil Chorus from *Il Travatore,* his favourite opera, in which he performed a few years before the war. I shared much feeling of sorrow for Dilys, to whom Jack had been engaged some months before he was shot down. I know how difficult it was when Dilys joined my homecoming party that evening and I will never forget her courageous presence at that time.

It was a good party, despite the limitations of food rationing at the time, and I was particularly pleased when Mr and Mrs Davies, Nita's parents, joined us later in the evening. My thoughts were now a whirl as my loved-ones fired me with so many questions, particularly about life behind the wire in Hitler's Germany. Later that evening I remember walking in the garden and admiring the colourful woodland behind our house. It was great to be home and with my loved-ones again.

Later, as I walked with Nita to her home, we marvelled at the heavens and God's contribution to our lives. I walked slowly, using a stick and Nita reassured me that all would be well. As I slowly returned home later, that quarter of a mile was not easy but I looked forward apprehensively to my future, full of hope. Now, with the ghastly experiences of the past two years behind me, and with the immediate anticipation of my twenty-first birthday just one week hence, I seemed to have had such an eventful life already that I was unable to contemplate the long future ahead of me.

6.   Recovery and Resettlement

My prayers of thanks were coupled with much joy as I slept well in my own bed that night. The previous day had been very exciting and emotional and I awoke in the safety and simple comforts of my home. There was much mail to read and I also commenced contacting the sixty-odd addresses of fellow prisoners' families, to fulfil the promises I had made before leaving Stalagluft VI. I expected that, allowing for visitors and other activities, this commitment would take about a month to complete.

Amongst the many callers was the head of the Neath Branch of the Red Cross Society, who was most interested in what I had to say. I also undertook to attend their next Sunday night concert, when they would be entertaining members of the forces in the Neath area. This was a wonderful evening and I was cheered wildly as I addressed the audience of about two hundred soldiers, airmen, and even a few naval chaps who were on leave in the area. They were most interested in what I had to say. I issued a challenge to all present, and asked them to make every effort to quickly release the many thousands of our comrades behind the wire in the hands of a tyrannical regime, which could not be relied upon to ensure their safety.

On my return to the UK, I kept abreast of the progress of the war via the BBC news and the daily papers. The valiant airborne attack at Arnhem had been a courageous attempt to capture the bridges over the vast River Rhine. This had started on September 17th. That day, the frequent interjection of radio news items about the vast airborne armada of RAF Transport Command, USAF DC3s and the massive glider-borne force was wonderful as I went about obtaining the necessary passes, money and railway vouchers for my journey home the following day. There was a confident mood, initially, in anticipation of a successful outcome of the battle, but over the following days, as reports unfolded, it became less optimistic. When, eventually, news of the withdrawal of the remnants of our airborne forces across the river south of the Oostebeck perimeter was announced, I felt very depressed, particularly over the thousands of casualties sustained in this abortive operation. A large number of wounded were left behind to become prisoners of war. This, inevitably, reminded me of my own involvement in Northern Holland two years previously, and of the tragic death of six of my crewmates. Events then had raised questions in my mind about the Dutch section of SOE, and the underground resistance organisation in Holland. Was it just a coincidence that the German flak was present at our dropping zone that night in December 1942?

Now, two years later, Northern Holland was again the scene of the unexpected involvement of German forces.

Was the decimation of the First Airborne Division at Arnhem due to a failure of intelligence? There has since been much written on this subject to suggest that there had been a lapse in intelligence in the planning and execution of the operation. Could there have been exceptional difficulties in maintaining secrecy in the Netherlands at that time? Did pre-war, cross-border relationships with Germany result in the wartime successes of Nazi Espionage and Counter-Espionage facilities?

My own experiences made me sceptical, and as I quietly reflected on these during my home leave in September 1944, I resolved that at some future date I would seek out the truth behind these events.

Some years later I was to read *The Venlo Incident*, which described how, at the outbreak of the war in 1939, a failure of intelligence (omitting to report the disposition of SS officers, in civilian clothes, near the Northern Dutch border with Germany) resulted in the capture of two British diplomats, Captain S. Payne-Best and Major R.H. Stevens, who remained prisoners of the Germans until the end of hostilities in 1945.[3]

However, for the moment, the excitement of being free and with my loved-ones outweighed everything. I could now walk a short distance unaided, but with a partially-locked left ankle joint and a painful left knee, walking and standing were always difficult. To walk any distance I needed the support of a stick, which for a young man of my age was a cumbersome inconvenience. But my feelings of inadequacy were always dispelled by Nita when we were together. She was proving a wonderful companion and had withstood the pressures of our two-year

---

[3] Details of the incident at Venlo only came to my attention when Payne Best's book was published in 1950, although newspapers reported some details of their capture in the early weeks of the war.

separation, between the ages of 19 and 21. During these war years many suitors had advanced their affections in Nita's direction, but I was never in doubt about her love for me or her loyalty. It was so different for me being in enforced confinement for this important period of our lives. During the four weeks in my home village we spent as much time as possible together and our strong affection for each other grew as we shared many invitations to join friends, who were interested in my exploits in the Royal Air Force and as a prisoner of war.

I remember an occasion when we were invited to a whist drive at my former technical school. We had an enjoyable evening and were both successful with prizes, although being a non-smoker, my prize of cigarettes was disappointing, except to my father, who had a steady desire for the wretched weed!

I thoroughly enjoyed being home with my parents, who were reassuring and plied me with as much food as the meagre ration system allowed, which helped me recover some of my weight loss of the past two years. This wasn't helped, however, by a feeling of nausea and sickness each morning, when I was unable to hold down breakfast; it was as if my stomach was re-adjusting to 'proper' food, as opposed to the meagre rations we had received from our German captors.

Apart from my parents, the only other family members who shared our home at that time were my younger sister, Winifred, who worked as a secretary in the Local Health office, and my brother, Walter, who had just completed his "O" levels at Neath Technical School. This was a very commendable achievement in view of the grief and distraction at home as a result of Jack's death and my being wounded and a prisoner of war. We spoke of events in the past two years and discussed the war situation. This was particularly interesting to Winifred, whose sweetheart, Trevor, was serving in the RAF ground staff in the Middle East; this resulted in several years of separation for them.

During that month at home I had many visitors, among them Penry Rice, a former classmate at Neath Technical School, who was on leave from a RAF Heavy Conversion Unit, where he qualified as a Flight Engineer and was about to commence operational flying with a Lancaster Squadron. He was keen to hear of my experiences. I was so sorry to hear later that he had been shot down and killed over Germany.

Another classmate at Technical School was Alan Hill, who went up to Halton with me in 1940 and later became a Flight Engineer with 617 Squadron. His aunt told me of his award of the DFC and that he was continuing on operations over Europe, which, of course, I knew to be dangerous at all times. Alan was a good friend at school and a keen swimmer whilst at Halton. I was pleased to hear of his success. Our paths didn't cross during the war and it wasn't until we met at a reunion of the 41st Halton entry in 1990 that we exchanged experiences and I learned that he had done much successful post-war flying with BOAC.

During the war Nita was called up to war service by the Ministry of Labour and National Service. Her talents for "sticking to the rules" were well directed to carry out accurate inspection work at a Neath factory. The manufacturing process was carried out on the three-shift system, which involved night work every third week. Nita was unhappy with these arrangements, but nevertheless continued in the job until the effects of evil smelling lacquer used in the process brought on a nasty nausea and frequent sickness. Her condition deteriorated, eventually resulting in her leaving the job.

She was still recovering from the illness when I spent my four weeks home leave. She was then asked to go to the Birmingham area and be involved in electrical work. There was much demand at the time for female workers in electronics, radio and electrical manufacture, but her medical condition confined her to her local area. After a period of convalescence, she was fit enough to undertake light work and fire-watching at the nearest town, Neath, which was on the main railway line from Paddington to Swansea and West Wales. There was also a main road and a rail bridge over the river Neath, which had become a vital link in the conveyance of a large amount of weaponry and men involved in the June 1944 invasion of Normandy.

The build-up of American forces for final training in the area had continued after D-Day and particularly in the Morriston area. Swansea docks and ports in West Wales would be used extensively for the large supply of war material for the fierce battles in Normandy to free France and the Low Countries.[4]

---

[4] This explained the heavy censorship of my sister's letter to me whilst I was a POW.

My four weeks' leave passed quickly as there was so much to do and so many people to see in connection with their loved ones still in captivity. Among them was my cousin Janet, whose husband had been captured by the Japanese in the Far East and of whom news was scarce. Nita and I spent a few days visiting her and other relatives in rural Oxfordshire, which provided an opportunity to see Janet at Addebury and her parents Uncle Joe and Aunt Annie at Bodicote. They were so pleased to see me and were delighted to meet Nita for the first time.

We enjoyed the warm Cotswold countryside, which showed much evidence of the recently-completed grain harvest. This was one of the main topics when we called in on Aunt May and Uncle Norman at Wykham Mill Farm, about two miles from Bodicote. This had been my holiday home for many pre-war years when my brother Len and I had happily worked on the harvest of wheat, oats and barley in the daytime and enjoyed a pleasant ride on the horses in the evenings.

They were thrilled to meet Nita, who enjoyed the farm environment, except for the manure-heap at one end of the yard, awaiting distribution on the fields!

I heard the latest news of cousin Philip, now a Flight Lieutenant pilot on a Coastal Command Squadron, flying Mosquito aircraft and based in West Wales. I was subsequently to make contact with him and we shared a pleasant time together when he managed 24 hours away from his squadron and stayed at my parents' home.

I noted how well the Italian POWs, assigned to work on the farm, were looked after by my Uncle and Aunt, whose other employees had been called up, with the exception of the foreman, Charlie, who had taught me so much about farming methods during my many visits in the late 1930s.

I was also pleased to enjoy church services again in my native village, where I thanked God for my preservation and safe return. The parish church had been a tower of spiritual strength throughout the war and Nita was warm in her praise for the regular prayers, seeking God's help and sustenance for the wounded and safekeeping for all servicemen on land, sea and in the air.

It was with mixed feelings that I walked slowly home on that last night of my month's leave. Nita and I had sat next to mother at Evensong earlier that afternoon (the 6.30pm services had been brought forward to 3pm as a wartime measure, to avoid church-goers trudging home in the blackout). I had been entertained to supper at Nita's but the evening had passed all too quickly, before a loving kiss was followed by a difficult parting. I was due to catch an early train the following morning, for Blackpool, to report back at RAF hospital, Weeton.

As the train sped north that morning, I sat alone in the compartment and worried as I contemplated further treatment on my left leg and a strengthening of my right leg, which was slow in recovering. I was also concerned about my future in the Royal Air Force. Would the powers-that-be accept a disabled flier back on operations with the situation in the Far East looming as a serious threat? There had already been one casualty in the family in that theatre of war, when Nita's cousin, Mervil Smith, a Hurricane Pilot, was shot down and reported missing over Malaya in July 1943. I remembered how, in 1941, my Christmas leave from Halton was extended by a week as our quarters in No.1 Wing had been occupied by a contingent for the Far East, who were being kitted out and inoculated before sailing. On my return to Halton I had been upset to find that my cricket bat had been removed from my locker and completely ruined by the frolicking airmen, having a last fling before sailing. Little did I realise at that time that most of the chaps from that contingent would be killed or captured by the Japanese in their march through Malaya, Singapore and the East Indies.

By the time I reached the end of my solitary journey that day, my mind had travelled through a maze of possibilities about the future, reflecting on my medical situation, which I hoped to resolve soon at the RAF hospital. Regarding my future career prospects, much depended on the air force appraisal of my suitability to continue in service. At the same time, I was pleased with the loving welcome home from Nita and felt secure in my future relationship with her, but I pondered on the potential difficulties that would arise from an overseas posting and its effect on our future together.

I was reunited with my fellow ex-POWs at Weeton Hospital and all had much to say about how good their homecomings had been – except one young air gunner who had suffered a spinal injury when he baled out of his blazing aircraft. He was now busily contacting the RAF legal department to help him obtain a separation and divorce. He had undergone the appalling experience of contracting venereal disease from his young wife at the commencement of his leave, who had then been compelled to admit that she had been unfaithful during his enforced absence as a POW. It was fortunate that the hospital was now able to treat him for his disease, as well as deal with his disabling back problem, but his profound disappointment left me with a deep sympathy for the difficulties he faced in the future.

Conversely, it was with much happiness that Don told me of his continuing loving relationship with his sweetheart, Daphne, whom he had much exalted whilst we were together in Germany.

The injuries to Don's leg were similar to mine (although he had additional head injuries) so it was no coincidence that our medical appraisals by the doctors at Weeton resulted in us both being advised that no further surgery was necessary and that we would therefore be sent to a Royal Air Force Rehabilitation Unit within the next few days. This unit, where remedial work was carried out on aircrew members who had suffered wounds in operational flying and training, was based at Hoylake, on the Wirral peninsula. There the Ley's school, occupied during the war emergency, provided the facilities for orthopaedic cases to be treated with physiotherapy and carefully-controlled exercises and sporting activities. Such activities also assisted in the psychological recovery of the damaged minds of downed airmen, aiming for a successful return to flying duties wherever possible.

I enjoyed my three months of rehabilitation, which involved much exercising of my damaged leg to strengthen the reduced muscles. An attempt was also made to increase the limited movement of my locked left ankle. Gymnasium exercises, cycle riding and dancing resulted in a strengthening of my leg, regrettably accompanied by excessive swelling at the end of each day's activities. I was advised that this was due to extensive damage to veins and nerve ends in the lower leg and ankle joint, although further surgery was not contemplated.

Life was very pleasant, in a splendid environment, at "The Ley's", with plenty of female presence in the shape of WAAF assistants in all departments and some local ladies, who attended once a week to help with the dancing exercises for leg cases. This suited some of my colleagues, who dated company fairly regularly, but despite the many opportunities, I remained loyal to dear Nita, who had faced many similar advances, especially when the RAF Balloon Unit was based in the village.

There was much to do in the evenings, with bridge, whist and plenty of reading material in the library. There was also an abundance of air force literature, enabling me to bring myself up to date with the flying news, so well written in *Flight* and *Aeroplane* magazines.

A visiting padre enabled us to have services each Sunday and these were well attended, as most Church of England services were in my Royal Air Force experience. They provided an opportunity for some thankful solitude in which to think about my future career, which was very much dependent on the Air Force medical authorities, who were continuously monitoring my progress. At the same time, I was conscious of a strengthening of my love for Nita. We decided to talk over the situation during my next leave, which soon followed in December 1944. We found mutual agreement, during a most enjoyable Christmas at home with my family and Nita, and on a Warrant Officer's pay I could afford to exchange better presents.

There was disturbing news during the pre-Christmas period of an unexpected German breakthrough in the Ardennes, only thinly occupied by the American army. It became apparent that the German thrust to the Meuse, aimed at Antwerp, was extremely dangerous and the threatening 'bulge' in the allied lines was only stopped and reversed by the timely intervention of the British 21st Army Group in the north and west and the Americans in the south. Within a few days there followed a massive attack by the Luftwaffe on the advanced allied air bases in the Low Countries. Again, there followed cheerful news that during these attacks, despite the loss of many allied fighters on the ground, the Luftwaffe's losses of fighters was excessive. The failure of these two major efforts by the Germans was to prove decisive and I felt confident that the war against Germany could not last much longer.

I was now walking greater distances, with a slight limp but less pain, although the strain of this very limited activity resulted in a painful swelling of the limb each day. I continued remedial treatment at Hoylake for a further week or so, until, after consultation with the senior medical officer, I was advised that no further operations were necessary and that I was to report to a holding unit at RAF Innsworth, near Gloucester, to await posting instructions. There, I was told that my re-assignment would be delayed and I could go on indefinite leave. Despite this uncertainty, I enjoyed being home again and resolved that I would now take a vital step in life and ask Nita to marry me. After spending much of my savings on our engagement ring, it was pleasing to overcome the cold and snow on January 26th 1945 with Nita's warmth and acceptance, when I proposed. That evening of our betrothal we discussed the future and resolved that in view of the fact that we both only twenty-one years old and the need to save funds for setting up home together, we would not marry for at least two years. We wished for an early summer white wedding at our parish church and set our sights on Thursday June 12th 1947, come what may. In the event, and after consulting with our parents, we set out, with much discipline and planning, to fulfil our wishes. We were clearly in love with one another and looked forward to the future with much optimism. We prayed that God would bless us and help us at this vital stage of our lives.

In a few days I received instructions to report to RAF St Athan, where I was to undertake instructor's duties at the same Flight Engineering School where I had received my own training just over two years before. This posting pleased me, especially since I could dispense my knowledge and experience at a school I knew, and only thirty-five miles from home. This would enable me to see Nita often at weekends. I was treated well at St Athan and with due regard to my physical condition I was not required to do any of a Warrant Officer's duties that necessitated marching or standing for long periods and I was issued with a bicycle to enable me to get around the large station. I had my own private room and an orderly was allocated to maintain a clean and tidy quarter for me.

After a short refresher course on the later versions of the Halifax and some training in the techniques of instruction, I was let loose to give lectures to the young volunteers being trained as Flight Engineers. All the while I hoped that they would not have to undergo my wretched experiences of a terrible crash, being wounded or becoming a prisoner of war. In the event, there were many casualties on bombing operations, right up to the day of of the German surrender in early May 1945. Those were followed by other losses of aircraft on training flights and during bomb disposal. The worse disaster was when twenty-four army ex-prisoners of war were being flown home on May 9th by a Lancaster of 514 Squadron. The aircraft crashed near Juvincourt, killing all the ex-prisoners and the crew of six – a terrible blow to all the grieving families, especially those of the POWs, whose return had been expected, perhaps after many years of captivity. Thankfully, this was the only crash among many hundreds of flights bringing back ex-prisoners at the end of the war.

Other trainees on the Halifax Mark III with whom I had been involved, were destined for Far East operations against the Japanese in Singapore, Malaya and the East Indies. There was much flying to do in preparation for the planned assault from Ceylon, but, mercifully, the Japanese surrendered in September 1945 and these endeavours ceased. Bomber aircraft were soon engaged in recovering and bringing home large numbers of Far East prisoners of war who had suffered and starved far more seriously than we had experienced in Germany. The Japanese, like the Russians, did not adhere to the Geneva Convention in their treatment of prisoners, neither were Red Cross supplies accepted by these belligerents.

Although my leg was strengthening slowly, I was still walking with a slight limp and could only achieve short distances. Towards the end of April, I received instructions to report to a medical board in London. This was a blow, as I was enjoying my duties as an instructor and the frequent weekends at home with Nita and my family, including worshipping at the village church, where the bells were now being rung regularly. Dad was so happy to be able to resume his lifelong hobby and Nita and I took great pleasure in the beautiful sound from the ancient tower on Sundays and practice nights on Fridays.

The medical board chairman, an Air Commodore, informed me that my condition was unsatisfactory for air force requirements and regretted that I would therefore be discharged from the service. He added that I was young enough to embark on a new career. This was staggering news. I had been committed to service life until the age of thirty and there was every probability of promotion beyond that age, if I had felt so inclined. This, and the thought of my future with Nita, exercised my mind as I journeyed home.

My parents were not surprised when I broke the news and seemed reconciled to my future in God's hands. They knew that my sickness attacks in the morning were not only due to a change in diet after prison camp food but also to the psychological results of my wartime experiences.

Whilst Nita was also aware of these effects, she was very gracious in her prognosis and assured me that all would turn out well. She was blessed with good parents, who supported her in all ways, and they were kind and considerate with me. I was now given leave to await my discharge papers, which arrived within a week or so, and I duly reported to a discharge centre at Wembley, where I exchanged my service clothes for a civilian de-mob suit and a trilby hat. It was now VE day and I made haste to catch an early afternoon train home. I was not happy in crowds of people and the celebrations in London did not appeal to me. I just wanted to be with my loved-ones, who had survived the double blow of having two sons missing in operations over enemy territory.

Events had passed so quickly since my return from Germany and during the re-adjustment to life with a disability I was unable to pursue my investigations into the mystery that had changed my life so dramatically in December 1942. I did, however, learn that extensive clandestine operations had been continued by 138 and 161 Squadrons from Tempsford right up to 'D' Day and beyond with a stepping up in their frequency in the early months of 1944. These were supplemented by the support of 90 Squadron, transferred from RAF Tuddenham in 3 Group Bomber Command, where they had been involved in bombing attacks and mine-laying operations.[5]

Despite various enquiries, no information was divulged about SOE operations during the war and I was left in the dark about events that had brought an end to Halifax 'R' Robert and my crew. I was now living with my parents in Wales and without a telephone it was more difficult to seek out and follow up likely sources of information.

I met up with a friend who just returned to Llantwit Major from a prisoner of war camp, who told me of the terrible experiences of former colleagues, who had been marched out of POW camps in Poland and Eastern Germany, ahead of the approach-

---

[5] Had my brother Jack not been killed in an attack on Berlin with this squadron in August 1943, it would have been an interesting co-incidence that we would both have served at Tempsford. Regrettably, it was not to be. Jack was initially buried, with five other members of his crew, in the Eastern zone of Germany. After the war, their graves were transferred to the Commonwealth cemetery in West Berlin.

ing Russian armies. In the depth of winter, with no proper food, often dug raw out of the fields as they trudged on, they often slept in the open and there was a high degree of dysentery and other illnesses. Some were force-marched more than five hundred miles to reach Stalag 359 at Fallingbostel and other camps west of Berlin. I learned that my colleagues at Stalagluft VI had been transported in the dirty and cold coal-holds of tramp-steamers from Lithuania and the Eastern Baltic to Stettin and other ports in Northern Germany. They were then force marched, in atrocious conditions, until they were eventually released by the Allied armies approaching from the west and flown home by RAF or USAF bombers.

I was also told of many unfortunate deaths amongst my POW friends, who were accidentally shot up by our own Typhoon fighter/bombers engaged in attacking enemy troop movements and assembly points for their mobile defences. I also recall hearing of the discovery by our advancing troops of Buchenwald and other death camps, where the wholesale slaughter of foreign workers, Jews and other unfortunate souls had been carried out by their German captors. I was not entirely surprised at these announcements by the Government and in the world press, as I had observed with my own eyes many train-loads of these unfortunate people, being transported from south-east European countries to Germany. In the railway sidings, where we often stopped during our travels, these smelly wagons, crammed with screaming people, were sometimes shunted nearby. I also saw what appeared to be pits of lime at intervals by the track, presumably awaiting the corpses of the unfortunates who died as a result of these squalid conditions.

In those early months after 'VE' Day I continued to make contact and meet up with as many of my returning friends as possible. I was particularly grateful to Mr and Mrs Coleman for entertaining me at their home in Downley, Buckinghamshire when visiting their son Don and other addresses in that area. In early June, Nita and I made a train journey to London and met up with Sgt D.R. Johnson, the mid-upper gunner and sole survivor of my brother's crew. He was able to describe the attack by a German night-fighter over Berlin on August 31st 1943. He thought Jack was fatally wounded and went down, along with five of their crew, when they crashed South East of the German capital as they were flying away from Berlin on their return journey. He said that they were a busy, happy and experienced crew and had been approaching the mandatory thirty operations during the highly-intensive bombing campaign in the summer of 1943. He described Jack as the eldest in their crew and quite popular at their base, Wratting Common in Cambridgeshire.

Nita and I returned home with the sad confirmation of Jack's death This was accepted by everyone in the family except my dear mother, who still retained her doubts and feared that he might still be wandering around in the now-defeated Germany, with head-wounds and loss of memory. It wasn't until 1968, when she accompanied me to the British Commonwealth Cemetery in West Berlin and saw the well-kept tombstones of Jack and his crew, that she finally came to terms with the sad loss of her eldest son.

The well-kept cemetery in West Berlin revealed the highly efficient and thorough work of the Commonwealth War Graves Commission, created by Major General Sir Fabian Ware in 1917. This organisation, which is responsible for the care of the graves of some of my crewmates at the village church of Ijhorst in Northern Holland and others throughout the world, does an outstanding job in preserving the memory of gallant servicemen who sacrificed their all for our benefit.

On my return journey to Wales from London on 14th June 1945, I was stirred by a report in the *Evening Standard* headed "Secret flyers beat Gestapo in night game" by Jane Stuart. This was a glowing summary of the work carried out by 138 and 161 Squadrons from Tempsford. They were not able to include details but mentioned the hundreds of individual operations carried out using Whitley and Halifax aircraft over long distances, delivering agents and/or supplies for resistance groups, and Lysanders and Hudsons for shorter distances, with their ability to land and take off on small, improvised airfields. Such details were still secret and remained so for many years after the war. The vital connection that the Tempsford Squadrons had in the secret war was now exposed, but I was not happy with the headline in view of the fiasco that took place with the Netherlands resistance in 1942 and 1943, in which I and my fellow crewmembers were so disastrously involved. During the rest of my journey home that day I pondered my future actions in view of my undertaking to maintain secrecy before I started operations at Tempsford.

In the summer months of 1945 my life was in a whirl as, following my medical discharge, my future career occupied much of my time. In those months I renewed contact with many friends with whom I had shared the wretched POW experience and with the families of former school and RAF friends who paid the supreme sacrifice.

I had a difficult experience when I visited Mrs Lewis, the mother of Warrant Officer Ernest Lewis, who was shot dead by the Gestapo after his recapture near Danzig in August 1944. 'Taffy' Lewis had broken out earlier from Stalagluft VI, on the border between Lithuania and East Prussia, and planned his escape down the coast via the contacts set up at Danzig by earlier escapees from our camp. Mrs Lewis had earlier been advised by the Red Cross that her son had died of wounds while attempting to escape. In fact, shots to his head had brought about his cruel death, but I avoided revealing these details when giving my commiserations to Mrs Lewis. Her son had been a wireless operator on a 10 Squadron Whitley V, shot down on a bombing operation to Bremen on the night of 27th/28th June 1941. He hailed from Crynant, just a few miles from my home village.

During the summer I attended an interview at Hatfield, whereupon the De Havilland Company offered me a student apprenticeship, leading to a career in aeronautical engineering. I had already completed much of the ground during my earlier education at Neath Technical College, followed by my Halton apprenticeship, and then part-time study of advanced mathematics at Cardiff Technical College, whilst at RAF St Athan, plus some work achieved whilst a POW. I was readily accepted by the college at the interview. However, medically I was not yet fit enough, as my constitution had not readjusted itself. Despite mother's capable handling of my diet, I had periods of vomiting most mornings. I could not expect similar care away from home. At the same time there was no further improvement in the condition of my leg. This left me with pain and swelling each day after a minimum of standing and walking. I therefore wasn't able to accept the college's offer.

Regrettably, I also turned down an opportunity to attend Swansea University, where I was offered an undergraduate course in Mechanical Engineering. On reflection, I realise that uncertainty and lack of confidence had invaded my mental attitude in the summer of 1945. I was, meanwhile, enjoying the loving presence of Nita in my life. Whilst I felt I had some catching up to do, having courted her little in the past five years, she always encouraged me to take my time and come to the right decision. It was now late summer and I feel sure God intervened and guided me in my mental dilemma. I was approached by a friend, who was manager of the local office for the Ministry of Labour and National Service, who offered me a temporary job. The resettlement of men and women into employment following victory in Europe and the Far East was a mammoth task, and they needed additional help to deal with the extra workload.

My work at Neath Labour Exchange involved the unemployment benefit entitlements of a number of former coalminers, suffering from the dreaded *silicosis* and *pneumoconiosis*. These men had spent their working lives down the pits in the Glyneath and Resolven areas, but due to ill-health were now unable to follow full-time employment. Their plight disturbed me; I felt they deserved as much medical and financial help as the nation could provide, but regrettably there was inadequate support and the delays in their medical examinations were excessive. This failure was one of the many reasons why the area has remained a Socialist bastion until today, despite the cessation of deep-pit mining two generations ago ago. The scars still remain, in memory of the damaged lungs of their forefathers.

I soon learnt the procedures and found my own experiences invaluable in dealing with ex-service people of comparable age. My ability with figures and statistical work was quickly recognised and I was offered an appointment, with promotion, at the Government Training Centre being set up at Swansea. About this time I passed the Civil Service examination for Clerical Officers. Thus, as a permanent Civil Servant, I became the Assistant Accountant at Swansea GTC, where we occupied a temporary factory and office space at Cwmbwrla. Under the control of the accountant, Mr Alan G. Hart, and the temporary assistance of a mature civil servant sent down from London, who helped in the setting-up of the organisation, we commenced the training of ex-servicemen in the building trades. With a small administrative and accounting staff, trainee members were soon up to two hundred in carpentry, bricklaying, plumbing and ancillary trades.

I found my technical training background and experience of mixing with all branches of HM Forces whilst a POW most beneficial in settling down to the new tasks. Alan Hart was proving a most capable head of our department and I learnt much from his knowledge and experience in the finance department of the Wales office of the Ministry. His ability in labour relations, in particular, was most pronounced. My association with him developed into mutual trust and friendship, which Nita and I enjoyed with him and his wife, Winifred, for forty or more years until Alzheimer's disease overtook them both. I will always cherish the fact that they both put their Christian principles into practise in their conduct towards those around them.

I was also most fortunate to meet up with Mr W. Arthur Griffiths at this time, who was appointed office manager for the newly-opened Training Centre at Gors Road, Swansea when we vacated our temporary accommodation. Arthur Griffiths, with long experience as a manager in the labour exchange service in Wales, proved an outstanding colleague, and our friendship strengthened during our shared daily train journey from Neath to Swansea. As a long-time secretary of Neath Rugby Club, his interesting stories made the daily travel far too short and his wealth of experience in departmental affairs was most helpful to me in my new role.

It was now 1946 and I had progressed in my new career and with higher income Nita and I were able to save as our great promised day in June 1947 became ever nearer. There was also the saving of ration coupons for household goods, furniture and bed linen which started as we planned to set up our home together following the big day.

Throughout this time my meagre attempts to unearth the truth behind my wartime debacle were not succeeding and there was no explanation forthcoming from the authorities. The SOE organisation had been disbanded when the wars in Europe and the Far East were concluded, with no apparent report on their work, and I was too remote in Wales to make any personal calls on the London power-base. My wretched experiences of 1942 to 1944, however, remained at the back of my mind.

But for now, thoughts of my career and forthcoming marriage crowded out such thinking. My confidence and health improved and my leg was now much stronger. Despite the rationing and the rigours of the post-war years, the country was getting on its feet. I was, however, very disappointed when Winston Churchill was defeated in the first post-war election. In fact, Nita and I were particularly disturbed when visiting the cinema at Aberavon, where the audience booed loudly when Churchill was shown giving a speech on *Movietone News*. To us this seemed a disgusting show of ingratitude after the outstanding achievements of the Prime Minister throughout the war, but it reflected the attitude of a people whose forefathers had been ruthlessly exploited by the their employers during and after the industrial revolution. Poor working conditions, poor pay and no attempt to introduce pension schemes for the large workforce of miners, steel and tin plate workers and other related industries had resulted in feelings of bitterness and resentment.

My own political thinking, since I had been old enough to understand, was influenced by the corruption and arrogance that had developed in local government while under Socialist control. Nita and I were very much in the minority and both our parents favoured the liberal approach of Lloyd George and his supporters. They remembered well his contribution in the First World War.

My work in the Ministry provided a broadening of my political understanding and opportunities for advancement became apparent. I remember taking a week-long course on labour relations, in London, during the early months of 1947, when a fuel crisis had led to strict control of the use of power and light and even hot water levels in baths at hotels were restricted. These were tough times, during a very cold spell of weather.

There was, however, a crumb of comfort when the cricket clubs restarted, most having abandoned their activities during the war. In the spring of 1946, work on village, town and county grounds took place and players began donning their whites, after a long lay-off. Such activity did not go unnoticed by me and I was itching to have a go, but my desires were thwarted by my inability to run. I visited the Ynysygerwn ground and watched them play a few times, and during the intervals between innings I handled a bat for the first time since 1944. This was a great thrill and I vowed to improve my physical condition so that I could partake once again.

Time marched on and in the winter of 1946/47 Nita and I firmed up our plans for our marriage, which was to take place the following June. We were very much in love and joyously planned for the wonderful occasion. The Vicar welcomed us warmly when we proposed the date of Thursday 12th June, followed by a honeymoon of a few days in Taunton before moving on to the Crofton House Hotel at Torquay for a week's stay. Both our families were loyal members of the village church, enabling the ceremony and wedding breakfast to be well organised around the church. Helpful members of the Mothers' Union served the 125 guests to a splendid meal in the church room. Nita and I had prayed earnestly for God's help in furthering our unison and the whole village rallied round with food coupons and much goodwill. The marriage service, carried out in the presence of a full church, was well conducted by the Vicar, the Reverend Ishmael, supported by our Curate, Rev Curtis Morgan. We chose meaningful hymns, including our favourite, which resounded through the ancient church and set the right tone for what we had prayed and longed for – a long and happy marriage, filled with joy and happiness.

Hymn 671 (*Ancient and Modern*) sung to the tune *Tranter*

> *Breathe on me, Breath of God,*
> *Fill me with life anew;*
> *That I may love what Thou dost love*
> *And do what Thou wouldst do.*

> *Breathe on me, Breath of God,*
> *Until my heart is pure;*
> *Until with Thee I will one will*
> *To do and to ensure.*

> *Breathe on me, Breath of God*
> *Till I am wholly Thine,*
> *Until this earthly part of me*
> *Glows with Thy fire divine.*

> *Breathe on me, Breath of God*
> *So shall I never die*
> *But live with Thee the perfect life*
> *Of Thine eternity.*

These words beautifully encompassed our deepest thoughts on our wedding day and have provided Nita and I with much solace in the sixty years since.

Nita's parents were generous in their warmth for me and most kind in making available in the village two rooms and shared use of a bathroom and kitchen. The other residents in the semi-detached residence were on a short-stay lease, so we were able to start our young lives together soon on our own. After a splendid honeymoon we returned to our new abode – 'Brookdale', Cadoxton, near Neath – all set up for us, despite the absence of a stair carpet, as our stock of ration coupons was insufficient. It was many months before we could accumulate the coupons to afford this luxury. However, one day I returned from my work to find the soft comfort already laid; a further step forward.

After watching some cricket during our short stay in the West Country I was developing an urge to get started again. Later in the 1947 season I saw a few matches at Ynysygerwn, where my brother-in-law, Frank Gordon, had played with distinction before the war. This wetted my appetite and I ventured to see a game or two at the Gnoll, played by the Neath eleven, where Frank had also opened their innings many times in the late 1930s.

Regrettably, his cricket career was curtailed by the onset of tuberculosis, which was a virulent disease in the late 30s, and he spent a long time at Craig-Y-Nos sanatorium. This was formerly the castle occupied by Madame Adelena Patti, the Italian opera singer, who, at about the turn of the century, used the spectacular setting as a temporary home whilst in the United Kingdom. She was a great attraction and a friend of royalty. The single-track Neath and Brecon railway line used to carry the famous to the beautiful landscaped estate, where the River Tawe flows down from the Brecon Beacons. Latterly the castle has been used for a variety of events, including Neath Opera Group's use of its intimate theatre, with little space for an orchestra, seating only about 100 or so enthusiasts, as in Madam Patti's day.

The smell of the linseed oil on the willow and of the mown grass, accompanied by the sight of the players all in white, was becoming a great attraction, and I vowed to make myself fitter and participate in a few games in 1948. I was encouraged to these activities by Nita, who knew my potential and that such activity would help me recapture my youthful involvement in a sport I loved. We were still just twenty-four years of age and I encouraged Nita to get out her tennis racquet and renew her interest in the game she enjoyed so much.

After the very cold early months of 1948, I visited the Ynysygerwn club and started practicing batting and fielding when the season commenced. I was not very mobile, but I was soon playing good shots in the nets and fielding at the slip catcher, despite the pain of my damaged leg and other exercise pains from muscles and joints that were not quite fit. To my great satisfaction, I was selected to play in the second eleven and, after achieving some good results, was soon opening the batting for the first eleven. Although, at that time, the club was not in the top cricket league in South Wales, the standard of the team and the opposition was quite good. Both Nita and I were so pleased that I had not lost my enthusiasm or ability, following the fate that had befallen me 1942. My parents, too, were pleased with my progress and we all thanked God for his mercy and guidance in our lives.

No one was more pleased that I had enjoyed some success at Ynysygerwn than Arthur Griffiths, who, during our daily travel together, persuaded me to look further afield the following season. He had some friends connected with Neath Cricket Club and I was approached to join them in the spring of 1949.

In the meantime Nita and I were blessed with the arrival of our baby son, Philip Roger, who was born on 25th January. Despite a normal pregnancy and careful preparation, the birth proved most difficult. The complications necessitated a surgical birth at Neath General Hospital, where Nita was detained for about ten days and not allowed to see her new-born for five days. He was isolated in the children's ward after the birth, seriously in peril. In fact, Vicar Ishmael came with me to the hospital with Nita's mother and mine, to pray for the life of both our child and Nita. It was a hard time for her, which negatively influenced our attitude to increasing the size of our family.

However, Jesus was ever-present with us and mercifully helped both Nita and Philip survive their suffering. Our prayers had been answered again. I had repainted the child's bedroom in time to greet my loved ones on their return and baby Philip soon settled in for a happy childhood and a most interesting and absorbing life ahead.

I was very busy in my job at Swansea GTC, as large numbers successfully concluded their training after military service and unemployment. I was granted leave of absence for one day when Nita and Philip Roger returned home; a normal amount of time in those days, as opposed to today, when people can take six months or even a year away from work, which I think is unnecessary. I also believe that the mother being home with the child for as long as possible is preferable for the development of our youngsters.

With a young child to rear, Nita and I found meeting all the financial needs more difficult and we resorted to careful budgeting of our income and expenditure. At the time, Civil Service annual pay reviews were miserly and I recall writing to the staff magazine, complaining of the "frozen weight of the Treasury impinging on the situation". My efforts were rewarded with a book prize from the staff association. Nevertheless, I became conscious of the inadequacy of pay in Government Service at the time and this remained with me for further resolution.

Within the next year I was pleased to be selected by my employers to undertake a part-time study in Economics and Industrial Psychology at Cardiff University. One day a week I attended lectures by Professor Brinley Thomas, the gifted head of economics at the University, and his younger colleague, who provided interesting enlightenment, particularly with regard to people's motivation and attitudes towards work and their fellow men. I grasped this opportunity with enthusiasm, despite a very early morning start and a late return in the evenings. I found lying alongside Philip, who had been reluctant to sleep, most rewarding as I related stories of my travels, including one about "the Cowbridge cows" who made a habit of delaying the Neath-Cardiff coach as they crossed the road after milking each day.

Meanwhile, Nita rejoined the operatic society, after a short interval, and was soon singing Philip to sleep with arias and absorbing music from *Martha*, a delightful opera, based on *Richmond Fair* by Flotow. During practice evenings, we were blessed with the presence of Nita's mother, Dolly, who lived about three hundred yards away. With a fond love for Philip, she was only too pleased to be with him as often as necessary. He had an alert mind from birth and we found that evenings were always a time when other interests prevented him from settling down early.

I was able to follow through my introduction that summer to the Neath Cricket Club, where I found a warm welcome from Cyril Michael, the first eleven skipper, and a most capable left-arm bowler and vice-captain, Phil Griffiths. Both had been pre-war stars with the club who, after returning safely from war service in the Army, were now both headmasters of schools in the neighbourhood. Consequently, they both had a keen interest in youth development. The other members at the Gnoll were all congenial and I soon settled in with batting and fielding practice. They were conscious of my inability to run properly at first, but with help, encouragement and the psychological impact of a sound batting technique, I found myself chasing around in fielding practice and using the slip-catcher. My abilities with the latter, and my batting, were sufficient for me to be selected for the second eleven, initially under David Samuel, whose character and genuine love of people were prominent. After a couple of good scores and successful matches I found my name appearing on the First XI team list, along with John Shaw Williams, a young ex-serviceman also promoted to play under the guidance of Cyril Michael, our able and amenable captain, and his outstanding spin-bowler, Phil Griffiths.

Thus followed an interesting and rewarding phase of my life in a successful club participating in the South Wales and Monmouthshire League. In my first season I was pleased to achieve moderate success, which continued in subsequent years. During that time I made lasting friendships with, amongst others, John Shaw Williams, Huw Morgan, Terry Shufflebottom and Stan Trick, who moved on to obtain greater honours for Glamorgan County and the All-England Amateurs. His business connections in his father-in-law's car dealership, were instrumental in his decision not to play professionally; he continued into retirement with Neath CC.

At this time, a youngster in a green cap was making his way in schoolboy cricket and, whilst he was still at Neath Grammar School and under the careful tutelage of Cyril Michael and Phil Griffiths, developed into a splendid batsman, with whom I opened the batting many times for our First Eleven. The talented youngster was A.R. (Tony) Lewis, who went on to play senior cricket successfully for the Combined Services whilst doing his two years National Service in the Royal Air Force and was later the first grammar school boy to captain Cambridge University. After graduation his prowess was recognised by Glamorgan County CC, which he captained to victory in the county championship. He was a successful member of the MCC, touring as their captain, and later became their president. We are so proud of our prodigy of the Neath Club, who surpassed even the achievements Cyril Walters, another former member of the town eleven, who, when captain of Worcestershire, also captained the national eleven in test matches. Their two photographs still proudly adorn the cricket pavilion at the Gnoll, having brought great distinction to the town and club.

During the 1949 season, I was also pleased that my cricket performances came to the notice of my employers and I was chosen to represent the Wales region of the Ministry of Labour and National Service for a couple of seasons. These were most enjoyable mid-week matches, played with some other first division league players, including Reg Webb of Newport, Cliff Tamplin, the Cardiff wicket-keeper and other well-known names in South Wales and Monmouthshire cricket circles. We played at Trent Bridge, against the Midlands, and lovely grounds in Stroud and Bristol, our home matches being played at Cardiff Arms Park, Barry and other good, fast pitches, which suited my batting technique.

With the continued weakness in my left leg, I was predominantly a forward-playing left-hander, allowing me to take my forward thrust on the good leg. Despite using such technique, the left leg was always painful and swollen, requiring a rest after each match. Our young son was introduced to the cricket scene at an early age when his mother would wheel him, in his Silver Cross pram, to our home matches at the Gnoll, and I would snatch a few minutes with them in the tea intervals. He was keen from the start and I gave him a little cricket bat, with a handle small enough for his two-year-old fingers to grip.

These were great times, which we all enjoyed. We also had the benefit of the warmth of Philip's grandparents, who showed such Christian love to us all. We used to take pleasure in our outings after church on Sunday mornings. We would drive out with Nita's parents to quiet locations, within about an hour's journey from home, such as the beaches on the Gower Peninsula, or the Brecon Beacons, with their abounding beauty, which were among our favourites.

I was becoming increasingly conscious of the limitations of Civil Service methods of financial control employed at the Training Centre, some of which were well-intended but very restrictive on individual initiative. I was good at figures and estimating, but felt these qualities were not being exercised to the full. I was supervising a small staff of ten and enjoyed the organisation and supervision of their work. I had a good introduction to implementing financial control of an industrial canteen, providing daily meals and services for about 350 people. I preferred an industrial environment, which was more interesting and better suited my technical background.

I realised the limitations of rewards in my position and knew that a qualification in industrial accountancy was essential if I was to achieve my potential and improve the quality of life of my family. A study of the alternatives indicated that membership of the Institute of Cost and Works Accountants would be an excellent prospect, as it combined my flair for mathematics and statistics with my technical background. It was late in 1949, the cricket season had finished and I applied for student member-ship; this was quickly granted, with exemption from preliminary examination due to the educational standard I had already achieved. The School of Accountancy in Glasgow had an excel-lent syllabus and I based my course planning on a minimum of twenty hours per week. I prepared myself well and within about a year was successful in the intermediate examinations, which I took in two halves. I was now fully immersed in the subject of industrial control and the economics of industry; I read avidly and knew this was my vocation. However, apart from passing the final examinations, I needed to gain a minimum of three years' practical experience in the profession. Whilst my work as Assistant Accountant in the Training Centre had some merit, I knew that experience in manufacturing industry would be essen-tial. I therefore resigned from the Civil Service when a suitable opportunity arose.

My application for the post of Foundry Accountant, requiring a minimum of intermediate standard in the professional exami-nations, was accepted at the South Wales Aluminium Company's plant near Resolven, a location just twenty minutes by bus from home. In the next two years my work provided excellent experi-ence and I passed the final examinations of the Institute. I was already better paid and found the long hours of study most rewarding. I was also fortunate in having the wonderful support of Nita, who understood how focused I was on my studies.

As a qualified member of the Institute I started to look further afield for a more responsible job with better opportunities to exercise my knowledge and interest in the financial control of industry. That opportunity soon came when, after two interviews and overcoming capable competitors, among them Bill Wil-liams, who was a highly-skilled colleague on the staff at the

Aluminium Company, I was appointed Works Accountant at Imber Research Limited, Pontardawe. They were setting up a new plant to manufacture oil heating and lighting products for Aladdin Industries Limited, the parent company, based at Greenford. My interviewers were Messrs Robert Imber, Director, Leslie Finlinson, Accountant, and Gordon Casselton, the appointed General Manager of their new venture, who, among other senior executives, remained good friends for many years.

This was my first executive appointment in industry, which I enjoyed immensely. We occupied an empty factory building that had been built post-war in the Wales Development Area – a government initiative that provided financial grants for capital expenditure on plant and buildings, which we utilised to the full. I was fortunate to find Gordon Casselton, an able General Manager who had experienced a lifetime with Aladdin Industries, latterly as General Manager of home sales. The company was also successful in overseas markets, which accounted for about forty percent of their annual turnover. A newly-appointed Works Manager completed an initial executive team and we were soon, with technical help from Greenford, assembling domestic and greenhouse oil heaters from components of our own manufacture and supplies from the parent company.

I often visited Greenford, to receive advice and compare notes as I set up the new systems of financial control and budgeting. It was a happy and rewarding experience, with a splendid working environment, and we were soon employing about 300 local people, of whom a third were women, who, along with most of the formerly unemployed men, required training in their appointed tasks. With a nucleus of experienced toolmakers, plant maintenance and office staff, we set up an efficient organisation, which was soon in its stride, accompanied by a canteen that supplied wholesome midday meals.

With a thorough training programme and technical support we made excellent progress, with steady growth of factory space and employees. I was given plenty of scope with the introduction of the accounting and costing system and involved myself in control statistics for the manufacturing processes. Some innovative ideas for recording scrap and quality control were introduced and I recall having a paper published on the subject in the accounting institute magazine. They kindly rewarded me with a book for my effort.

During these eventful years in my career, Philip had made excellent progress and in his infancy showed an alert and enquiring mind, which Nita and I both fostered. We were improving our lot financially and, after success in a driving course, I bought our first car – a beige Austin Somerset family saloon – which provided the means for more travel and an opportunity to repay Nita's father, who had been so generous in our early married years. Nita and I continued to worship faithfully at the village church, joined often by young Philip, who was brought up in the principles of our Lord Jesus. I felt that our prayers for success in my examinations and career progress had been answered by a loving God.

7. Discovering the Truth about Operation 'North Pole'

Now much fitter and with a greatly more settled and rewarding life, my thoughts turned increasingly to the fateful events of my wartime years. My frequent visits to Greenford and the London area gave me the opportunity to seek more information regarding SOE activities in the Netherlands during the war. These efforts were thwarted, however, by the effects of the Official Secrets Act, which drew a curtain over what had been secret operations, setting up and aiding the resistance organisations in Europe. Then, early in 1955, I experienced a remarkable break-through and was startled to learn that the events of 22nd/23rd December 1942, in which I had been severely wounded and six of my crewmates killed, were contrived by German intelligence and that we, in fact, had set out on our mission under a full moon that night at the behest of the enemy.

My suspicions at seeing German armed troops in the immediate area of the crash in Northern Holland were now confirmed by information obtained from German and Dutch sources. They had awaited the arrival of our Halifax with the ground signal lights in the correct geometrical pattern. As we circled near the dropping zone, with our propellers in fine pitch, aligning ourselves to drop our canisters and bags of supplies in the meadow as arranged, the German light flak unit assigned to the task of interception cocked their guns, ready to blow us out of the sky. We had no warning of the enemy presence and were unable to defend ourselves or take evasive action. We were sitting ducks – making the survival of Frank Tierney and myself all the more remarkable.

Similar enemy actions in Holland during the months between September 1942 and October 1943 resulted in the loss of twenty of our four-engined Halifax aircraft and the loss of 150 trained and experienced Royal Air Force aircrew. Lt Col Giskes, head of German Abwehr in Holland, also claims to have arrested 54 agents during that period as they parachuted into the arms of the awaiting enemy.

Operation "Nord-Pol" was a successful achievement of deception by the Abwehr, which had started in November 1941 by the betrayal of the Dutch resistance for financial gain by a man called "Riddenhof". He was a dealer in diamonds living in Holland and said his business had foundered when he met "Willy", an agent of the Abwehr. "Riddenhof", in trouble with the German authorities for diamond smuggling, spoke Dutch, Spanish, German and English, and knew a Dutch Reserve Officer Captain Van der Berg, who was already in touch with two Dutch agents operating with the British. Riddenhof wanted to be a "V" man, paid by the German secret service, and sought protection against the German currency authorities, with whom he was in trouble. His information was sufficient to influence Lieutenant Col Herman Giskes, head of Abwehr in Holland, and by March 1942 Operation North Pole was secretly in action to thwart the SOE Dutch section in London, in their plans to organise and arm loyal Dutchmen. Coded messages between London and agents in Holland, using key-tapping techniques, were a vital link, and the Abwehr and other German Naval and Military RDF (Radio Direction Finding) units were utilised to the full against them. This led to the detection of a transmitter near Arnhem and the arrest of the wireless operator, William Van de Reyden.

Hermann Giskes succeeded during Van de Reyden's interrogation and the Dutchman eventually divulged information about the codes that were employed, but he did not reveal his security checks. Giskes used Van Reyden to transmit coded messages to London without his security check, resulting in a negative response. Some weeks later a new secret transmitter was tracked down in The Hague, which led to the arrest of Dutch operator Hubert Lauwers and his agent companion Thijs (or Taconis), the latter having already contacted a branch of the resistance, which had been penetrated by an agent of the Abwehr. Their secret code for deciphering wireless messages to and from England was also seized, and this information, along with other intercepted transmissions, was enough for Giskes' plan *'England Spiel'* (England Game) to be activated.

He was supported by Leutnant Heinrichs of the radio interception department of the German police, responsible in Holland, following its occupation in 1940, for the suppression of clandestine radio links. He was successful in tracking down and

deciphering coded messages received from the Dutch section of
SOE in England.

Giskes was able, by clever interrogation and promises of
safety from the clutches of SIPO, to undermine the passive
resistance of Lauwers and Thijs, who eventually broke down.
This enabled the Germans to control the messages transmitted to
the Dutch section of the SOE in London by Lauwers and a
further fourteen radio links which were not detected by the
British, despite the safety checks included by Lauwers at great
risk. This, coupled with a failure to recognise the different touch
and individual characteristics of the German operators on the
transmission keys, was a serious lapse by SOE.

Lauwers' transmissions between March and October 1942
included his security check, which should have been a clear
warning to the receivers of the messages in England, who thus
knew that he had been captured by the Germans. Lauwers ci-
phered these himself, to confirm that his German captors had not
tampered with them. Later transmissions were carried out by
German operators using the captured codes and these also were
not picked up by SOE Dutch sections before 31st March 1944.

During this 18-month period they continued to send out
agents and supplies of arms and other resistance materials,
involving dangerous flights carried out by the Tempsford Squadrons. About fifty agents and large quantities of supplies were
parachuted straight into the arms of the awaiting German SIPO
squads, who arrested the agents and passed them over to Giskes
for interrogation. SS Sturmbannfuhrer Schreieder was in charge
of those members of SIPO, who must have been present at the
scene when my aircraft was shot down in Northern Holland on
that fateful night of 22nd/23rd December 1942. I have now concluded that it was one of these security policemen who dragged
me clear of the blazing wreckage which was about to engulf me.
Whoever it was wore civilian clothes, as did the enemy official
who carried out the first interrogation of Frank and I at the
Bonifatius Hospital in Leewarden. I thanked God, at the time,
for the sudden intervention that saved my life and now record
my grateful thanks to this stranger. May his soul rest in peace.

I have also been able to confirm from records of 138 and 161
Squadrons' casualties, sustained as a result of operations over
Holland in the period of Operation North Pole that German
claims of twenty aircraft succumbing to the cunning wiles of the

Abwehr are correct. Regrettably, during that 18-month period, the Royal Air Force aircrew losses on secret missions over Holland were 150. These were clearly due to a series of clever deceptions by the Abwehr. For most of that period these were not picked up due to a serious weakness in SOE Dutch section's ability to maintain the security of codes used in their transmissions to agents in the field.

An important feature of the Giskes' plan was to allow all the aircraft conveying the agents and canisters to drop their valuable secret cargoes to the apparent Dutch loyalists. The Germans then shot down only one in three of the vulnerable aircraft, hoping that the frequency of aircraft lost on Dutch operations would not raise suspicion. Nevertheless, the rate of losses on these missions was higher than similar operations over the Western and Scandinavian countries under German occupation. I recall an extra concern was shown by the aircrews in 138 Squadron when operations to Holland were ordered. These instructions emanated from SOE Dutch section, whose continuous requests for such missions demonstrated, in my view, a terrible lack of control by the officers responsible.

Against the background of higher-than-average RAF losses over Holland, two other factors were present. First, notwithstanding the powerful radio transmissions from Grendon, Bedfordshire, agents across Europe regularly requested confirmatory (i.e. second) messages; very few, if any, such requests were received from Dutch agents. Secondly, agents under pressure in the field often sent indecipherable messages or made occasional mistakes in their transmissions to the UK. In those received from Holland, however, this was not the general pattern, the messages usually being suspiciously error-free.

These phenomena were noted by a young Londoner, Leo Marks, who, at the age of twenty-two, had been selected for a course of training as a cryptographer in the Government Security Service. The talents of this young genius had been observed during an earlier interview when, despite his apparent flippancy, his answers to the head of the code-breakers school, Major Masters, were adequate to ensure his selection for the eight-week training course. This normally led on to an appointment at MI8, the headquarters of the cryptographic department at Bletchley in Buckinghamshire. Our base at Tempsford was also conveniently sited in Bedfordshire.

The highly secret activities at Bletchley Park have only been divulged in recent years, following the 30-year rule for the disclosure of secret documents. This rule has enabled an abundance of writers and historians to reveal to the world much of the commendable secret intelligence activities that sustained our country through the ups and downs of World War Two. There is no doubt in my mind that weaknesses at the London end of SOE's Dutch Section were one of the serious downs. They led to the tragic deaths of my crewmates and to many other casualties among my RAF colleagues of the Tempsford Squadrons, not forgetting, of course, the 50-odd courageous Dutch agents who fell into the traps set by the Abwehr during the best part of two years. Only since 1998 has the British end of the code war between SOE and German counter-intelligence in Holland been revealed to the public. I am, therefore, finally in a position to see the whole truth behind the events that culminated in my wartime experiences at the hands of the enemy.

The logical mind of Leo Marks and the painstaking analysis of hundreds of coded transmissions received, enabled him to discover that many messages from Holland were being transmitted in code without any errors. This was very suspicious, as all agents made errors during their training in the UK. When such messages were being composed and transmitted under extreme pressure and danger in enemy-occupied territories, there was every expectation that even more errors would be made. This was the case in transmissions from all the countries under occupation, with the exception of agents under the control of the Dutch Section.

A report to his seniors, Dansey and Owen, the Head and Deputy of Secret Codes for SOE was soon followed by one presented by Marks to Lieutenant Colonel Nichols of the War Office Signals Directorate and his deputy, Heffer. In the interview that followed, the brilliant young Marks was subjected to a searching examination of the many months of intensive work which had led him to conclude that the Germans had been using the SOE codes for their transmissions for a long time.

Mercifully, his report was acted on and, in a reorganisation of the signals traffic, Leo Marks was appointed to control the ciphering and coded transmissions of the agents' codes, now separated from the main line codes under Dansey and Owen. Colonel Nichols was appointed Head of the Signals Directorate and two other signals officers were dismissed for being inefficient, while others were posted back to their units and two army captains with responsibility for Dutch Section SOE affairs were relieved of their posts and sent to the Far East. This was a clear recognition of failure in the Dutch Section and of the success of Giskes and his Abwehr team in the secret war. Meanwhile, there was an increasing need for SOE activities in all the European countries, as the activities of underground resistance organisations were being stepped up prior to the impending invasion of the continent, which was inevitable before the German domination could be defeated.

One of Leo Marks' discoveries was that, hitherto, poems had been used to incorporate the coded messages between Headquarters and agents in the field. He proved that such coding could be broken easily by clever cryptographers and interpreters. The captured agent Boni acknowledged the safe arrival, on the night of December 22/23 1942, of new poems for himself and agents 'Parsnip' and 'Cabbage', who had also been swallowed up in the Giskes' web. This was the fateful drop by our Halifax "R" Robert on operation 'Marrow 12'.

But it was now Christmas time, a year after I was shot down, and whilst the code operators at Grendon House had some leave, the commendable Marks stood in and had a surprise visit from Colonel Nichols. This enabled the indefatigable young cryptographer to explain all that was wrong with the poem method of coding and the merits of the use of his newly-created WOK – a small piece of silk cloth on which a series of pre-printed transposition keys were provided, which would be burned by the agent immediately after use. Sufficient keys were provided for one hundred messages to be sent to and from the agent in the field using one WOK; a distinct improvement in the security of coded transmissions. This led to the use of random numbers as transposition keys on the WOK which was tried out on Flight Lieutenant Yeo Thomas, a leading member of the resistance organisation in France, parachuting in on many occasions. Later when a Wing Commander and known as the "White Rabbit" he was captured and suffered death at the hands of the Germans. Later in this narrative you will note reference to his widow Barbara, with whom Nita and I shared many happy times at reunions with members of the resistance organisations who survived the war. Members of the Tempsford Association, formed some years after the war, enjoyed the company of such gallant survivors.

Foremost among the French resistance survivors is my friend Gilbert Mûs who, after a period as a prisoner of war following the German victories in the 1940 campaign, escaped and eventually joined the Free French in the UK. He trained as a parachutist and sabotage agent and was subsequently dropped from a Whitley of 138 Squadron in 1942. he carried out many courageous and successful missions with the Jean Moulin circuit before it was betrayed, when he was rearrested by the Gestapo. He was detained in the notorious Fresnes Prison in Paris. This was a most gruelling experience, followed by incarceration at Mauthausen concentration camp, where he awaited the dreaded death sentence. Thankfully, however, he survived long enough to be freed by advancing American troops.

Free again, he returned to France where he and his charming wife Marie were married. A long and successful period in the Foreign Service of his country followed, and he and Marie were joined by a growing family. He retired to Bolbec in Normandy and was an active member of the ex-French resistance organisation. Whilst on our reunion at Amboise, a delightful town on the river Loire, Nita and I had much pleasure in meeting Gilbert and Marie. A close friendship ensued and we shared many holidays and reunions together in the UK and France. We found ourselves completely compatible and enjoyed Gilbert's sense of humour at all times. Marie's interest in and knowledge of historic buildings in her native country was always helpful on our many journeys. Sadly, with tired legs disabling our chums in France, and my own lack of mobility nowadays, we have to depend on other means to keep in touch. It has been a lasting friendship which we much cherish.

Members of the Special Forces Club also attended these many happy yet poignant reminders of the events of wartime.

One uplifting story to emerge from the sorry history of Operation North Pole was of the courageous and successful escape from imprisonment of two of the 52 Dutch agents captured during the operation. Pieter Dourlein and Bernard Ubbink were parachuted into Holland on 9/10 March 1943. On this occasion, the Tempsford-based Halifax that delivered them returned safely, but the agents and a large number of containers of explosives fell into the waiting arms of Herr Krimilinalrat Schreider and his SIPO Security Police.

After their capture, Dourlein and Ubbink were held at Haaren, a seminary in North Brabant converted into a high-security Gestapo prison, where the other 50 captured Dutch agents were also held. The two courageous and very determined Dutchmen made their daring escape on a moonless August 29th 1943, a Sunday, when, with the help of the Lord's intervention and an inattentive guard, their long, dangerous journey down the escape line to Switzerland and freedom began. It ended when they were flown by a RAF aircraft from Gibraltar to England on 1st February 1944, after nearly six months on the run.

They were immediately imprisoned by the authorities on suspicion of being German spies and it took a further three months of imprisonment and interrogation, including that by the Head of Dutch resistance in the UK, before the whole truth about Operation North Pole was accepted. This delay occurred despite a message sent via the British Embassy in Switzerland many weeks before they arrived in England. Such safeguards were deemed necessary by the British in order to combat the cunning measures employed by German Counter-Intelligence.

Such was the exemplary courage of Pieter Dourlein that in the last few months of the war in 1945, he trained and flew operationally as an air gunner in No.320 (Dutch) Squadron in the 2nd Tactical Air Force. This remarkable Dutchman, who was honoured as a Knight of the Militaire Willemsorde in 1950, thus started the war in the Dutch navy and ended it flying with the Royal Air Force. In between came the dramatic period serving in British Intelligence as an agent of SOE (Dutch Section).

These revelations in the 1950s provided me with sufficient confirmation that the disasters that had befallen our Tempsford Squadrons over Holland in 1942 and 1943 were primarily due to the failures in Dutch SOE operations and the success achieved by the Abwehr. But I was determined one day to revisit the scene of my crash, where I would hopefully find some local Dutchmen who remembered events of 23 December 1942.

It would be another 45 years before the outstanding work of Leo Marks was revealed in the release of documents under the 30-year rule, which confirmed that Operation North Pole could have been thwarted had mistakes not been made by the Dutch Section of SOE in London.

8. New Horizons

My job as Works Accountant at Pontardawe in the second half of the 1950s was proving successful and I enjoyed the environment under the splendid leadership of Gordon Casselton. His able secretary, Mrs Marjorie Brook, typed my confidential correspondence and final accounts to my complete satisfaction. We were a good management team and successfully introduced new products in an expanding factory and workforce. We overcame difficulties in training both male and female employees in a wide range of new skills and achieved levels of quality by disciplined inspection procedures. With the introduction of cost control and mechanised accounting techniques, I was also able to develop statistical methods, which enabled management to be constantly aware of inefficiencies and wastage rates that required correction.

I was developing wider interests in financial management and control in industry. Being an avid reader of the *Financial Times* benefited me greatly and further exposure to the more experienced practitioners in budgetary control and standard costing and forecasting was achieved by attending the annual summer schools of the Institute, held at Cambridge University. As my own confidence grew, I felt able to impart my knowledge and experience to students of the Institute of Cost and Works Accountants, as well as more mature students studying for membership of Chartered Institutes of Electrical, Mechanical and Civil Engineers, who required knowledge of financial control and business practices. I was able to do this by spending two evenings a week lecturing at Neath Technical College.

The few winter sessions between 1955 and 1959 provided me with exposure to the academic world and conversely I knew that my interaction with other tutors at the college was of benefit to them in furthering their knowledge of industry. I remember during this period attending a discussion on the post-war development of industry in Wales, conducted by Edward Heath and Keith Joseph, two leading politicians with responsibilities in the field of government assistance. They encouragingly accepted the suggestion that periods of interchange between university lecturers and industrial and commercial executives would mutually improve their knowledge and experience. I also learned much by attending the monthly meetings of the Welsh Engineers and Founders Association, whose management committee headed the negotiating body that set wage rates throughout engineering industry in Wales. This was an area deeply immersed in trade union activity, and I recall that, despite the innovative introduction of a works committee at our Pontardawe factory, within two years of introducing our new venture in the Swansea Valley, an area of high unemployment, we were approached by a trade union based in Cardiff, which proposed to organise our labour force. Their involvement resulted in the introduction of a level of militancy we did not want, and interfered with management progress in the field of good healthy labour relations.

We were proud of the working conditions and relationships that had already been achieved under Gordon Casselton. We rightly took exception to the many disruptive demands that emerged from trade union interference, based on outdated attitudes which stemmed from the development of trade unionism in the coalmining and metal processing industries that emerged in the late 19th and early 20th centuries in South Wales. Their outlook was not shared by our departmental foremen, who were mainly from the locality, and had a restraining influence on investment decisions in the area. I felt we needed a more cooperative and understanding attitude from the men and women on the shop floor. Our persistence with the monthly meetings of the Works Committee, in which all departments were involved, did, however, have some favourable results.

I was happy with my professional progress, which was accompanied by an improvement in my family income. This enabled Nita and I, by careful control of expenditures, to improve our quality of life. We were also able to save, for we expected young Philip Roger, who was growing in intellect and general knowledge, would need to be assisted into further education when in his teens. He was always very interested in the history of the United Kingdom and the United States of America, and questioned his mother and me regularly about important historical events. At the same time, he excelled at all ball games, and was always asking me to play cricket in our back yard. He was a well-disciplined lad, which reflected his mother's careful upbringing, and he modelled his behaviour on his fond maternal grandfather. He excelled at school and it was no surprise when he later was successful in the eleven plus examination, qualifying him for entry to Neath Boys Grammar School.

Throughout the fifties I played cricket as often as my damaged leg would allow and made many runs for the Neath first and second elevens. However, being so busy with work at Pontardawe and part-time lecturing at the college left me with no time for cricket practice; it was therefore not unexpected that my form suffered and I found myself opening for the second eleven, which was less competitive.

Meanwhile, Nita and I were looking for better accommodation with more garden space. We were most pleasantly surprised out walking one Sunday evening we chanced upon a detached house at Pen-Yr-Wern, which we had always admired. This was displaying a 'For Sale' board and all three of us set our hearts on this well-positioned property, nearer my work at Pontandawe and less walking distance for Nita's shopping expeditions and Philip's school. With the generous help of Nita's father and with a modest mortgage, we launched out and bought the handsome 'Sunningdale'. We were over the moon with our good fortune and busily made improvements to the layout of the kitchen and redecorated several rooms. Throughout this time we continued to worship in the Parish Church of Saint Catwg and consistently thanked God for his many blessings.

Then came a very important series of events, affecting all the family. The parent company wished to promote me, and offered me an appointment as Chief Cost Accountant, based at the company's headquarters and main factories at Greenford in Middlesex. We had hardly completed the work of redecoration to our lovely new home when I returned one evening in late autumn in 1959 with the news. After much discussion, when I explained the advantages, for my career and the family, Nita was quick to say that she was delighted for me and would support the move. Philip, who had not completed a term at the Grammar School, was at first a little apprehensive, but looked forward to new opportunities in a new environment.

We had been about two and a half years at Sunningdale and were well settled, but I felt this was a wonderful opportunity to work with the directors and senior executives with whom I had become familiar in the past five years. It would mean leaving Pontardawe and the happy relationship I had developed with my accounting and other staff and the splendid General Manager. I suspected that, despite the fact that my departure would leave an important role vacant in his organisation, Gordon must generously have had a big say in my promotion. The interim plan was to appoint an immediate successor to me and we were successful in the appointment of an experienced Chartered Accountant from the Swansea area who was seeking a challenge in the field of Management Accountancy. He proved an excellent choice and I was able to spend much time at Greenford, where I would be joined at weekends by Nita. On these visits we sought a new home within reasonable daily travel from Greenford. We wished to continue living in a village environment, which eventually led us to Farnham Common, a pleasant rural setting situated equidistant between the excellently developed Beaconsfield and Gerrard's Cross and near to Slough, with its wide range of shopping opportunities.

Our new home, 'Red Tops', was a modern detached property with a pleasant and easy sized garden for my limited ability in maintenance. This was a lovely environment, leading to many years of happiness in the Buckinghamshire countryside. It was where Philip Roger developed into a young man and was successful in his studies and sporting endeavours. A major factor was our selection of a school at which he could continue where he had left off at Neath Grammar School. Buckinghamshire supported the Grammar School system and there were three such schools within similar travelling distance form home. There was also a strong recommendation from his earlier Headmaster to seek a place as a boarder at Dulwich College, situated in South London. However, Philip wished to live at home and, after much deliberation, the decision went in favour of Slough Grammar School, where he was duly admitted in the Easter term of 1960. We moved home early after the Christmas holiday in 1960 and quickly celebrated at the Farnham Common village church where we were happily greeted by the priest in charge, David Jones, a very warm-hearted native of Wales.

With our family now happily settled in our new environment, I was strengthened in my resolve to make a success of my new responsibilities at the headquarters of our company. I quickly integrated into an experienced organisation, and had the help of Leslie Finlinson, who I was replacing before his move to retirement on the Sussex coast. With my advancing knowledge of management accounting practices, I was soon providing fresh ideas and introducing more mechanical, and later automatic, accounting for production costs and work in progress. Whilst at Pontardawe I had used my technical background and become skilled in the accurate measurement of performance and wastage and I was able to bring innovative measures to my work at the Greenford factories and their growing subsidiaries, involved in the manufacture of engineering and electronic components.

Within a year or so I was involved in the monitoring of the performance at the company's operations in Teheran. There, after some years of successful exporting from the United Kingdom, it was decided to manufacture certain products locally. A factory was built a few miles west of the capital, at a location in the desert where new industry was being encouraged by the Shah's regime and where a new airport was also planned. The company employed a Works Manager from the UK, but the remainder of the staff, including Mr Assaturian, a capable General Manager, trained in law, were all Iranians citizens. I made several visits to Iran in the 1960s and, apart from the absorbing work at an expanding business in the Middle East, I developed a renewed interest in the history and culture of the region. This had been a prominent feature of our General Studies when at Halton. Then, the prime purpose was to educate us in the development of the strategic oil producing countries and of the British involvement. It was most interesting to learn, at first hand, of the plight of the Armenians in the 1920s when their small country was occupied by the Russians and the Turks. Then, a large proportion of the predominant Christian population sought refuge, crossing the mountain region into what was then Persia. This resulted in the settlement of a large Christian community in that country.

The years following the Second World War saw the introduction and rapid growth of both digital and electronic technologies. This followed the outstanding success of the mechanical and electronic breaking of secret codes at Bletchley Park during the war, to which I referred earlier. Initially, there was greater emphasis on the central processor unit or 'hardware'. Our company had already used mechanical accounting machines at Pontardawe and Greenford, where systems were developed for a wide range of volume transactions, which proved accurate and labour-saving. However, the company's financial links with Aladdin Industries Incorporated of Nashville, Tennessee, enabled me to take advantage of their better progress in this field of financial control and business methods.

I visited their splendid plants, manufacturing both engineering and electronic products, on many occasions and I was warmly invited to study their control systems, which involved the use of punched-card techniques. They were an excellent company, enjoying good labour relations and working conditions. I learnt much on my visits, which also enabled me to understand what made this large country become so successful. I was particularly impressed with the mammoth development under the Tennessee Valley Authority, which opened up great opportunities for industrial development and solved their serious unemployment problems earlier in the century.

My visits were sufficiently long to have the benefit of weekend breaks, enjoying well-attended church services and visits to the Blue Mountains at the southern end of the Appalachians, where I was sorry to see the plight of the poor whites, struggling to make a living in some of the remote areas. One particular trip that has always stayed in my memory was a most interesting visit to the space museum at Huntsville, Alabama. The advance in flight and space technology was very impressive. My experiences in engineering and flight whilst in the Royal Air Force remained a strong influence throughout my life, despite my concentration on professional advancement and other interests down the years.

The remarkable events of 1942-45 were constantly in my thoughts. Since then, at regular intervals of six to eight weeks, I suffered from disturbing dreams in which the appalling disaster I had been involved in was recalled. I only became aware of this phenomenon after I was married, when Nita would tell me at breakfast that I was again calling for help from the blazing aircraft. Apparently, I used the same pleading expressions on each occasion, although I was never aware that I had been dreaming of such horrible events. Later in this narrative, I will be describing the astounding cessation of such dreams, which have not recurred since. I have tried to understand what triggered them in my subconscious, but there is no logical explanation such as seeing a war film or reading about the subject during the evening before retiring to bed. It seems it was a subconscious reaction to the terrible events of 1942.

The pressure of work and frequent overseas travel combined to prevent cricket practice, thus my involvement with the High Wycombe Cricket Club, to which I was introduced by wartime fellow-POW Don Coleman, was limited to a couple of seasons in the second eleven. With increasing pain and swelling in my damaged left leg, I decided to hang up my boots and retire from competitive cricket. An exception was during our Church Parish week, when the Rector at Farnham Royal would arrange a fixture with us at Farnham Common, under David Jones's captaincy. He found it difficult to raise a competent eleven and, joined by Philip, who was performing well at the Grammar School, I was persuaded to turn out. The battle of the Royalists against the Commoners usually resulted in victory for the latter. They were invariably a close call, with plenty of refreshment afterwards, courtesy of the Rector, who maintained a very active church and always an enjoyable week of lively events.

Philip, to the joy of his parents, was making excellent progress with his studies, achieving high marks in his examinations. He was also successful in making the school cricket eleven whilst still a junior. There was no rugby in the junior forms, but to our surprise he was successful in making the under-13 and under-15 school soccer teams. Meanwhile, he was making good progress at tennis at the Farnham Common Club. Whilst still a junior, he represented the club as one of the senior first pair. It was no surprise when we heard he had been selected to play in the Buckinghamshire County Juvenile Tournament and Schools' Wimbledon.

We had much for which to thank God for his help through life and we continued our regular attendance of the Sunday services at our local church. Philip had been confirmed, Nita was very active with the Mothers' Union and I was a member of the Parochial Church Council and for a short while held the fort as Church Treasurer, although this was curtailed when my frequent overseas business visits prevented regular attendance to matters of importance. However, during my PCC membership we were actively involved in financing and building a new church at Britwell, a newly-built area of expanding housing on the northern fringe of Slough. This was quite an achievement, ably led by a leading member of the PCC and the owner of a building company. Much financial support was given by Mr Jubb, a Local benefactor and leading member of our church.

Frank Tierney and I kept in touch and annually exchanged Christmas cards. I was able to tell him of the information now available, which provided answers to many of our outstanding questions about our wartime experiences. I was also able to advise him that the bodies of our unfortunate crewmates lay in a country churchyard at Ijhorst in Northern Holland.

We were also pleased when Frank and his wife, accompanied by their youngest son Jim, spent a short time with us at Farnham Common, en-route to a holiday with his wife's family in Dorset. This provided me with the opportunity to set up a long weekend visit to Holland for myself, Frank and Don Coleman.

Thus it was that in July 1962, in a hired car, we toured the area, found the graves of our crew and, after much searching and local assistance, were able to find the field where we had crashed in our Halifax in December 1942. We were fortunate that the son of the farmer, in whose field our aircraft had burnt out, was visiting his ageing parents that weekend. He remembered the events he had seen as a boy, when the German gunfire and our crash in flames at about midnight had awoken everyone in the farmhouse. We were some distance from the nearest village, but some of the older inhabitants also recalled the events of that night. For some time after the crash, there had been very active involvement of Luftwaffe personnel and other troops, guarding the wreckage before its removal some weeks later.

I understood that the Luftwaffe provided a military burial for the six deceased crewmembers and we found the graves of our six comrades in a neat, well-kept line near the church at Ijhorst. We understood that the British Commonwealth War Graves Commission maintained them in their fine state. This was an emotional occasion for Frank and me and brought tears to our eyes as our thoughts turned to the young men who had flown with us and given their all for their country, victims of the successful tactics of a determined enemy. It saddened me to think how so many intelligent and clever German minds had been hoodwinked by the dastardly wiles of those who swept to power in the 1930s and adopted policies which eventually brought devastation to their nation and death to many millions of innocent people before they were finally defeated in 1945.

We had a similar sombre feeling when we paid homage to Don's gallant crew at Bergen-op-Zoom, where their graves, alongside those of other Royal Air Force airmen, paid silent tribute to their supreme sacrifice.

Frank's visit to England enabled Nita, Philip and me to meet Maureen, who had shared Nita's wretched experience twenty years earlier when Frank and I were taken prisoners of war, the hardship for Maureen, of course, being much greater, as she was carrying her first-born at the time. Fortunately, with God's help, her pregnancy was successful and Nita and I had the pleasure, later, of meeting her eldest son, when on our first visit to Canada in 1970. Regrettably, he later sustained a crippling injury, in a road accident, which left him seriously disabled.

During Frank's holiday we were able to attend a Royal Air Force's Ex-POW Association function in London, when we had the opportunity to reunite with many of our former inmates at Obermassfeld and Heydekrug. This was a wonderful experience, sharing tales with former comrades, with whom we had experienced adversity in earlier years. These included Dixie Dean and Nat Leamon, two of the leading men responsible for the Tally-Ho organisation at Stalagluft VI. It was also pleasing to meet up with Larry Slattery, our violinist friend, who was 'POW No.1' in the Second World War and the devoted secretary of our association. It was no surprise that later we, in the Royal Air Force Ex POW Association, set up the "Larry Slattery Memorial Fund", with charitable status, for the assistance of promising young musicians who needed financial support in their endeavours.

The happy times we were enjoying at Farnham Common were somewhat interrupted by the disabling effect on our son Philip of an attack of mumps, followed by a serious malfunction of his pancreas. He was fifteen years of age and a prolonged illness, which required a strict non-fat diet, meant he was absent from school for much of a critical year at school when "O" level examinations were due. However, in his determination to succeed, and with the excellent cooperation of Dr Long, his headmaster, and fellow schoolmates, he worked at home and recovered sufficiently to have good "O" level results. We were all very pleased that he now had an excellent basis on which to tackle the "A" level syllabus and thanked God for his spiritual help and guidance to us all. It was also a merciful step when we were able to embark on a normal diet once more in our household!

Nita and I were to resume frequent visits to Covent Garden and enjoy many wonderful opera events, usually accompanied by Norman and Betty Ellis. Norman was Aladdin's Home Sales Manager and a great chum, whilst Betty, a mezzo-soprano, was splendid company on these occasions. For some years we set a pattern of alternating our bookings and enjoyed several enjoyable shows a year.

Then, our domestic situation was considerably interrupted. I was asked by our Managing Director to undertake a new challenge, which I was happy to undertake. A new manufacturing venture of the company at Seaton Carew, near West Hartlepool, had run into serious difficulties. I knew the situation well, as my financial control responsibilities at company headquarters embraced the activities at this modern plant for the production of vacuum flasks.

It was a fine plant, employing similar machinery and production methods to those used at the Aladdin plant in Tennessee, from which senior production staff were on temporary loan to initiate the processes and help train the newly-employed departmental management and foremen, many of whom had been recruited locally, along with about three hundred production workers. Regrettably, the venture was foundering and after a year or so of failure to achieve the desired results, the General Manager resigned and, at short-notice, the Board of Directors asked if I would take on a temporary assignment away from my headquarters responsibilities. This was indeed a challenge to my professional and management skills.

With Nita's blessing, I set out one Sunday afternoon in November 1966 on the long journey, ending in an early fall of snow. I settled in to my temporary accommodation at the hotel in Seaton Carew, which I had previously used, along with our managing director, on many a short stay during the early days of the new venture. I estimated that it would take about two years to turn the plant into an efficient unit and appoint a successor before returning to Greenford and continuing my duties with the company.

It was not an easy decision, as I knew I would be away from home most of the time for the next two years, when Philip would be deeply involved with his 'A' level studies at Slough Grammar School. Fortunately, Nita's father had long since retired and he and Nita's mother enjoyed visiting us at Farnham Common. This freed Nita, who made many a long train journey to join me at Seaton Carew, where I had been able to find a comfortable furnished flat. In her absence, I was able to devote most of my time, including weekends, to company affairs, but when she visited we used to enjoy an occasional foray to the Black Swan at Helmsley, or to spend a few hours at the motor racing circuit at what had been a wartime Bomber Command airfield at Croft. We also renewed contact with Malcolm Thomas, the former Welsh and British Lion Rugby player, who was involved with the supply of packaging material when I was at our Pontardawe factory. He now had a countrywide marketing role with his company and we enjoyed many a convivial evening when he and his wife were in the area. He was later to introduce me to John James, who was subsequently appointed my successor before I completed my assignment in the North East. A fellow Welshman and a graduate in mathematics and physics at Cardiff University, John had, since graduation, been a management trainee and subsequently a works manager and was well suited to deal with the many problems of technical and personnel leadership in industry.

The manufacture of vacuum flasks involved a range of tech-niques, which I found most interesting and absorbing. The most critical work involved the production of the vacuum vessel itself. In those days, most domestic vacuum-ware used a glass vessel, which ultimately enabled the user to maintain liquids in either a hot or cold state. The vessel was made by welding together two very thin clear glass vessels of different diameters around the mouthpiece and then extracting all the air from the space between the glass bottles via a nozzle at the base of the outer bottle. This was a highly technical process, involving specialised machinery and heat treatment of the glass envelopes, which were loaded in a vertical position on a circular rotating platform, enabling thirty or forty vacuum bottles to be manufac-tured simultaneously. We obtained the very thin glass bottles from a manufacturer mainly of glassware for electric light bulbs, conveniently situated in Yorkshire. This provided good continu-ity of supply of the different sizes required to meet our varied production schedules.

Once the machinery was set up for a particular size of bottles, they were loaded onto the machine by hand, after which the heat processes that achieved the welding of the glass around the top rim and then sealing the nozzle through which the air had been expelled, were automatic. There were many reasons why the factory was making large financial losses, but the main one was the high rate of wastage through the malfunction of the high speed rotating glass welding process. To achieve high volumes of good quality vacuum bottles, the equipment required very careful setting, and control of temperature during the welding process was critical. Failure to do this resulted in frequent breakages of the thin glass shells during the production processes. Regrettably, early production runs produced a very low throughput of satisfactory end-products, with a very high percentage of breakage and waste.

As the new General Manager, much of my time and thought was focused on this major problem. The costs of quantity manufacture required three shifts, operating within a twenty-four hour continuous production cycle, to achieve the best results. We arranged a thorough inspection and recording of each shift's results and by careful analysis of each hour's achievements we narrowed down the period when wastage was at the highest level. The latter came by noting the critical temperature of the glass weld during these hourly cycles and we found there was a particular time each day when wastage rates were the highest. The heating of the glassware utilised town gas as the fuel (this was before North Sea gas was made available). Discussions with Gas Board technical experts and numerous tests indicated that the high level of failures was due to the calorific properties of the gas in the mains supply to the factory not being consistently maintained at the critical limits demanded.

It was finally established that the town gas supply to our mains was sourced from a number of different gas works in the area, which were not all producing gas with the same critical sulphur content. To change the sourcing was apparently not economically possible for the Gas Board. Eventually, after a long process of detecting failures and varying our inspection procedures, coupled with much deliberation with the gas suppliers, we were able to achieve satisfactory results, but we had to resort to an alternative source of gas that had consistent calorific properties and sulphur content to meet our critical demands.

This was an expensive correction of a technical error made in the original selection of heat source, which had resulted in exceptional losses of production. However, it was gratifying that

I had been able to use my knowledge of statistical methods to solve such an important problem.

The welded vacuum bottles were put through a silvering process before moving to an assembly line, where they were fitted accurately inside attractive outer casings of metal or plastic. The manufacture of the latter demanded highly accurate tooling and machine setting to ensure the successful final assembly and incorporation of screw-on seal of the flask. This required the employment of skilled toolmakers and setters and continued maintenance to high tolerances.

I was much absorbed in my work, which brought together my technical and accounting backgrounds, in order to exercise control over an interesting range of manufacturing processes. The administration of the factory was not a serious problem, but difficulties in the timing of supplies, avoiding excessive stocks whilst at the same time meeting the production schedules, exercised the minds of the buying staff, with whom I kept in close contact.

I remember our sales department reported an excessive rise in demand for a new product for the Christmas market. This was more than expected and demanded an urgent rescheduling of supply and production. This was a well designed vacuum jug, in four different colours. The jug body was made in thermoplastic material with high quality finish. The raw plastic powder was imported and our normal supplier could not, at short notice, meet the extra tonnage required. The only other supplier at that time in the second half of the 1960s was in the United States of America. By resolute and intensive communication we were able to trace, at short notice, the source and fly it over by cargo plane. Timing of the operation was critical, but we didn't bargain for a heavy snowfall in the vital weeks, when the road transport conveying our supplies from London-Heathrow airport was interrupted within about fifty miles of our factory. The roads were impassable for heavy vehicles for some days and we had to convey our consignment in smaller lots by lighter vehicles. Eventually we managed to meet most of our marketing demands for the Christmas market, which was deemed vital for the company's image, although there were considerable cost penalties in meeting the customers' requirements at this time.

This was my first Christmas at the plant and lessons were learned in what was a new venture with relatively inexperienced personnel. With hard graft and much determination I was not surprised to see in the monthly management accounts that our losses were progressively reducing. One could feel the pulse of the organisation was beating more regularly. This had not been an easy assignment, but I did not regret taking it on. It was a wonderful opportunity to extend my man management skills in a North East development area where there was high unemploy-ment. With the keen supervision of the departmental managers we were able to train local men and women into an effective production team.

In due course, our chairman and I interviewed candidates to take over my responsibilities when my assignment was over. I was pleased when John James was chosen and was able, after joining our company, to share my flat with me. This speeded up the transition period, with our discussions often continuing into the night. I was so pleased when I was able to rejoin Nita and Philip once again and continue our happy life at Farnham Com-mon. They had maintained close contact with the church, the ladies group and Philip's school and sporting club, which had helped overcome Dad's absence for most of the past year and ten months.

I benefited greatly from this experience and moved on to ac-cept greater responsibility in the executive management of the company, with particular involvement in the financial perform-ance of the whole group, which now comprised many subsidiar-ies. It was interesting work, which involved visiting overseas countries, including a visit to Baghdad, where I carried out an investigation into the possible manufacture in Iraq of our heating and lighting products, along similar lines to our operation in Iran. I was joined on this exercise by the Works Manager of our operations in Teheran.

Whilst this was prior to the takeover of the country by Sad-dam Hussain, nevertheless, after careful study of the labour force and business conditions prevailing, we did not recommend manufacturing there. One of the major stumbling blocks was the insistence of the Iraqi government to own 51% or more of the share capital of the company. This was not satisfactory, as con-trol of the operation would have been taken out of our com-pany's hands. In the light of subsequent developments in that country, I have no regrets about my recommendation to our board not to proceed.

I developed an increasing interest in the requirements of Corporate Financial Control of the Management of Companies. There had been a progressive growth in the small company structure to one of concentration into larger combines or groups in the second half of the 1950s and into the 60s. My company, through acquisition and introduction into new ventures, had grown fast during this period, being involved in electronic components and plastics. I was consequently wrapped up in business matters and trying to keep pace with national economic affairs. With the aid of a walking stick, I managed some very pleasant walks with Nita to Burnham Beeches, which bordered our village to the south, and in other areas of the lovely county of Buckinghamshire, including the Thames area of Marlow. We were in touch with events at the village sports club, where we were family members, and Philip was excelling himself at cricket and tennis. He also became Grammar School captain of cricket and we were pleased with his outstanding progress through life. I was invited to captain the fathers in two annual cricket matches against the school first eleven. Whilst rather stiff and out of form, I managed decent scores on both occasions but, as Nita and Philip enjoyed pointing out at the breakfast table, we were beaten on both occasions by a better and more agile team, bolstered by our son's extra helping of runs.

As we moved through the second half of the 1960s we witnessed major changes as the country picked itself up from the wasteful years of the Second World War and the difficult post-war years in which the Labour Government struggled to build the National Health Service and deal with the increasing power of the trade unions.

Throughout this time, I was concerned that no attempt was made by governments of either ruling party to reform the structure of pensions for all levels of the workforce. The long- term effects of these failures were not properly appreciated in official circles and it was left to employers to institute pension schemes for their own employees, financed by joint contributions from the employing companies and their workforce. It was encouraging to note that our company, Aladdin, had the foresight to introduce such schemes for the management and all the workforce after they had been employed for a qualifying year, but a substantial majority of employing organisations did not enter into such schemes. In recent years, with the declining actuarial valuation of the invested contributions, many of our population and the National Treasury are regretting these failures to act during the early years of employment of today's pensioners. The basic pension for retiring people in the United Kingdom is not adequate and has to be boosted by various benefits, many of which are dependent on means-testing and similar regrettable measurements of people's entitlements.

The 1960s saw the exceptional advance of space travel, in which I took a keen interest and I marvelled at the advances in jet-powered aircraft. During this time, the state of Britain's national finances restricted many home-grown advances in such technologies, allowing Americans and Russians to overtake us. It was, however, encouraging to see the introduction of the De Havilland Comet, which was a great step forward in high-speed passenger travel. Nita and I had the pleasure of flying in the Mark IV version when we visited Canada in 1970. Meanwhile, thankfully, the Rolls Royce Company – which had manufactured the successful Merlin engines that powered my Halifax and many other aircraft types during the war – was keeping British engineering to the fore with its successful jet engine developments. Later in this narrative I describe our move in retirement to West Wittering and our purchase of a lovely property next door to where Sir Henry Rolls lived throughout the 1920s and into the 1930s. I have always been proud of British engineering competence and have decried the decline of so much of our industry in the latter half of the twentieth century, particularly in the production of locomotives, motor cars and motorcycles. I can recall the days when, in Britain, all these enterprises were among the best in the world.

During the latter half of the 1960s the demand for oil heating and lighting products in the home market suffered a decline following the introduction of North Sea gas supplies. There were also mishaps when appliances were misused or accidentally knocked over. The negative publicity that ensued from incidental damage to household properties, some occupied by large groups of immigrants, resulted in the introduction of additional safety measures. The resultant modifications added to the complication and costs of our products and the market for them reacted negatively. Manufacturers were busily engaged in modifications, where necessary, diverting production and sales efforts to other products that were introduced. There was much diversity in our company. Regrettably, after much deliberation, the Board decided against entering the gas industry, as the availability of North Sea gas spread through a new network of underground pipelines in the country. This, I thought, was a wrong decision, as our major competitor in the industry went on to design, develop and produce a range of successful gas products.

In the early 1960s, Gordon Casselton, the able General Manager at the Pontardawe factory, retired after long service with the company. He was replaced by the Group Engineering Manager, who left our executive management team at Greenford. However, he did not have the personal touch of Gordon and labour relations at the plant suffered, with increasing militancy at what had become a manufacturing and distribution operation employing a 100% AEU membership of hourly-paid workers.

Meanwhile, in a few tragic years, three of the controlling family died, including the founder of the company, who had more than fifty years at the helm, during which he had been a successful chairman, seeing the company grow from modest beginnings. The remaining full-time Managing Director became Chairman and two non-executive directors were appointed. These changes at the top occurred during the difficult period of reducing demand for the products and a worrying decline in productivity at the Pontardawe factory.

The nation, at this time, was experiencing increasing concern over the advances of the communist regime in the Soviet Union following the post-war realignment of Europe.

The twenty years or so since the war had been very difficult internationally, with increasing tensions, from the Berlin airlift in the late Forties, the Korean War in the early Fifties, Suez and Hungary in 1956, the building of the Berlin Wall in 1961 and culminating in the Cuban Missile Crisis of 1962.

Domestically, the UK struggled through these years and, whilst living standards improved substantially, the country continued to experience relative economic decline, due to a number of factors, but perhaps primarily, the crippling financial burden from two world wars, general lack of competitiveness, increasing and overbearing trade union power and an overreliance on the old, original, heavy industries.

This was followed in 1963 by the assassination of President Kennedy, which I found most disturbing. During these troubled times, it was my happy home life with Nita and Philip and the love of God, reinforced by continuing worship at our village church in Farnham Common, that sustained me.

Much to our great joy, Philip achieved very good results at 'A'-level and, after an extensive interview and written examination, was awarded a place at Keble College, Oxford, commencing in 1968, studying Philosophy, Politics and Economics. That year seven boys from Slough Grammar School were awarded places at Oxford and Cambridge universities. This was an excellent result for the school and we in the family were extremely proud of Philip, none more so than my father, who was of Oxfordshire stock, born on a farm near the neighbouring villages of Bloxham and Hook Norton.

Sadly, within a few weeks we were mourning the death of my father at the age of eighty-five. This was a severe blow to all the family, particularly my mother, with whom he had shared fifty-five years of marriage, including during the trying times of two World Wars, the loss of their eldest son Jack over Berlin in 1943 and also their youngest, who died prematurely of a heart-attack in 1957. Mother and Father had been loving Christians all their lives and, with the Lord's help, Mother was able to bear the grief she felt.

I was so sorry that Dad had died before I was able to fulfil my promise to take them both to see Jack's grave in the British and Commonwealth War Cemetery in Berlin. This failure jolted my conscience and I felt I should accompany mother to the graveside as soon as she felt able. I was pleased to achieve this in the summer of 1968 when, along with Nita and my elder sister Phyllis, we set out by car on a ten-day trip, crossing by ferry from Harwich to the Hook of Holland. After a couple of days in Holland I was also able to take my party of ladies to visit the graves of my crew at Ijhorst and the scene of my crash in 1942.

This was a moving occasion for us all and we were pleased with the well-kept condition of the six graves. As we silently prayed, the profusion of tears expressed our unspoken gratitude that I was not lying beside my crewmates in that quiet cemetery in Northern Holland. The following day I drove my trusted Cresta saloon through the border control to our stopover at a hotel in Hanover, where Phyllis met a friend who was serving in our Army of the Rhine. We left early the following morning and soon arrived at the border control between Western and Eastern Germany at Helmstedt.

I had been advised before we left the UK that the British Government did not recognise the communist regime of Eastern Germany and could not issue entry visas for this Soviet-controlled state. In the event, clearance through the very thorough and well-guarded border required the completion of forms, passport checks and the payment of a stiff fee for permission to drive on East German roads. The car was scrupulously searched before we were able to drive eastwards. We had travelled only about five miles on the autobahn before we were ordered to stop by armed soldiers, who ordered everyone out and searched the car and luggage again.

Eventually, with some trepidation, we drove off and I wondered what danger I had brought the ladies into. They showed determination as we moved on, only to be met by convoys of Russian tanks and troops moving in the opposite direction. We thought they were on manoeuvres, only to discover, when we met British guards at the West Berlin border post, that there had been a revolt in Czechoslovakia and the Russians were sending in forces to attempt to quell the Czechs, who were seeking freedom from their Soviet oppressors. I felt the danger of the situation but we pressed on regardless to find the Windsor hotel awaiting our arrival. We enjoyed a good dinner and a comfortable night in a four poster, only to be awoken by Mother, fully-dressed and ready to go. Remarkably, although seventy-five years old, she was up and ready first, as there was only one thing on her mind. She was anxious to visit her eldest son's grave for the first time since his tragic death twenty-five years earlier.

In due course we boarded a tram, which took us in a westerly direction. My heart was beating madly as we entered the Spandau district and soon found the cemetery. It was a relatively narrow entrance, which opened out inside to reveal a large number of gravestones in neat lines between well-kept grass-covered areas. Near the entrance we found a small office in which remembrance books detailed the names of approximately five thousand, mainly Royal Air Force, fatal casualties of the 1939/45 war. We soon found Jack's grave, in a line that included the other five members of his 90 Squadron Stirling, which had been shot down while leaving their Berlin target in August 1943. Mother, in tears, sat in silent prayer at the graveside whilst, in silence, we, her children, with lumps in our throats, admired her in peaceful solemnity. We remarked how well the graves and surrounds were maintained as we quietly moved through the rows of graves of the hundreds of our brave twenty-year-old countrymen, who had made the supreme sacrifice on our behalf.

It was another moving occasion when we found the grave of Pilot Officer "Chappy" Prince, Nita's young cousin from Hereford, shot down in 1944. I also came across the grave of Flying Officer C.J. Dineen, a fellow apprentice with me at Halton who had played in the pack of our successful Wing Rugby fifteen. He was a Flight Engineer in 35 Squadron, shot down leaving their Berlin target in March 1944. This came as a shock to me and, as I stood silently and pondered the good times we had shared in our Halton pursuits, I was determined that one day I would produce a roll of honour of our gallant comrades of the 41st entry. Later in my story I will describe the fulfilment of this endeavour.

Mother at last acknowledged that her dear son Jack was now in the hands of God, at rest, and had not survived the catastrophe, lost his identity, or was living in a foreign country.

Later that day we returned to Berlin and saw the grim Berlin Wall that prevented movement between East and West and was causing so much frustration for West and East German peoples. The Brandenburg Gate and other sites were visited before returning for a pleasant dinner and a very restful night for me, as I felt the mission had been accomplished. The following morning Mother had slept on a little, having come to peace with her maker before we set out on our return journey to the West.

Following my planned itinerary, after leaving the British zone of Berlin we retraced our drive over the flat terrain on the worn East German autobahn. A stop for a fill of petrol was frustrated by the unexpected requirement for West German marks. This was the period when our sterling currency was under pressure and we were limited to fifty pounds per person for foreign travel, necessitating tight control of the spending of our party. However, this did not prevent us enjoying some good wine at dinner in our stopover at Hamelin that evening!

I had planned a different route on the return journey from Hanover in order to meet Mother's specific request to visit Hamelin, a lovely town on the River Weser, which had fired her imagination since her younger days, when she had told the wonderful story of the Pied Piper to her pupils at the village school at Cadoxton.

A pleasant journey the following day, and an interesting stop-over in the old town of Munster, was followed, on the last day of our eventful trip, by a visit to Amsterdam. We then returned to the Hook of Holland, where our trusted Cresta was winched aboard the ferry for an uneventful crossing to Harwich. Then home, having fulfilled my long-awaited promise to Mother.

Shortly after our return, Nita and I attended a Royal Air Forces Ex-Prisoner of War Association Reunion in the West End of London. This association, which I had joined some years earlier when we moved to Farnham Common, included former members of the Commonwealth Air Forces and it was a great pleasure when we met up with many friends I had known whilst in captivity. This pleasure was capped with great delight when I met Don Morrison, with whom I had spent the best part of a year in hospital at Obermassfeld and Kloster Haina.

It was a great joy for Nita and Don to meet for the first time and we both had our first meeting with his lovely wife Jean. This proved to be a most successful meeting of personalities, born of a mutual respect and love that had begun during our long period of suffering in the prison hospitals. They spent a few days with us, before returning to their home at Don Mills, north of Toronto and down the years, until Don's tragic death in 1995, we enjoyed a great deal of their company in the UK, Europe, the Mediterranean, Canada and the USA. I fondly recall Don's wonderful sense of humour and the surprises he would spring on us during our many journeys through Canada and the US. As I write this script in the summer of 2006 we are still in close touch with Jean, who stayed with us at our Hampshire home only a two years ago. Don had a strong compassion for his fellow men and worked tirelessly for the Veterans' Association in Canada. There was also the occasion when he turned up at an Ex-POW function in London with a surprise gift of a wheelchair for our President, Dixie Dean, who had been struck down with MS and was very disabled.

Don's post-war occupation as an executive with Air Canada brought him frequently to London and there was hardly a month or two between his short visits to our home. It was always a pleasure to see him with some of our mutual ex-kriegie Canadian friends, particularly Howie Copeman, Brian Filliter, Dabby Dabous and many others. Jean would accompany him every four years to coincide with our International RAF Ex-POW Reunions. These quite large affairs, with about seven hundred attending, were held over a period of five nights, when, with our wives, we enjoyed company from all over the Commonwealth at a suitable hostelry or a place of learning vacated during the summer recess.

As the Association's auditor, I would prepare careful budgets of expenditure for these occasions, in order to break even on each venture, which would cost upwards of £250,000. With the capable accounting of our treasurer, Doug Endsor, and the shared responsibilities of our very active committee members, we successfully achieved a series of events through the 70s and 80s. These alternated, every two years, with similar successful reunions in various locations throughout Canada.

Our memories of these super occasions are filled with much joy shared with fellow airmen who, during 1939/45, put their lives constantly on the line. It was always such pleasure to share these occasions with our wives and on every occasion a highlight of the itinerary would be our attendance at a place of worship, when we unanimously thanked God for our deliverance from the dangers of wartime flying. On these occasions we were honoured to have the Chaplain in Chief of the Royal Air Force to conduct the service and preach a most apt message to us all. I was so pleased when the Venerable Weg Payton, my old cricketing chum of Halton days, did us proud at Winchester Cathedral during our successful reunion at Southampton in the 1980s. We enjoyed these reunions which will live prominently in our memories. Nita and I were also honoured to be hosts to Marshal of the Royal Air Force Sir Michael and Lady Beecham at an Albert Hall concert, following which the POW Association made a sizeable donation to leading charities.

Early in 1969 Nita and I were invited to dinner with the Company Chairman, who asked me to undertake another assignment that would mean moving back home to Wales. The Chairman and I both knew that the Pontardawe factory had run into many problems, was making losses, and that a turnaround in its performance was needed. I was asked to undertake the job as General Manager, for an indefinite period. I knew this would be a tough assignment and that it would mean me handing over my financial responsibilities at Greenford, but it was pleasing to think that the Board of Directors had confidence in my ability to recover the situation and take on a similar task to that which I had previously undertaken at the Seaton Carrew factory.

This would be another step forward in my career in industry and, after much consultation with Nita and Philip, I accepted the post. Philip had started at Oxford the previous October and had settled in happily at Keble College. Nita, with her usual warm understanding, was happy to go along with my decision, and at the prospect of a return to our native Wales.

Now aged forty-five, I was to return to take control of a much larger factory than the one I had helped to set up fifteen years earlier. The Pontardawe factory now had one thousand employees, of whom about one third were women. There were many familiar faces among the departmental managers and operatives, but many others were new to me. There was not the same degree of contentment amongst the workforce, the employer/employee relationship having deteriorated since Gordon Casselton had retired a few years earlier. I was soon aware that this would have to improve if higher productivity was to be achieved.

In order to be better informed, I set up weekly meetings of the six departmental managers and requested a written report from each of the departmental foremen to indicate what was needed in their areas to enable productivity and labour relations to be improved. Levels of absenteeism were too high and, after the personnel manager had produced some relevant statistics regarding the nature of illnesses reported and the departmental areas with the greatest propensity for absence, I was able to consult the part-time works doctor for his observations, whereupon I criticised the apparent ease with which medical certificates had been obtained in some quarters. Following a tightening up of procedures we achieved a marked improvement in attendance.

I was now faced with a 100% membership of the AEU amongst the hourly-paid male and female employees. There were active shop stewards in each department, under a determined convenor, who had too easy access to the works manager and made too many requests. The attitude of the workers was, apparently, guided by self-interest and they did not seem to accept any responsibility for good attendance or effort on their part. There was also little interest in the quality of output, resulting in the need for more inspectors and the levels of wastage and rectification of faulty production were too high.

I faced these many problems at the outset and, recalling my study of industrial psychology at Cardiff University many years earlier, I decided to seek the help of a lecturer on Industrial Relations at Swansea University. We had met socially since my arrival in our new home area on the Gower Peninsular, and he undertook to give lectures to groups of shop stewards and the convenor, who were duly bussed to the University. This was one attempt to provide an independent, learned opinion of the responsibilities of *all* employees towards the management and company that provided the source of their financial income and future prospects. I also stressed that I was Welsh-born, one of them, and that good results of our joint efforts would provide the prospect of future employment for their children.

Before the commencement of the works annual holiday, after much thought, I decided to have an open day, in which all employees were invited to bring their families and friends. We had the pleasure of the Chairman and one of our directors from Greenford attending and the Chairman, in a closing speech, having met many of the employees and their families during a tour through the various departments, said how pleased he was with the occasion and wished everyone success. That evening at dinner, he and the other director congratulated me on a successful day for all concerned, which augured well for the future.

Another of my more difficult problems was the introduction and development of new products, which involved alternative working methods and procedures. One I remember well was the production of an unusually designed reflector, for use with a new type of radiant heater, which involved pressing a large sheet of steel into a parabolic shape. The degree of accuracy required was a distinct challenge to the toolmakers, our most skilled personnel, but they eventually succeeded.

There had been criticism of the production bonus system in operation in all manufacturing departments, used in calculating the bonuses payable to supporting personnel in stores, maintenance and similar departments. An examination of factors adversely affecting productive performance indicated the need to review our payment methods and we decided to carry out an in depth work-study prior to the introduction of an alternative payment system. This was a mammoth task, spread over many months, but, combined with other measures, some of which I have previously described, it resulted in better productivity. The net result was a marked reduction in the labour force, which was mainly achieved by natural wastage.

I worked long and hard on these tasks, but was glad each evening to return to Nita and our new home on the beautiful Gower peninsular. We were happily placed at a high point between Mumbles and Langland Bay, overlooking Swansea Bay and the Bristol Channel and near enough to drive to the homes of my mother and Nita's parents in about thirty minutes. The change of environment was refreshing and helped me to maintain a good workload. Philip joined us during his college vacations and enjoyed the change from country village to the seaside, bringing many university friends to share in the fun. He also found a sweetheart locally. This, following his graduation and commencement of employment, led to the marriage of Philip to Lynne at Newton Parish Church, where Nita and I worshipped most Sundays, thanked God for all his blessings and I prayed for support in my increased responsibilities.

We renewed many friendships amongst the cricketing fraternity in South Wales and Philip, who had gained his half blue and scored many runs for Oxford University Authentics, joined the nearby Swansea Club during the summer vacations. He was quite successful and played the occasional game for Glamorgan 2nd XI and had the pleasure of being selected as twelfth man for the county side against the Pakistan Tourists at St Helens.

In the summer of 1969 Nita and I had much pleasure in witnessing the investiture of the Prince of Wales by Her Majesty the Queen at Caernarfon Castle. It was a moving spectacle with the sound of trumpets resonating around the ramparts of the ancient building. The singing was excellent and it was a very moving spectacle for the few thousand inside the castle walls. The ceremony was also relayed outside and on TV and radio. There was an added attraction for Nita and I as, following his investiture, the Prince sailed quietly around the Welsh Coast in the Royal Yacht. Well lit up, it anchored overnight in Swansea Bay, and this provided a splendid sight from our home. This was a big occasion for the Principality and one we will always remember.

Another event at about this time was the wonderful achievement of the US space program and the first walk of man on the moon's surface. The television coverage of the remarkable event was most striking. It showed a feat perhaps not to be achieved again in my lifetime. These aviation feats were so outstanding and their precise navigational skills filled me with awe, as I reflected on the dead-reckoning methods employed by the Royal Air Force in operations in the first three years of the 1939/45 war, just twenty-five years earlier. I also marvelled at the technological advances made in the sixty-odd years following man's first powered flight. These thoughts reminded me of the extraordinary technological advances achieved by all the major participating nations in the World War Two, particularly in aviation. The remarkable development of the Spitfire from the commencement of hostilities to their cessation focused on the continuous improvement of the Rolls-Royce Merlin engine. The twin-engined Mosquito and the four-engined Lancaster also played a vital role.

Despite their own excellent engineering and technological advances, particularly in the science of rocketry, radar, and the development of their own aero-engines, the Germans were unable to overcome the strategic policy mistakes of Hitler and his High Command. I liken the blunders of the Third Reich, which overreached itself in attempting conquests beyond its ability to control, particularly the attempted invasion of the mammoth Soviet Union, with a business entity suffering from the adverse financial effects of overtrading, embarking on an ill-conceived and costly takeover of another large enterprise. Such failures in business have regrettably become commonplace in the past twenty years or so.

Whilst I was completely immersed in my tasks at Pontardawe, many changes were taking place at our headquarters in Greenford. My earlier duties were now undertaken by a newly-appointed successor and the enlarged company, with its varied product range, was divided into three divisions, each with a General Manager reporting directly to the Chairman and Managing Director. This marked an attempt to spread the considerable workload that the latter had undertaken since the tragic death of three of his board colleagues. Whilst control of the company remained in the family, with some new participation of American Directors, it remained a private limited company. Regrettably, such a situation could lead to a limited availability of working capital and I foresaw difficulties ahead. With the declining market for our products in the oil heating and lighting field and the management structure changes, some of which I was not happy with, I became concerned about my future prospects within the company. With a total of six years in General Management and more than ten years' experience in the financial control sphere, at the age of forty-eight I felt there was the need for a change. Thus, after seventeen years of loyal hard work, I parted company with the organisation, with whom I had been happy and successful ... most of the time.

This event did not come as a great surprise to Nita, who had seen a change in my demeanour over a period of months. She knew I had continued to apply myself diligently to my tasks and had sufficient confidence in my ability to move on to new horizons in my profession. We knew that my experience had been in the engineering industry, where I had been successful, combining my earlier technical education with the management accountancy profession. It was my desire to continue in this field and, knowing that senior appointments were few in Wales, the family resolved to face a move of home if necessary.

After a couple of months' break, when I kept an eye on appropriate *Financial Times* and *Daily Telegraph* employment opportunities, I launched myself on the job market. In a short time I was asked to attend an interview with head-hunters in London, who also sought confirmation of my abilities and personal integrity from my former chairman. The interviewer told me the latter had given an excellent report on my performance and regretted my departure. Consequently, in a short time I was interviewed by the Directors of an engineering group of companies and appointed Financial Director designate. They were a larger company than my previous employers and the existing Financial Director was due to retire within a few months. In due course I was pleased to accept the full responsibilities of Financial Director, in which I found much interest, hard work and fulfilment.

My appointment was at the company headquarters and factory in the Wimbledon area. After a short spell in a Surrey hotel and several weekends when Nita joined me in the task of house-hunting, we finally were able to settle in a very pleasant house in Woodham, a village adjoining West Byfleet, on the direct electrified line to Wimbledon and central London. I travelled daily to work by road but was often delayed on the busy A3, where underpasses were being constructed. This resulted in my setting out earlier and returning later each day. After combating this inconvenience for about three years, we decided to move nearer my workplace and, with the aid of a *Sunday Times* advertisement, found a desirable detached residence near the Fair Mile in Cobham. We both enjoyed life there and worshipped regularly at the church in the nearby village of Stoke D'Abernon. We made many splendid friendships there and Nita was soon busy with the Church Ladies Group, which involved good companionship and many useful activities.

Meanwhile Philip, now married, was making good headway in his banking career where his Honours Degree in Philosophy Politics and Economics from Oxford provided a platform for entry into advanced promotion into executive management. He continued to play cricket in the Bristol area and represented his bank at various levels. Whilst resident in the West Country, he and Lynne provided us with our first granddaughter, Philippa Kate.

My work entailed responsibility for all the accounting of a company with several subsidiary manufacturing activities in different parts of the UK and overseas, where we were very active, exporting about 55% of our home production. Overseas sales were achieved in about forty outlets, with the accompanying problems of export finance and credit arrangements throughout the world. Our main competitors were German manufacturers, who took more risks than us when extending credit to foreign importers. We were highly successful manufacturers of a branded product with a uniquely designed feature and our profitability improved through the employment of firm financial control of our operations. Systems of budgetary control were extensively employed, with the executive directors and senior management fully involved.

There were continuing excessive inflationary pressures on the economy, particularly in the second half of the 1970s, when the annual percentage increase in UK inflation reached a mammoth 28% for a short time. There had been a rapid growth in this rate over a period of a few years, which called for continued vigilance over the company's selling prices and that of its subsidiary companies, to keep abreast of the crippling effects of inflation on our purchases.

I found my work most absorbing and enjoyable, attending to company affairs, which involved some foreign travel, when approving the budgets of our subsidiary companies and monitoring their performance. Company business necessitated visits to many European countries, the USA and Australia. I remember on one occasion the planned itinerary for my work in Sydney had been curtailed following the calling of a special Board Meeting in the UK.

To accommodate the new itinerary it was necessary to cut down my travel time to Australia and I was fortunate in securing the agreement of higher authority to book a flight on Concorde from London to Singapore. This was in the late 1970s, when this was a regular service run by British Airways, once a week in each direction. I saved the best part of two days on that journey, enabling me to achieve my planned schedule of work Down Under. This was my first flight at supersonic speed and I was thrilled to the core at seeing the machometer, displayed on the forward bulkhead, creeping up to very high cruising speeds. It was a super flight and I enjoyed the new experience, especially when I recalled cruising in the Halifax bomber at about 120 miles per hour, which was not much above stalling speed, over enemy territory with all its dangers. I was also pleased to successfully complete my business commitments in Australia, which included visiting Perth, a delightful city way out west in that large country.

Meanwhile, the company was engaged in improving its information technology. This entailed examining the alternative suppliers in the computer industry, where rapid developments in integrated systems involved keen competition among the producers of hardware and operating systems. I was fully involved with this work, which also required the recruitment of specialised staff and excellent support from our parent group. They had successfully diversified and grown, having taken ownership of our group of companies prior to my appointment. My relationship with the group directors was very good, two of them having been present during my original interviews with the company.

There was hardly a dull moment in the 1970s, grappling with company affairs in the deteriorating economic environment of the UK. This included, on one occasion, the hasty retreat of the Chancellor of the Exchequer back to his desk in the Treasury from London Airport, where he was about to board an aircraft for the USA, due to the declining state of the country's finances.

Meanwhile, life at our Cobham home was very enjoyable, despite my inability to play cricket or manage a few holes at Golf. Nita and I continued to enjoy regular visits to the opera at

Covent Garden with my former colleague Norman Ellis and his wife Betty. We were also able to manage annual holidays overseas, taking the opportunity to visit the Balearic Islands and many interesting European locations. One most enjoyable trip involved a car journey across France, then southern Germany and into the beautiful Alpine area of Austria. There, in the mountain village of Igls, we enjoyed our 25th wedding anniversary and our happiness embraced a splendid trip through the Brenner Pass to the awesome sight of the Dolomites. Our return journey through the Black Forest to Lake Constance was delightful and we were quite amazed with the successful recovery of war-torn Germany in just under thirty years of post-war endeavour.

Nita and I took great pleasure in the success of the Welsh Rugby XV during the late 1960s and 70s and were thrilled by the performances of Gareth Edwards, Barry John, JPR Williams, the Pontypool front row and many others. Tickets for international matches were like gold-dust, so we were fortunate to have the occasional ticket from contacts with clubs and, when Philip was captain of the Grammar School Rugby XV, we managed a ticket each for Twickenham. There was much friendly rivalry amongst our friends in Surrey, whose loyalty was always to the Twickenham gang. I always recalled my mother's piece of advice which, coming from a schoolmistress, had some weight throughout my life: "All work and no play made Jack a dull boy". I was so glad that Nita, with her wonderful sense of humour and interest in sporting achievements, shared my life and this common approach generated many long-term friendships, some going back to pre 1939/45 days, but the majority wartime and post-war, who we cherish.

Our company, meanwhile, was continually improving its profitability, introducing excellent new products and maintaining a high proportion of exports. The quality of the engineering was successfully being maintained and the works management team kept a capable control of labour relations, with a sound incentive scheme for all on the shop floor. I was very pleased with the performance of the company and the executive directors were a happy team. These results, however, were contrary to many other company performances in the UK, where a shortage of funds resulted in a disturbingly large increase in the public sector borrowing requirement during the 1970s. This meant that Central Government was borrowing heavily, as were Local

Authorities and Public Corporations. This situation was reflected in the decline of British Industry, indicating the failure of successive governments to encourage investment in the late 1960s. This led to a devaluation of our currency in 1967.

I was very concerned with the national outlook and decided to keep abreast of the situation by greater study of government and CBI statistics. I became a Fellow of my Institute in 1972 and, with my all-round ability and experience, was also accepted as a Fellow of the British Institute of Management and a Fellow of the Institute of Directors. I felt such steps would provide me with a constant update in the affairs of British companies and also provide me with better opportunities, should I desire further advancement in my profession.

With the introduction of the Industry Act 1972, the government assumed wider powers of intervention in industry than at any time in peacetime Britain and we Directors had to be on our toes to be aware of these powers. There had been the Industrial Relations Act, affecting the trade unions, but the latter were gaining more and more power, particularly under Labour administrations. The countries of the European Economic Community were our company's strongest export markets, especially Germany, Italy and Spain, This market needed protecting and nurturing and required us to be better informed about measures being undertaken on the continent.

It was a difficult time for industry and I sought the sanctuary of our lovely home at weekends, coupled with the refreshment of my mind attending the Sunday morning services, ably led by the Reverend John Waterson, who had a thriving church community at Stoke D'Abernon. There was also a revitalizing experience when I was among a group of fifty ex-RAF POWs invited to Buckingham Palace. Accompanied by our wives, we had tea with the Queen and Prince Philip, the latter correctly wearing the association tie for the occasion. We had presented the tie at a dinner occasion, previously held in the City of London, when he graciously accepted an associate membership of the "Ex-Kriegie" organisation.

The royal garden parties, held each July, have become a memorable institution, and our party represented just a few of the fifteen hundred or so guests on that occasion. We were quite thrilled when the Queen, talking to Dixie Deans, remarked how pleased she was to welcome fifty of us with our wives on this splendid occasion. Dixie, in his wheelchair, was very sick with multiple sclerosis. Shortly afterwards he suffered a fatal stroke and was laid to rest at a very solemn occasion. His wartime courage had been exemplary, only matched by his gallant acceptance of his long disabling illness. His services to the POW organisation could not be equalled and saying goodbye at St Clement Danes was a very sad affair.

There was also a very large attendance at the Royal Air Force church in the Strand in January 1978, when we said "happy landings" to another well-known and well-loved ex-Kriegie, Group Captain Harry "Wings" Day GC DSO OBE, a different character to Dixie, but revered by many friends since he had joined the Royal Marines in the 1914-18 war. He started flying in the Fleet Air Arm in 1924, transferring to the Royal Air Force in 1930. His exploits flying out in Persia (Iraq) pre-war were many, and he had been the Flight Commander when Douglas Bader crashed and lost his legs, flying a biplane, in the 1930s. He was, for many years, the senior member of the Royal Air Force POWs, having been shot down in September 1939 whilst flying a Blenheim with 57 Squadron on a reconnaissance of Western Germany to report on the suspected build-up of forces north of the Rhine. His Blenheim was no match for the three ME 109s that attacked him. He escaped from the blazing aircraft and became a prisoner of the Luftwaffe. His exploits as a POW in Germany for more than five and a half years have been well documented. He used his keen brain and strong personality to combat his captors. His survival was remarkable and so were his post-war activities. He was a keen member of our organisation and always popular with our ladies on the many social occasions we shared, both in the UK and Canada. He was always good for a lark and a laugh and our wives, including Nita, enjoyed his company. It was no surprise when, in black-and-white days, he appeared on the programme *This is your Life* on television.

It was around this time that the "old boy" organisation of the Halton Aircraft Apprentices Association was reborn and an occasional reunion at Halton brought much interest. I was able to attend on a couple of occasions, when I met up with my old chum Hugh Blissett, a fellow cricketer in the 41st entry. We decided to form an entry branch and so, with Hugh as Treasurer, I undertook, as Chairman, to arrange a meeting at the local hostelry at Weston Turville. It was a success. Denis Davies was an eager Secretary and, after many years and happy reunions, it is a pleasure to record that we three warriors are still at the helm, although in recent years, due to my failing health, I was elevated to Life President, passing over the work entailed to subsequent chairmen. Regrettably, our numbers attending reunions have declined in recent years, but it was a great joy to me when, in 1990, we celebrated our 50th anniversary of going up to Halton, when 150 members and a further 105 ladies attended a memorable occasion at RAF Halton. One of the most moving experiences was the dedication of the 41st Entry roll of honour plaque, by the Venerable Bishop Ashton, a former Royal Air Force Chaplain in Chief. This brought to fruition the promise I made to myself in the Commonwealth War Cemetery at Berlin when I visited there in 1968. The roll of honour, produced with much ingenuity by Mike McHale, lists sixty of our entry who gave their lives for our country and its citizens during the 1939/45 war. It hangs on the West Wall of St George's Church, Halton as a testimony to the contribution made by the 41st Entry in a vicious war that brought freedom again to our troubled world.

One regret that remains constantly in my memory is my great disappointment that a friend most dear to me and Nita was not able to attend the dedication. The Venerable W.E.G. Payton had been my cricketing companion and mentor whilst he was a young padre at Halton in 1940/2 and was latterly Air Vice Marshal and Chaplain in Chief of the Royal Air Force. He had agreed to carry out the dedication and preach at the service in the afternoon of the reunion, but sadly he died, after a short illness, most unexpectedly in September 1989. Whilst attending his moving funeral at Nailsworth, I met up with Bishop Ashton, who, without hesitation, agreed to dedicate our plaque and worship with us the following March on our 50th anniversary. In his sermon he spoke most generously of the sacrifices made by the young aircrews, who defied the elements and took on the enemy in the long struggle. Among the large congregation many a tear was shed that day, and those of us who survived the ordeal thanked God.

I regretted that Weg wasn't able to join us on that moving day, as I cherished his friendship and was inspired by his example to us all. His theology learnt at Cambridge was imparted so clearly to me at Halton and has helped me immensely as I steered my way through the many pitfalls that await us in life. Weg's wife,

Nita, who we met during our Farnham Common days, was endowed with a lovely disposition and my wife and I shared with them a loving friendship and a great deal laughter down the years from the 1960s.

There was a good deal activity amongst the RAF Ex-POW organisation in the 1970s and 1980s when we had the good fortune to be led for the first time by a senior serving officer, Air Commodore C.H. Clarke. Charles, a flying officer navigator, flew a Lancaster with 619 Squadron and had been shot down in 1944. He was incarcerated in Stalagluft III at Sagan before surviving the long forced march to Western Germany in 1945. Post-war he continued in the service and ended his career at the MOD. He enriched the Ex-POW association affairs through his many contacts and friends in the services, which brought forth many senior serving officers and others to express their appreciation of we former wartime fliers.

In 1978, the Old Vic theatre in London was the venue for one of these happy occasions. With the initiative and hard work of committee-man Vic Gammon, we staged a splendid show in the presence of Princess Alexandria and her husband, the Honourable Angus Ogilvy. It was a splendid occasion, enriched by the charm of the Princess who, after being met in the foyer by Charles and Eileen Clarke, was presented with a beautiful bouquet by our four-year-old granddaughter Philippa Kate.

The warmth of the Princess helped little Philippa, who handled the occasion with a child's simplicity, demonstrated when the Princess said she liked Philippa's dress. To everyone's surprise Philippa's response was, "I like yours too." The charming Princess then knelt down and said to Philippa, "Is that your grandmother with you? Ask her to show you the elephant design at the back of my dress." Nita gladly obliged, pointing out the shape of the elephant to much laughter, which remained the mood throughout a splendid evening of lasting memories.

The successful show enabled our POW association to make a generous gift to the Red Cross Society, one of our favourite charities. This was not the first time that Nita and I had the pleasure of being in the company of members of the Royal Family. During our ex-POW dinner at the City of London in 1977 we had the good fortune of meeting and talking briefly to the Duke of Edinburgh, who was our guest of honour. In his speech he expressed the thanks of the nation for the fortitude our members had shown in the face of the enemy, both in the air and later in captivity.

The declining performance of the UK economy and increasing government involvement in industry led to an upsurge in trade union activity. This was accompanied by the closure of a large proportion of our manufacturing industries and declining returns for shareholders in British companies. I was very concerned about the situation and, in order to enlighten myself further I made myself available for a four-week senior management course at Henley Administrative Staff College. This fitted in with what I considered my longer-term prospects within the company. I was therefore pleased when my educational background and industrial experience, along with a tough interview, satisfied the college management. Having prepared temporary communication links with the finance department of my company, I took up residence at the college in April 1979. This coincided with the dramatic election of Mrs Thatcher's Conservative government, from whom I was confidently expecting an improvement in the UK economy, particularly with regard to a reduction in inflation rates, which in the past had caused me much anxiety and extra work.

As usual, Nita was fully supportive of my involvement in this course to improve my knowledge of the business world. Fifty-six others joined me for very intensive lectures and discussions throughout the day, which continued after dinner in the evenings. My colleagues were all involved in senior management in their organisations, which included manufacturing industry, nationalised companies, major banks, the civil service, the military and all branches of commerce and exporters. There were also some African and Indian participants, all of whom spoke excellent English.

We were divided into four syndicates for close study and involvement with learned tutors, who set a high standard. Guest leaders of industry and commerce gave talks after dinner, when much was learned from their practical experiences in managing large enterprises. Once again, I found the involvement with academics most refreshing and, with two other course members, I was tasked with a study in depth of a Japanese trading company which, being very successful in one product group, was contemplating increasing investment in further product areas. The others in our team were from the engineering and chemical industries and our joint report would be required for presentation to the whole class of fifty members, plus our tutor and others from the college staff. We were given much information about the company's origins and successful expansion of manufacturing and trading over a period of many years since World War II.

The Japanese company was very cooperative and provided three years' final accounts and supporting schedules and requested a copy of our report as presented. Our team was much impressed with the high level of Research and Development expenditure incurred each year, expressed as a percentage of sales; this was higher than the average UK, European or American engineering company, which accounted for the excellent quality built into their products. This clearly had much influence on their trading performance and the fine reputation they had built up, particularly in the post-war resurgence of the Japanese economy. We also noted the relatively low rate of labour turnover during this period, which was a reflection of the national policy whereby companies were encouraged to provide living accommodation for their labour force.

Our team recommended that the product field into which they were contemplating expansion was highly competitive throughout the world and would therefore require an exemplary range of products and thus a great deal more investment in Research and Development. My earlier engineering studies and experience had taught me the importance of expenditure in controlled R&D, which figured strongly in our joint report at the completion of our study. This was well received and I would like to think some of our findings were useful when the Japanese company subsequently merged with a large organisation already established in the field they were aspiring to join.

At this time, corporation and company mergers were being affected with increasing frequency, especially in the USA, but also in the UK. They were not all successful and often indicated a lack of in-depth study of the merged or acquired company by the directors of the acquiring company on such occasions. The financial press frequently reported on financial losses incurred by such ill-conceived take-overs. There were also many reported cases of very large payouts to company chairmen and chief executives. The apparent greed portrayed in these cases concerned me greatly, as the tendency seemed to be so unfair and unchristian.

I thoroughly enjoyed the most interesting spell at Henley and learned much from the tutors and fellow course members. I was faced with an accumulation of work on my return to office, but with extra effort I was soon astride current problems.

Then came the disturbing news of my mother's failing health and, in June 1980, and at the ripe age of ninety, she passed away. I was very fond of mother, who, throughout her life, maintained her love and loyalty to her Maker, earning the respect and trust of all the family. She had faced her many wartime disappointments with courage and was an example to all around her.

Then, in the early 1980s I was faced with an ill-judged merger of my company with a slightly smaller company, manufacturing and trading in a similar product range but on a smaller scale. In my view, the decision made by our holding company was incorrect and should have included a more in-depth study of the company being purchased. Insufficient assessment of the level of redundant stocks, among other failures, resulted in an inaccurate valuation of assets, which in turn resulted in reduced profits in future trading.

I was frustrated and unhappy at this situation, which brought a considerable jolt to my professional career in management accountancy. My studies and experiences in company affairs had taught me that the most valuable assets were the people employed by the organisation. When merging two long-standing organisations, a close study of the personalities involved should be carried out, after all, good human relationships in all walks of life are of vital importance. I decided that I did not want to be a part of the 'rat race' that had developed and, at the age of sixty, I elected to retire.

Nita was pleased with my decision, as she knew I had been working excessively hard and that the failing condition of my war-damaged leg was causing me increasing discomfort. I had been a conscientious worker and it was therefore with some regret that I ceased to be a company executive director. I was determined, however, to maintain an interest in economic affairs and the financial control measures of industry.

In the meantime, the family was growing with the happiness of two new grandchildren. Louise was born in Berkshire in 1977, followed by Robert, in Hampshire, in 1981.

9. Retirement and Failing Health

I had long-since been unable to do much in the garden, as my left leg was bowing outward at the knee joint, resulting in constant pain whilst walking or standing. This required medical attention and I didn't need much encouragement from Nita to consult Mr William Murphy, a leading orthopaedic surgeon who lived in the neighbouring village. He gave me a thorough check up with x-rays and referred my case to a specialist in arteries and veins, as these had been severely damaged in my lower leg. In his final consultation Mr Murphy made it quite clear that, because of the condition, which in five years would require a wheelchair to maintain my mobility, the alleviation of pain and the restoration of my ability to walk and stand better would require major surgery of the left knee joint. He recommended the use of a fitted plastic support of my left ankle and lower leg as a temporary measure until he was able to operate.

Meanwhile, Nita and I were already intent on a move of home, away from the large garden at Cobham and the increasing traffic and housing development in this area, which had become part of the stockbroker belt, being within easy commuting distance of the City of London. Many of our neighbours were from the USA and an American school had been incorporated in the area. Cobham had grown from a small village to a small town in a very short time. We had grown up appreciating the relative quietness of village life and our sights were to be concentrated further south, in Sussex. We knew we would miss our regular worship at Stoke D'Abernon, but had sufficient confidence in our ability to find an alternative, where we could enjoy the opportunity to pray and touch the hand of our God, who had blessed us with so much happiness throughout our lives.

After some months of searching, we eventually found a lovely house at the village of West Wittering on the Sussex coast. The seventh century church and the schedule of activities and services in the village were most appealing and in November 1983 we declared our intent for this major move. The beautiful Cathedral City of Chichester was just seven miles away and the renowned theatre there was an added attraction. Mr Murphy, meanwhile, felt that it would be better to make our move and settle into our new abode before calling me in for surgery. We also thought it best to await the spring weather, which would allow Nita to make the 120-mile round-trip to visit me at St Peter's Hospital, Pyrford, where he would operate. We settled for a date in May 1984, when Mr Murphy would carry out major surgery, which he estimated would require a three-week stay in hospital. My membership of BUPA from the early 1970s enabled the surgeon and me to choose a suitable time in a private ward, so I had relative peace in which to effect a satisfactory recovery.

The operation entailed breaking and realigning the upper tibia and femur and correcting the alignment of the knee joint, difficult to achieve without stiffening of the joint. To avoid this, four sturdy stainless steel rods were inserted through the flesh and bones laterally and the securing nuts were tightened from time to time. Meanwhile, for the second time in my life, the leg was mounted on a cradle, but this time the knee joint was kept moving continually by the clever use of an electrically-powered flexing machine. I was able to control the machine through switches that enabled me to start, speed up, slow down and stop the knee movements. I was discouraged from using the latter control even at night, when sleep called.

I remember well seeing the televised programme at dawn on June 6th 1984 when the 40th anniversary of 'D'-Day was celebrated with a programme from the beaches of Normandy. This was a moving occasion and I was reminded of the valour and tremendous organisation entailed in the successful landings of the British, Canadian and American troops against an enemy that had four years to prepare their defences. As I lay on the hospital bed, with my left leg flexing on its cradle through about thirty degrees every minute or so, I was reminded of my own catastrophe in December 1942, which had changed my life so dramatically.

After three weeks in hospital I was advised by Mr Murphy that I could return home, but that the stainless steel rods would have to remain in position for a further three months, when I would return for examination and, if my recovery was satisfactory, they would be removed under anaesthetic. I hastened to master the use of crutches again and Nita modified pairs of trousers, enabling me to be up and about in our delightful home.

Fortunately, it was a good summer, which enabled me to enjoy lovely sunny days outside. The handicap of taking thirty-two tablets daily, which required the use of mathematics to space out, was ably overcome by the warm caring love of Nita, who nursed me through that trying period. She also didn't show her bitter disappointment when, for the first time after many applications, we had been successful in obtaining two tickets for the opera at Glyndebourne, but were unable to attend. Fortunately, our next door neighbours, Doctor Tony and Anne Conyers, who had passed on useful advice during my rehabilitation, were also opera lovers and were able to replace us for a wonderful evening of Verdi.

Our detached house at West Wittering had been built in 1972 on grounds that had formerly been the orchard of Sir Henry Royce. As I lay basking in the lovely sunshine of 1984 my thoughts often settled on the tremendous success of the Rolls-Royce Merlin engines, which powered the Halifax in which I flew and many other more successful aircraft in World War II. These included Hurricanes and Spitfires, which helped to save the nation in the Battle of Britain in 1940, the magnificent Mosquito and the heavy bomber force that paved the way for victory over the evil forces of Germany in 1945. I again thanked God for his mercy and for my deliverance and prayed for a satisfactory improvement in my physical condition.

Following two further visits to the hospital at Pyrford, the rods were successfully removed and soon I was able to dispense with the crutches and other paraphernalia that had aided my recovery. This enabled me to join Nita for Sunday morning services at the ancient church of St Peter and St Paul.

I was now able to participate in the lively atmosphere at West Wittering and a few weeks later I met up with John Wright, the Secretary of the Parochial Church Council and an active member of the village sailing club. He and his wife Dorothy, both former Cambridge graduates and devout Christians, decided to form an Abbeyfield Society in the village and I was approached by them to join their worthy venture.

Local meetings were called, funds were raised and, with the financial aid of the Housing Corporation, a roomy detached house in the village was purchased. After minor modifications we were able to house eight elderly, lonely people in a happy home, under the care of a paid housekeeper, a part-time cleaner and a part-time gardener. All the other work was carried out by volunteers and the whole operation controlled by John as chairman and a volunteer committee. In due course, I was able to use my talents as secretary, treasurer, in house maintenance and eventually succeeded John as chairman for eight years.

The Abbeyfield organisation was a most worthy contributor to the social life of the community and provided a comfortable home where each individual had their own room. The cost for occupancy was about half what one would pay at a nursing or retirement home. The parish clergy carried out regular communion services at the home and some of the residents were able to attend Sunday morning services at the church. I felt the guiding hand of God in our Abbeyfield home. Nita was also involved in organising support activities at the home or outings for the residents. We appreciated the tremendous help from so many volunteers, not least Mrs Joy Hillary, who was a caring matron at the local nursing home and a very capable Vice Chairman, succeeding me in the hot seat when I retired.

Meanwhile, I was invited to join the Parochial Church Council at St Peter and St Paul and after a few years, during which I carried out sidesman's duties on Sunday services, I became a church warden. Having served on Church Councils in previous parishes I had an inkling of the duties of a church warden, but the more I studied the responsibilities and duties involved, the more I realised the full extent of the commitment I had made. I was fortunate to have George Lord as my fellow warden; he had already been in post for a few years and was a devout churchman. His wartime role as a pilot in Royal Air Force Coastal Command enabled us to share experiences of operational flying, with all its dangers.

George, well supported throughout his long married life by his wife Kathleen, made a considerable contribution to our village church, although he and I did not always agree on which course of action to take. Our most trying period was when we were faced with a disturbing situation that led to an interregnum. This involved decisions by the Bishop and Archdeacon of the diocese, who were a great help to us as we steered through the unfortunate machinations that affected our parish life. We were relieved when the situation was settled and we had God's help in guiding us to the successful appointment of an able successor, the Reverend John Williams, as our rector. All connected with the church helped in maintaining good attendances at the weekly services. I can therefore reflect on a happy and successful period of twenty years in which Nita and I were associated with a warm and loyal church at West Wittering, around which we built many lasting friendships.

As soon as I was on my feet again, I was able to journey to London for monthly meetings of the Ex-POW committee, which met under the capable chairmanship of Dixie Dean until he was too ill to participate.

We had a most enjoyable Ruby wedding party in our house and garden on 12th June 1987, when forty guests and family joined us on a beautiful summer's day. Our family had now grown to three grandchildren, and they were all thrilled to under-take minor tasks for the occasion. Philippa, the eldest, greeted everyone on arrival and conducted them to the garden. Louise made an excellent job of keeping the background of recorded music in enchanting continuity and young Robert kept his young cousins happily playing around the shrub beds. Linda Baker, a caterer of repute and a friend at church, provided an excellent meal and with the champagne flowing it was a memorable occasion.

The 1980s had seen a great deal activity in the Tempsford Association, with its annual reunions, held mainly in London and later at the Anchor Hotel on the Great North Road, a favourite watering hole for our squadrons at Tempsford. Here I was able to meet friends from 138 and 161 squadrons, among them Brian Atkins, a navigator, shot down on an operation over Denmark and a fellow POW, and Tom Russell a 138 pilot who completed a tour of operations and went on to pilot a Government minister. He was a good chum, living at Bognor Regis, and accompanied me to monthly meetings of the Aircrew Association, held at Arundel. There we relived the memories of many experienced flyers, who had served in all the varied commands of the air force and had much to tell. Regrettably, our meetings brought the news of the increasing number of wartime comrades who had passed on. At every meeting there were moments of silence as we prayed for their souls, now in the safe hands of their Maker.

The Tempsford Association was ably led by retired Air Chief Marshal Sir Lewis (Bob) Hodges, who had commanded 161 Squadron and flown a Halifax and a twin-engined Lockheed

Hudson, the latter having the ability to land in enemy territory and retrieve agents and important resistance personnel from under German noses. The hard-working secretary of our association was an ex-aircraft apprentice and station engineering officer, Squadron Leader Sid Firth, who had ensured that the ground staff maintained our aircraft in good shape for the hazardous operations they were called upon to undertake. Our mutual Halton training resulted in a close bond down the years. Amongst our members were many who had achieved considerable success in defying our determined enemy on many dangerous operations.

The distinguished Lysander pilots, many who recorded their exploits in outstanding books, were great chums, perhaps the foremost being Group Captain Hugh Verity, who, along with Group Captain Ken Batchelor, was my sponsor when I was made a member of the Special Forces Club. This organisation comprised members formerly employed on secret operations against the enemy and provided overnight accommodation and a meeting place in Knightsbridge, London. There, I was able to meet up with Colonel Maurice Buckmaster, Barbara Yeo Thomas and many others who had carried out secret work during the eventful war years. But despite many conversations, little was said about the German 'North Pole' operations and a great deal of the SOE Dutch section activities remained secret. I came to the conclusion that in war, the side making fewer mistakes won the conflict.

Regular attendees at the Tempsford Association reunions were outstanding Halifax pilots, who impressed me greatly with their wartime achievements. Group Captain Ron Hockey led the aircraft which dropped SAS forces to bring about the destruction of the heavy water plant in Norway. He also flew two Czech agents to their native land on a mission to kill the notorious head of German interests in that country, Gauleiter Heydrich. This resulted in the heavy punishment meted out to the Czechs by the Germans at Lidice. Ron was a great companion at many of our post-war reunions and visits to former resistance groups, particularly in France. The other was Group Captain Frank Griffiths, a north Walian who joined 138 after I had been shot down. He flew Halifax's and crashed, due to engine failure, near Annecy in Alpine France. Unlike some of my more unfortunate and heroic chums, he evaded capture and successfully returned to the UK after a six month ordeal, only to be rebuked by Air Commodore Fielden, the Station Commander at Tempsford, with the question "Where the hell have you been?"

Griff was quite a character and great company. Many of our ex-Tempsford regulars received high awards for bravery and success and many, including Lewis Hodges, Alan Boxer and Robin Hooper, were also knighted for wartime or post-war Royal Air Force or diplomatic service. They were a splendid team, whose outstanding clandestine work had made such a marked contribution to our country's war effort.

With a series of visits to Royal Air Force stations, regular re-unions of the Ex-POWs, organised under the energetic chair-manship of Charles Clark, and my other activities in our home village, the time flew by. But Nita and I were able to enjoy many holiday cruises on the splendid P&O Liners, sailing out of Southampton. The most memorable of these was in 1998 when we joined the *Aurora* for a musical cruise in the Baltic. This included Richard Baker and other talented artists, who provided an outstanding feast of music each evening, which we thor-oughly enjoyed after an excellent dinner. If only my health held good for Nita and I to enjoy more of these splendid occasions!

Following the major surgery on my wounded left leg in 1984, with the aid of a walking stick, I enjoyed many short walks of just a few hundred yards in Elms Lane and Nita and I would often drive the half a mile to the seafront from our home. There we would absorb the sea atmosphere and enjoy walking short distances along the grassy hinterland. As shareholders we util-ised our season-ticket passes to take in the well kept grassland at the sea's edge, which enabled us to look across the Channel to the Isle of Wight on a clear day. This was a splendid sight and these were happy times.

Although we missed the visits to Covent Garden Opera, we were able to enjoy regular visits to Chichester Festival Theatre and often entertained friends for short stays with us, taking in a theatre show. Weg and Nita Payton and Hugh and Hazel Blissett from Halton 1940 days were regulars, who reciprocated with splendid opportunities for us to visit the Cotswolds and the delightful village of Dingley in Leicestershire. We thoroughly enjoyed these outings with fellow Christians, whose attitude to life we much admired.

There followed, in the 1990s, a serious deterioration in my health. Apart from a worsening condition of my left leg due to wear and tear, and my limited walking ability, I found difficulty in standing for more than short intervals. In February 1992 trouble with my waterworks and a painful bladder required an endoscopic resection of the prostate. This was carried out by Mr Ashby at King Edward VII hospital, located on a hill just outside Midhurst, formerly used to treat RAF personnel suffering with Tuberculosis during and after the Second World War. I was pleasantly surprised to be provided with some aeronautical literature from the hospital library whilst recuperating after my operation. This, incidentally, referred to the high achievement in technical training attained at Halton, on which much of the success of the Royal Air Force was based.

I also had a significant reminder of the fine service in which I was privileged to serve when I was fortunate to be amongst those attending the presentation of Her Majesty the Queen's Colour for the Royal Air Force in the United Kingdom. This spectacular 75th anniversary event was held in April 1993 at RAF Marham, an active Bomber Command Station throughout the war and since. I remember it rained heavily and the capable management at the station switched the ceremony at short notice to be held inside one of the large hangars. We, the spectators, were seated around in several tiers of seats, with the Queen on the dais at the centre of one of the long sides. My companion for the day was Squadron Leader Hugh Blissett, an old chum from my Halton days and one of my best companions.

Sitting the other side of me were two German Luftwaffe Officers, who were in a party conveyed from RAF Cottesmore, where they were on flight training for the Tripartite Typhoon aircraft. The German air force has financed and developed this modern jet, along with the Italians and ourselves. It was interesting to exercise my modest knowledge of German, when we discussed our visitors' view of the Russian-made fighter aircraft they had known while serving in the East German air force, prior to the destruction of the Berlin Wall and the integration of the West and East German air forces. The maintenance and backup facilities at the latter bases were considered inferior when the West Germans took them over after the amalgamation of resources, but the performance of some of the Russian-built aircraft, now in the German Luftwaffe, was considered of a high standard by them. I enjoyed chatting with them but the highlight of the occasion was the disciplined march by two representatives of each of the seventy active squadrons in the RAF. These young Flight Lieutenants carried their Squadron colours around the perimeter to musical accompaniment, played inspiringly by the Royal Air Force Band. These marching young airmen were a shining example to the youth of our country and one felt that the nation was safe in their hands for the future – a memorable occasion.

Such occasions as the 75th anniversary, the happy reunions with former RAF POWs at home and in Canada, and get-togethers of the Halton 41st, all revitalised my feelings of pride in Britain and in the RAF, in which I had been privileged to serve. Our common bond, forged when facing danger in war, has had a lasting effect. The comradeship, between fellow kriegies is even stronger and more compassionate, because of the shared hardships and suffering that imprisonment by the enemy entailed.

Early in the 1990s I received a most pleasant surprise when a letter dropped through our letterbox from a middle aged Dutchman, who explained that he had been looking for me for many years. Jan Mennink lived in the Staphorst area of northern Holland, which was in the neighbourhood of Ijhorst, where my aircraft had crashed in 1942. As a youngster he had been inspired by the courageous activities of the Royal Air Force in World War II. He was so grateful to the British airmen for their brave fight against the enemy that had forcibly occupied their country for five years, inflicting so much treachery and misery on the Dutch population, that he was now researching and compiling details of all wartime aircraft activity in his area. He was particularly interested in knowing more about my six fellow crewmembers, buried in his local churchyard near Ijhorst. He was also interested in the clandestine operations of the Tempsford Squadrons and was much relieved when I was able to provide this for him. This was the commencement of a friendship with Jan and his wife Janet and we are thankful to receive Christmas greetings from them each year, containing references to the Christian vigil they make to the graveside of my comrades each 23rd December on the anniversary of their demise. With Jan's help, Nita and I were able to tour the area later, enjoy the hospitality of our hosts and learn much of the wartime resistance activities in the area where they had grown up after the war.

The 41st, which I have been proud to lead down the years, enjoyed many annual reunions in the UK, but none more so than the smashing trip we made when a party of about eighty members and wives spent a couple of weeks in Cyprus. We were fortunate to have Eric Barrett and John Davies, two of our group who in retirement were resident on the island. They, with their wives, were able to do much of the organisation for a splendid trip which we all enjoyed so much in delightful weather in March 1993. However, there were some difficult periods for Nita and me when I suffered several painful and breathless periods with attacks of angina. This had been earlier diagnosed when, with difficult breathing, accompanied by chest and shoulder pains, I returned from a short walk into the wind at West Wittering. Our doctor advised me against strenuous exercise and walks in windy conditions. He then prescribed Glyceryl Trinitrate spray to treat or help prevent an attack of angina. This has helped me preserve some measure in the quality of my life since these attacks started.

With the constant pain and deterioration in my left leg, I was throwing more weight on the right and about this time developed a painful right hip joint, which added to my standing and walking difficulties. With the pain developing into my right groin, it came as no surprise when, following 'X' rays, I was strongly advised to undergo a right hip joint replacement. Without delay, because I had maintained BUPA membership in retirement for Nita and myself, I was admitted to their hospital at Chichester and in March 1996 I emerged with a new hip, and it was back to the physiotherapist before walking correctly. It was a very successful operation and helped me press on with my life and I thanked God for his continual help in preserving my spiritual and bodily health.

After much organisation and planning Nita and I decided to celebrate fifty years of happy marriage together with many of our family and friends. We needed a long booking period for use of the Memorial Hall at West Wittering and on June 12th 1997 we were able to greet them at a hall lined with the inner lining for a marquee, a carpeted floor and an abundance of flowers. It was a super occasion and I thanked God for his help in sustaining Nita and me to this landmark in our lives together! We were so pleased when so many of our friends from the war years and since, travelled long distances to share with us and those of our family and friends from the village in a joyous occasion. Philip, in his humorous and able way, gave his parents a most glowing oration, which we cherish. So another important milestone in our lives passed bringing much pleasure to all the family.

This pleasure turned into grief when on Christmas Day 1997 we were shattered with the news of Nita's mother's death at the West Wittering nursing home. She had been a patient there for the past seven years and had achieved her 100th birthday on the 26th July of that year. Nita was her only child, who missed her immensely, having visited her every day at the nursing home, except when we were away from the village. There were many from Dorothy's native village of Cadoxton at the church of St Catwg when she was laid to rest with her loving husband Godfrey on January 3rd 1998. Dolly, as she was known, was a keen churchwoman and popular in her village, having left there to join us at West Wittering fifteen years earlier.

Life continued at a lively pace, with a large number of visitors to the delightful beach area during the summer months and two plays a year excellently performed by the village theatre group, ably led by Dorothy Chapman. But all was not well with me; I was feeling increasingly tired and breathless and requiring more relief from the pains engendered by attacks of angina. Then, suddenly, in 1999 I was diagnosed with cancer of the bowel. The surgeon to whom I was referred at Chichester said I was fortunate to have discovered the symptoms early and the operation to remove the offending cancer was successful. Before this was finally confirmed I had a series of follow-up checks, which went on for a period of years, resulting in a colonoscopy in May 2005. It is of much relief to know that I am clear of the haunting disease as I write these final pages of my autobiography.

Regrettably, I was becoming a frequent patient at both Saint Richards and the Nuffield Hospital in Chichester. In the year 2000 I was diagnosed with an enlarged heart and, additionally, two main arteries were closing up. This diagnosis followed x-rays and extensive tests, including a coronary arteriogram. It was explained to me by the heart specialist at Chichester that the condition of my heart was serious but there was too much risk of carrying out remedial surgery. It was therefore a case of frequent checks and extensive medication to control the blood supply to the many body functions. Consequently, I am currently receiving frequent tests of blood content and pressure, coupled with twice yearly consultations with the coronary specialist. My medical condition had become a serious worry to Nita and the family and, after several emergency admissions to St Richards Hospital, including one to a hospital at Portsmouth to arrest excessive bleeding, I felt it necessary that we should be living nearer Philip and family. This would provide greater assistance and security for Nita in the event of my departure from this life. We have sought God's help throughout these very trying times and thankfully the Holy Spirit has provided great comfort to us and sustained us throughout these difficult few years.

The onset of the cancer in 1999 led to a cancellation of a P&O cruise and I was subsequently advised, because of my dangerous heart condition, to refrain from further cruises or overseas holidays. We came to terms with such advice and have confined ourselves to short holidays at UK locations in recent years. My condition has also curtailed my activities with the Royal Air Forces Ex-POWs, the 41st, the RAF Association, the Aircrew Association and the Bomber Command Association, but I still manage to attend occasional meetings. It is a great pleasure for Nita and I to meet up with the surviving members of these five organisations, whose numbers are declining, inevitably.

Meanwhile, we are enjoying peace and happiness in our new home in rural Hampshire. Philip and his wife Glenys (he remarried in 1991) live just 7½ miles away and are frequent visitors and a welcome comfort to us. The grandchildren (and now two great-grandchildren, Lindsay and Eddie) are only half an hour away.

We had many regrets in May 2003 when we vacated our lovely home at West Wittering. The many churchgoers at St Peter and St Paul treated us to a feast of our favourite hymns as we said cheerio for now, and our many loving friends there have maintained contact. In fact, we have been invited back to many enjoyable parties in the village since our departure. We have found splendid friends in our new Parish, and enjoy the warmth of our loving fellow members of All Saints Church at Awbridge. We attend Sunday worship and our spirits are uplifted in the presence of Jesus, which, coupled with our many friends, provides the sustenance for meaningful living.

I am an avid reader, and regular copies of *Aeroplane* and *RAF News* keep me abreast of new developments in the world of aviation. I was sorry to note the cessation of Concorde flights, as this was a considerable achievement of British engineering in cooperation with French designers. The Concorde flight I made to Singapore in the 1970s and the flight we made with the Morrisons over the Grand Canyon in January 1994 were my most memorable post-war flying experiences. The New Year celebrations at Las Vegas were spectacular but I was not impressed with or tempted by the excessive gambling opportunities that arose.

Before we moved from West Wittering I was able to make a journey in 2001 that I had been wanting to make for a few years. Nita was not keen to do the trip, so along with Stuart Hillary, a neighbour from our village at West Wittering, I flew out from Southampton to Frankfurt-am-Main and revisited some of the places in Germany where I had been imprisoned during the war. Stuart is much younger than me but always interested in the experiences of wartime fliers; he also wished to visit the small town of Dobeln in Eastern Germany where his grandfather was born. This was located within a short distance of Colditz, which we also included in our itinerary.

As we flew out over the channel on a clear spring day, my thoughts returned to wartime flying and the events that overtook me. The aircraft descended from a high cruising altitude and circled in the Frankfurt area, preparing to land, and my desire to undertake the trip Stuart and I planned seemed to strengthen. Somehow, I felt it was something I had to do; it was a strange feeling. We duly collected a hired car for the journey, due to end five days later. Our first objective was to travel just thirteen kilometres north-west to Oberursel and revisit Kurklinic Hohemark, the hospital situated a mile away from the dreaded Dulagluft, the Luftwaffe transit camp where all downed airmen were brought to be interrogated, as I described in Chapter 2.

As we passed near Dulag I noticed that the hutted accommodation had been demolished and initially converted into quarters for American Camp David, an intelligence headquarters for the American occupying forces. Latterly, a new housing estate replaced that, but no doubt some of the Luftwaffe barn-like buildings remain. The Kirk Clinic is an imposing building on higher ground and is still used as a medical centre. Entrance was not possible for us, but we admired the carefully kept grounds and photographed the occasion. The view over the trees to the distant forest reminded me of the splendid view that had cheered me as I lay in my bed there forty years earlier. This tended to mollify my fearful thoughts of the many interrogation sessions I endured.

We then set out eastwards and enjoyed a comfortable night in a hostelry in the delightful countryside, en route to our planned visit to Obermassfeld the following morning. In due course, after traversing a winding route and noticing remnants of the wretched border fence, we crossed into what had been Eastern Germany, near Honfeld. We immediately noticed the inferior upkeep of buildings and roads east of the border. After a picturesque route over the hills in the Thuringwald, we suddenly arrived at the small village of Obermassfeld, spanning the river Werra. We quickly found the old hospital building between the two river flows and pulled into the forecourt, now giving access to various shops and the local post office, housed in the building that during the war had been the POW hospital of Stalag IX AH.

No sign, now, of barbed wire or guardhouse as we viewed the old place from the bridge which I had longed to cross to freedom during those long hours of boredom in 1943. Memories came back swiftly of the old steam engine in the back yard, of many comrades and our shared experiences, of the room across the road where we enjoyed the frolics of the concert party, and of the days of pain and anguish suffered in the hospital.

We stopped off for lunch at the pleasant town of Meiningen, then carried on, across the less interesting, flat, Saxon countryside to spend the night at Dobeln, where Stuart was able to search out his grandfather's birthplace and see where he had lived before emigrating to England in the 1930s.

The following morning we set out for Colditz, where we found an English-speaking guide, who conducted us around the imposing 950-year old castle, on the hill overlooking the town. Some limited investment from the state of Saxony, with its high unemployed percentage, had enabled a start to be made in the renovation of the old building. The very thick stone walls were evidence of the notorious prison camp, where political enemies of the Nazis were incarcerated in the 1930s and later allied prisoners during World War II. I was now more impressed than ever with the courage and determination of Pat Reid, who made his successful escape in October 1942 from this grim place.

A quick lunch and a glass of ale in the town below and we were on our way across the River Elbe on a novel ferry, which was hand operated by a system of ropes. This was situated, as I recall, on a quiet road near Torgau, the much-exalted meeting point of the American and Russian armies in April 1945. Then we travelled on across flat countryside to the small town of Annaburg, where the castle in which we repatrées were held for three months in the hot summer of 1944.

It was still an imposing structure, but seemed to have deteriorated under the communist regime after the war. Again the sight of the place reminded me of many events that had taken place there. I was able to recognise the small open area in front of the castle where we beat the Aussies, and New Zealanders in those memorable cricket matches and to locate the second-floor window of our room, from which Richard Pape was saved from falling during one of his minor encounters with tense roommates.

From Annaburg, we drove north across the flat plain, passing the former airbase at Wunsdorf and the town of Zussen, then on to our stop at Potsdam, where we checked in for two nights' stay. The following morning it was just a short journey near Wannsee, the location of the notorious meeting of German functionaries under Heydrich when the extermination policy was laid down. We passed the colourful Havel Lake before reaching the Spandau area of Berlin, where, in the Heerstrasse, we visited the next key item on our itinerary, the 1939-45 War Cemetery, where my brother Jack lay at rest. Having visited previously on my memorable trip with members of my family in 1968 I was soon able to single out the neat line of graves of Jack and his former crew members.

The Commonwealth War Graves Commission maintains a high standard of upkeep, which impressed my colleague Stuart immensely. He was moved to see so many tombstones of former flyers, with an average age of about twenty, who had laid down their lives. We prayed silently and I solemnly thanked God for my deliverance in the dark days of 1942. The following day we toured Berlin in an open-top bus and visited as many sights as physically possible, with my legs now feeling the strain. Stuart made his own way for an hour or so while I rested and was surprised at the remarkable degree of recovery that had taken place in the business centre of the city.

After a splendid dinner we turned in early, contemplating a prompt departure the following morning.

We set out speedily westwards as we had set a busy itinerary for the final day of our journey. Our hired car was quite quick on the autobahn and we were soon turning south near Brunswick, where our repatriation train had been halted in an air raid 56 years earlier. There we joined the secondary road, linking to another motorway near Hildesheim and by-passing Gottingen and Kassel, a highly industrialised section. We left the fast road for the hilly and more interesting countryside to reach our first destination, the Eder Dam, where we halted for lunch. We then observed how difficult the task had been for former comrades of 617 Squadron to descend steeply to the 60-foot bombing height and then climb sharply, avoiding the steep hillsides. The dam was breached, but with heavy losses of courageous airmen, who in May 1943 achieved much in the quest to defeat a determined enemy. The countryside now looked peaceful and pleasant as we moved on a few miles south to reach Kloster Haina, where, nestled in the hillside, was the hospital where I had been sent from Obermassfeld in 1943. I had some pleasant memories of Kloster Haina, where my recovery made a stride forward.

I noted that Kloster Haina had been developed into a large medical area and access was not possible to the section where I had been incarcerated so many years earlier. This was our final planned destination and we moved on rapidly south to Frankfurt-am-Main, where we turned in our hired car and boarded the evening flight back to Southampton and home to Nita.

It had been an interesting journey, with a pleasant companion, and had fulfilled a personal desire that had been building up for some years. There had obviously been some psychological incentive for the trip. This phenomenon was brought home to me when, a few months after my return, Nita commented that I had not experienced the awful recurring dreams of wartime events since my return. Five years later, this is still the case; I seem to have purged the demons that were lurking inside me and occasionally emerging during sleep.

Occasional contacts with visitors from Germany and a study of current reading matter, indicate the success of the efforts made in rebuilding the shattered country and educating the young people more about the sins of their forefathers, which brought so much death and misery in the two world wars. There is an awareness amongst young German folk of past failures, which augurs well for the future relationship between our two countries, Europe and NATO. Let us hope the lessons have been learned and the large cuts in aircraft and personnel in the Royal Air Force are justified ... although we must keep on our toes.

The commendable efforts of the Royal Air Forces Ex-POW Association resulted in the need to legally dispose of surpluses made from our activities for charitable purposes. Our hard working committee, which had been successfully welded together by James (Dixie) Dean, resolved to establish two charitable trusts. Along with Dixie, in 1978 Charles Clarke, Maurice Butt, Carlton Younger and myself were appointed trustees of "The Charitable Trust" to carry out exclusively charitable objectives and the "Larry Slattery Memorial Fund" which would assist promising young musicians who needed some financial support to help them on their way. Following Larry's untimely death there had been strong desire in our hearts to remember the loyal and loving Larry, who not only suffered the mental torture of five and a half years loss of freedom behind barbed wire but also was a most energetic secretary of our association, just prior to and after its formal constitution in 1963.

As I write these memoirs in 2006 I can record the outstanding work carried out by these two trusts, particularly the unstinting work of Calton Younger and our hard-working Treasurer Doug Endsor, both dear friends of mine and both always ready to help others and show truly Christian principles in their lives. Cal, an Australian of quiet disposition, flew as a navigator in a Wellington IV of 460 Squadron and was shot down on a raid on Gennevilliers (France) on 29th/30th May 1942. He has given more than forty years of devoted service to the Ex-POW Association, editing the "Kriegie" news-sheet, and especially managing the two trusts. I have much admiration for Cal, always an Aussie, and a loyal friend. His loving wife Dee supported POW wives and widows gallantly to the end of her days, earlier this year.

Doug, raised in North London, was a Hampden pilot of 50 Squadron and was shot down in a raid on Kiel on September 7th/8th 1941. He suffered four years as a POW. Appointed treasurer in 1971 Doug has given thirty-four years of time in excellently maintaining the association's books of account. A devoted Christian and assisted by his most loyal wife, Mary, he hasn't failed to help POWs at all times and as the association's auditor since 1972 I experienced his meticulous integrity and book-keeping, which was always most reliable. Despite the sad death of Mary a year ago, he continues in his work for the association.

We in the association salute the outstanding work of our current president and chairman, Air Commodore Charles Clarke. A Flying Officer navigator with 619 Squadron, Charles was shot down while flying in a Lancaster from Woodall Spa on 24th/25th February 1944, when the target was Schweinfurt, the centre of Germany's ball-bearing industry. He opted to continue service in the Royal Air Force after the war. He has been a loyal member of our association, well supported by his wife, Eileen, first serving alongside Dixie Dean then succeeding Maurice Butt, who followed Dixie as chairman. Since Larry Slattery's death in 1975 we have had a succession of industrious general secretaries, currently the loyal John Banfield, but the social activities of our group have been studiously maintained by Harold Batchelor throughout this most active and rewarding period. Batch was shot down on 17th June 1942 while piloting a Halifax with 102 Squadron and became a POW.

These colleagues have been the loyal core of a very efficient committee for more than thirty years and are an example of long devoted service to a fine association. Born out of circumstances when we were all volunteer airmen and fellow prisoners more than sixty years ago this is a splendid example of Christian men in action and I am proud to be one of them. My efforts for, and continued interest in, the work of the association would not have been possible without Nita's loving help at all times. This, and the unfailing support from Philip and family, has enabled me to refresh my thoughts as I recall the disappointing decline in the manufacturing industry of our country.

Whilst I retain a real concern for the country's future, economically, politically and morally, Nita and I remain in happy contentment. I trust that in the years ahead our love for each other and our Maker will survive. Meanwhile, the winning of the Ashes last summer enlightened my life. This, coupled with the Welsh victories in the Six Nation Rugby contest last winter, was very encouraging. I now feel refreshed as Nita and I continue on the long haul together.

~ End ~

Nita on holiday, 1949.

The Author ~ age 22.

Mum and Dad at their Golden Wedding celebration 1963.

My brother Jack, RAF Wratting Common 1943.

*My brother Jack (extreme right) at de-briefing after a raid
on Berlin on 24 August 1943 with 90 Squadron.*

Jack's grave, Berlin.

41st figured strongly in Wing Cricket Final, August 1940.
Author end right front row.

Inmates awaiting repatriation at Stalag IV DZ,
Annaburg, September 1944.

*"Victory over the Aussies" A cricket memory from Annaburg:
Lieutenant Colonel Lester Le Sauef, Australian Army Medical Corps.*

Six graves of my fellow crew members, IJhorst, Holland.

Ward 3 inmates, Stalag IXc Obermassfeld Hospital, 1943.

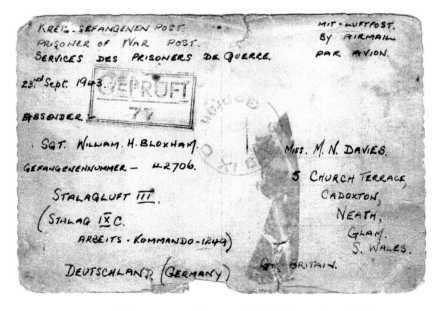

Front of above postcard, sent to Nita in September 1943.

Medical officers at Obermassfeld, 1943.
Major Bill Tucker extreme left of front row.

Roommates at Stalag IV DZ Annaburg, August 1943. Richard Pape second from right, alongside Author (3rd from right) in front row.
Don Coleman behind self and Richard.

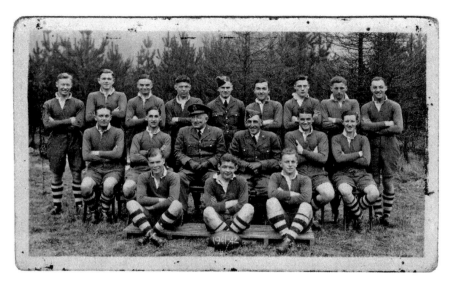

Successful Wing rugby XV, No.1 Wing, RAF Halton, Winter 1941/2

Winning the 'Ashes' at Annaburg Castle, August 1944.
Author with borrowed cravat.

Christmas cabaret, Obermassfeld 1943.

'Makers of Magic' – Obermassfeld 1943.

Annaburg Castle revisited, 2001.

Kirklinik Hohmark near Frankfurt, revisited 2001.

Over the bridge to hospital, Stalag IXc Obermassfeld.

Author (left) with Don Morrison, former inmates at Obermassfeld.

Author in interesting interlude with HRH the Duke of Edinburgh.
Nita near right shoulder, Eileen Clark facing, MD of AV Roe at rear.

Philippa Kate presents a bouquet to Princess Alexandra. The Hon Angus Ogilvy
and POW chairman Charles Clark looking on.

Merry 41st at RAF Halton Reunion, 1999. Author front row far left.

'Tribute' memorial to Aircraft Apprentices at RAF Halton.

Author at home in West Wittering with 41st committee.
Note: Sir Henry Royce's former home next door.

Annual celebration of Sir Henry Royce's life at West Wittering.
Cherry Mead through trees next door.

Nita [right] with Marie & Gilbert Mûs
at Cherry Mead, West Wittering 1984.

Nita at home with Weg and Nita Payton, West Wittering, 1980s.

Bescheinigung

Der BRITISH   Kriegsgefangene BLOXHAM, WILLIAM
(Nationalität)   (Zuname)   (Vorname)

geb. 25.9.23, Dienstgrad SGT   Erk. Nr. (Gef. Nr.) 42706

wurde am 4.5.44 der Gemischten Ärztekommission vorgestellt.

Seine Heimkehrberechtigung*) wurde bejaht*) — verneint*).

Er ist der nächsten Kommission wieder vorzustellen*).

Er ist in der Befundliste des Lagers*) — Res. Laz. (Kgf.)*) STALAG LUFT Ⅶ

vom 1.5.44 unter lfd. Nr. 14 eingetragen.

Der Vorsitzende der Gemischten Ärztekommission.

Major HRMy. wauward

*) Nichtzutreffendes streichen.

208 (Ⅴ) 2.44

Road to freedom... the coveted Repatriation Certificate.

The Author in 1970 [general manager, Aladdin industries Ltd].

*Author with fellow volunteers cutting turf for extension to
Inglenook, Abbeyfield, West Wittering 1990.*

*A memorable last trip together.
1994 with the Morrisons at the Grand Canyon.*

Grandson Robert with his father.

Grand-daughters Philippa (left) and Louise.

Son Philip, enjoying retirement.